Professionals' Ethos and Education for Responsibility

Moral Development and Citizenship Education

Series Editors

Fritz Oser (*University of Fribourg, Switzerland*)
Wiel Veugelers (*University of Humanistic Studies,
Utrecht, The Netherlands*)

Editorial Board

Nimrod Aloni (*Kibbutzim College of Education, Tel Aviv, Israel*)
Marvin Berkowitz (*University of Missouri-St.Louis, U.S.A.*)
Pietro Boscolo (*University of Padova, Italy*)
Maria Rosa Buxarrais (*University of Barcelona, Spain*)
Helen Haste (*University of Bath, U.K./Harvard University, U.S.A*)
Dana Moree (*Charles University, Prague, Czech Republic*)
Clark Power (*University of Notre Dame, U.S.A.*)
Kirsi Tirri (*University of Helsinki, Finland/Stanford University, U.S.A.*)
Joel Westheimer (*University of Ottawa, Canada*)
William Wu (*Hong Kong Baptist University, China*)

VOLUME 14

The titles published in this series are listed at *brill.com/mora*

Professionals' Ethos and Education for Responsibility

Edited by

Alfred Weinberger, Horst Biedermann,
Jean-Luc Patry and Sieglinde Weyringer

BRILL
SENSE
LEIDEN | BOSTON

All chapters in this book have undergone peer review.

The Library of Congress Cataloging-in-Publication Data is available online at http://catalog.loc.gov

ISBN: 978-90-04-36731-9 (paperback)
ISBN: 978-90-04-36730-2 (hardback)
ISBN: 978-90-04-36732-6 (e-book)

Copyright 2018 by Koninklijke Brill NV, Leiden, The Netherlands.
Koninklijke Brill NV incorporates the imprints Brill, Brill Hes & De Graaf, Brill Nijhoff, Brill Rodopi, Brill Sense and Hotei Publishing.
All rights reserved. No part of this publication may be reproduced, translated, stored in a retrieval system, or transmitted in any form or by any means, electronic, mechanical, photocopying, recording or otherwise, without prior written permission from the publisher.
Authorization to photocopy items for internal or personal use is granted by Koninklijke Brill NV provided that the appropriate fees are paid directly to The Copyright Clearance Center, 222 Rosewood Drive, Suite 910, Danvers, MA 01923, USA. Fees are subject to change.

This book is printed on acid-free paper and produced in a sustainable manner.

CONTENTS

Preface ... vii

1. Professionals' Ethos: An Introduction ... 1
   Alfred Weinberger, Horst Biedermann, Jean-Luc Patry and Sieglinde Weyringer

2. Metaethics and Moral Education ... 11
   Edgar Morscher

3. The Professional Ethos of Teachers: Is Only a Procedural Discourse Approach a Suitable Model? ... 23
   Fritz Oser and Horst Biedermann

4. Situation Specificity of Discourse ... 41
   Jean-Luc Patry

5. Promoting Conceptual Change through Values *and* Knowledge Education (V*a*KE) ... 63
   Dimitris Pnevmatikos and Panagiota Christodoulou

6. Democracy, Responsibility, and Inquiry in Education: Relationship and Empirical Accessibility Using the Criteria of Inquiry Learning Inventory (CILI) ... 75
   Johannes Reitinger

7. Responsibility as the Principle Denominator of Pedagogical Ethos: An Empirical Analysis of Pedagogical Responsibility from the Vocational Trainers' Perspective ... 89
   Sarah Forster-Heinzer

8. Education for Professional Ethos through V*a*KE (Values *and* Knowledge Education) in Teacher Education: A Cognitive-Affective Process System Analysis of Pre-Service Teachers' Moral Judgments Concerning a Socio-Scientific Issue ... 107
   Alfred Weinberger

9. The Dark Side of Teachers' Behavior and Its Impact on Students' Reactions: A Comprehensive Framework to Assess College Students' Reactions to Faculty Incivility ... 127
   Yariv Itzkovich and Dorit Alt

CONTENTS

10. Commitment to Develop Appreciative Relationships in School: Nonviolent Communication as an Approach to Specify a Facet of Teacher Ethos 137
    Karin Heinrichs and Simone Ziegler

11. Professionals' Ethos and Education for Responsibility: Teachers' Ethos as an Example of Professionals' Ethos 151
    Brigitte Latzko and Anne-Cathrin Paeszler

Index 163

PREFACE

This book originated from the EARLI SIG 13 conference *professionals' ethos and education for responsibility* which was held in July 2016 in Salzburg, Austria. SIG 13 addresses questions of moral and democratic education from a scientific perspective with a particular focus on theoretically founded empirical research. Moral education means education to improve the learner's moral competence and actions, and democratic education deals with the furthering of democratic knowledge, attitudes, and actions in all their facets. Moral and democratic competences are key issues in today's society. Competencies of this kind are topics in the school curricula of most countries; however, moral and democratic education mostly play a minor role in teaching, and where it is considered as necessary, it is usually not based on research outcomes but on traditions which often are quite questionable from a scientific point of view. The aim of SIG 13 is to promote warranted moral and democratic education, i.e., moral and democratic education that capitalizes on research in learning, development, and education, both in school and outside.

The conference theme focused on *professionals' ethos and education for responsibility*. Very broadly, professionals' ethos is seen as considering moral issues when interacting with each other in a professional context. Responsibility means, on the one hand, complying with some external requirements (e.g., legal norms, authoritative prescriptions, rules) and on the other hand, complying with one's own conscience or values system (internal requirements). Education for responsibility, finally, means, first, an ethically justified requirement to consider the target person's responsibility as an educational goal, especially fostering the students' internal requirements (values system). Secondly, it means that adequate means are addressed how to achieve this (and other) goals.

Based on an internal review of the organizers and editors of this book ten out of 58 papers of the conference were selected and the authors were invited to submit an extended version of their presentation as a chapter of this book. All chapters have undergone strict peer review. The chapter authors attempted to draw from established concepts of professionals' ethos and education for responsibility and build from the base of empirical literature to push the field forward and offer new insights.

This book is useful for researchers, methodologists, students, and practitioners from different disciplines with interest in professionals' ethos and education for responsibility as well as in moral and democratic education in general.

Alfred Weinberger
Horst Biedermann
Jean-Luc Patry
Sieglinde Weyringer

ALFRED WEINBERGER, HORST BIEDERMANN,
JEAN-LUC PATRY AND SIEGLINDE WEYRINGER

1. PROFESSIONALS' ETHOS

An Introduction

ETHOS – LINGUISTIC ROOTS AND MEANINGS

It is acknowledged that ethos is an essential element of a professional's work (e.g., Baumert & Kunter, 2006; Beckenförde, 2011; Francis, 2001; Senghaas-Knobloch, 2008; Tenorth, 2006). However, in the literature also appears widespread disagreement about the definition and meaning of professionals' ethos. The chapters of this book also indicate the variety of meanings of ethos. Moreover, as McLaughlin (2005) points out with respect to the lack of research on teachers' ethos, "[e]thos is relatively underexplored as a form of educative influence by educational researchers, philosophers of education, educational policy makers and teachers and educational leaders at classroom and school level" (p. 306). This introduction aims at first bringing light to the term "professionals' ethos" by analyzing its linguistic roots and meanings. Then the key themes and conclusions of every single chapter of this volume are summarized.

The term profession is used in different senses. In the Oxford English Dictionary (OED) eight different meanings of *profession* are distinguished. According to the OED, the first time that the word appeared in the literature was at about 1250 denoting the declaration, promise, or vow made by a person entering a religious order, hence the action of entering such an order. *Profession* in the sense of relating to professional occupation was first mentioned at about 1450 designating to an occupation in which a professed knowledge of some subject, field, or science is applied. According to OED, it describes a vocation or career, especially one that involves prolonged training and a formal qualification. According to Greenwood (1957), the attributes of a profession in the sense of a professional occupation are (1) a systematic body of (academic or research-based) theory or knowledge, which is continually increased through research, (2) authority and credibility, (3) community sanction, or regulation and control of its members through professional licensing, minimum criteria to enter the profession and apprenticeship, (4) a code of ethics, which describes proper client-professional relations and proper professional-professional relations, and (5) a professional culture, or a culture of values, norms, and symbols. Carr (2014) points to two further attributes of a profession: (6) The occupation in question provides essential valued public service, which refers to basic human needs in any tolerable human society, and (7) it is characterized by the criterion that its workers have appropriate scope for the exercise of independent ('autonomous') thought and judgment in complicated circumstances, such as in decision situations. Professions are divided into true professions (e.g., law, medicine) and semi-professions (e.g., nursing, teaching). Semi-professions lack or fall short of some of the key characteristics of professions (Hodson & Sullivan, 2007, pp. 259f; Ingersoll & Perda, 2008). A professional is a member of a true or semi-profession.

The term *ethos* was mentioned the first time in the 8th century BC in Homer's *Illiad*. In this epic poem about the Trojan Wars *ethos* refers to an accustomed place of activity ("haunt") or accustomed practices ("customs") (Worman, 2002). It originally designates the places where animals are usually found. Homer used the word in plural and never for humans but only for animals (Sobiech, 2014). Chamberlain (1984) elaborates on one simile in the *Illiad*, in which a stabled horse breaks out to return to "the ethea and nomos of horses" (p. 97). Chamberlain claims that this usage of the word contains the foundation of *ethos's* later meaning as character, for here the word has "the idea of 'belonging in'" (p. 97). A wild horse does not belong in a stable, which is not its habitat. Rather, it belongs in the place where wild horses are usually found (Sobiech, 2014, p. 13). The emphasis on habituation is a key point in Aristotle's discussion a few hundred years later in the *Nicomachean Ethics* about how *ethos* or character is developed in a person. Since "every action has its roots in character" Reale and Catan (1987, p. 11) point out that *ethos* is strongly related to character.

In the works of Hesiod and Theognis who lived in the 7th and 6th century BC *ethos* is used in its singular form and it is now also used for people (Chamberlain, 1984). According to Chamberlain (1984), it is now an "arena in which people [...] move", and also, it is an "essence" that "resists the imposition of outside influence. Here [that is in Theognis], as in Hesiod, ethos refers to the range or arena where someone is most truly at home and which underlies all the fine appearances that people adopt" (p. 99). Moreover, according to Worman (2002), Theognis uses *ethos* sometimes as an internal state while in some passages *ethos* appears as a visible behavior. Zulick (2004, p. 20) acknowledges that "[one] can perhaps see how the name has traveled from 'lair' to 'habit' (via 'habitat') to 'character' in the sense of the constellation of habits of thought, manners, and reputation that constitutes a rhetorical subject". Chamberlain (1984) points to further nuances of meaning including a political usage in which "ethos refers to the peculiarities which people of a certain polis acquire of being brought up under its particular laws and customs" (p. 101). According to OED *ethos* also denotes the "characteristic spirit of a culture, era, or community as manifested in its attitudes and aspirations". Frobish (2003) contends that *ethos* in its original meanings is not seen in moralistic or ethical terms but rather as a particular excellence of mind or body. Another meaning appears in the work of Heraclitus (500 BC). He used *ethos* in the sense of "human nature", how we are made up by nature (Geldard, 2000, p. 92).

Aristotle (4th century BC) refers to *ethos* in more detail in two of his works: *Nicomachean Ethics* and *Rhetoric*. In *Nicomachean Ethics (NE)* he distinguishes between *ēthos* in the meaning of character and *ethos* in the meaning of habit. The latter refers to righteous acts one repeatedly performs. Righteous acts are acts that are in accordance with moral virtues. "For the things which we have to learn before we can do them, we learn by doing: men become builders by building houses, and harpists by playing the harp. Similarly, we become just by the practice of just actions, self-controlled by exercising self-control, and courageous by performing acts of courage" (*NE*, I, II, 1103a, 31–33). For Aristotle, everyone has *ēthos* whether it be noble or ignoble (Smith, 2004). To develop *ēthos*, it is necessary to do righteous acts (*ethos*) repeatedly. The formation of *ēthos* takes place from the collective *ēthos* to the individual one. It is developed through education (*paideia*). In *Rhetoric (R)* Aristotle describes *ēthos* (along with pathos and logos) as a persuasive proof that consists of three components (Frobish, 2009; Smith, 2004): virtue, wisdom, and goodwill. The first component of *ēthos*, virtue, is the ability to produce and preserve the good (*R*, 1362b1) and it is a "state of character" concerned with 'choice'" (*NE*, II, 1106b, 36–40). Virtue aims at the ultimate good *eudaimonia* which means a sense of fulfillment or human flourishing and which Aristotle describes as a comprehensive state of being when living a good life. Virtuous actions are actions based on "a mean between two vices, one by excess and the other by deficiency; and while some of the vices exceed while the others are deficient in what is right in feelings and actions, virtue finds and chooses the mean" (*NE*, II, 1107a, 3–5). *Ēthos* "is reflected in deliberate choices of actions and [is] developed into a habit of mind" (Kennedy, 1991, p. 163). The second component of *ēthos*, wisdom, consists of theoretical and practical wisdom. Theoretical wisdom (*sophia*) refers to "scientific knowledge, combined with intuitive reason of the things that are highest by nature" (*NE*, VI, 1141b). Practical wisdom (*phronēsis*) refers to knowledge of contingent facts that are useful to living well. "Now it is thought to be the mark of a man of practical wisdom to be able to deliberate well about what is good and expedient for himself, not in some particular respect, e.g., about what sorts of thing conduce to health or to strength, but about what sorts of thing conduce to the good life in general" (*NE*, VI, 1140a–1140b). This practical knowledge is learned through experience (Loughran, 2013). Choosing wisely demands that we are guided by proper aims or goals of a particular activity. Aristotle's word for the purpose or aim of an activity is *telos*. For example, regarding the professional ethos of teachers, the *telos* of teaching is to educate students. According to Brezinka (1992) education is defined as "actions through which human beings attempt to produce lasting improvements in the structure of the psychic dispositions of other people, to retain components they consider positive or to prevent the formation of dispositions they regard as negative" (p. 40f). Ethos-based decisions of a teacher aim at the development and growth of the whole person. Dunne (1993) claims that "phronetic action can't exist without both intellectual and moral conditions of the mind" (p. 264). Aristotle draws attention to phronesis as a form of reflective practical wisdom that complements *techne*, technically oriented knowledge, and *episteme*, scientifically oriented knowledge, in considerations of what it might mean to develop and enact professional knowledge (Kinsella, 2012). The third component of *ēthos*, goodwill, is wishing good for others for their sake (*NE*, IV, 1167a). Goodwill is not based on reciprocation. Aristotle's account of *ēthos* in *Rhetoric* rests entirely upon the idea that one's *ēthos* is a perception which depends upon an audience's moral judgment of one's abilities, which could vary from one interaction to the next (Frobish, 2003).

Ethos and *ethics* are related. Warnick (2011) points out that "*ethikos* [...] or 'theory of living' comes from the same Greek root [as ethos] and from there we derive the modern English word *ethics*" (p. 24). However, while *ethos* and *ethics* are related, they cover distinctly different ground (Sobiech, 2014). According to its Greek roots "habit, custom, and character" *ethos* cannot be translated as "ethical" (Reynolds, 1993). *Ethics* as philosophical discipline substantiates and critically reflects a particular *ethos*.

Based on this analysis of the terms *profession* and *ethos* the following core issues can be summarized:

- A professional's work is characterized by autonomy and complex decision situations which call for deliberate choices of action. These choices of action reveal the *professional's ethos*.
- Ethos-based decisions aim at the *telos* of a particular profession. The *telos* for teaching is *to educate,* and it refers to actions which foster the development and growth of the whole person.
- *Ethos* cannot be translated as "ethical" or "moral", although it raises ethical and moral questions. A professional unavoidably encounters involved situations in which he or she must decide on how to act. As each action followed by the decision made by professionals has consequences for other persons, *ethos* then needs to be thought of in the realms of morality. The professionals, therefore are responsible for these persons and can be held accountable for their actions.
- A *professional ethos* can be learned. The formation takes place through education which emphasizes the practice of decision-making in typical situations of the respective profession. This decision-making grounds in the knowledge and (moral) norms or values of the particular profession. Applying this assumption to the idea of teachers' ethos one crucial ability would be that teachers learn to reflect upon the different decision choices.
- A professional shows excellence in his or her practice which means that he or she bases activities on the knowledge and the (moral) values and norms of his or her profession. Only a professional with a highly developed ethos can do the righteous and excellent in a particular situation for the sake of his or her client without thinking about his or her benefit.

The chapters in this book draw on some or more of these issues. They present an original contribution to the exploration of a relatively underexplored facet of a professional's work. The next section summarizes each study and presents the main conclusions the authors draw from their analysis.

THE CHAPTERS – FINDINGS AND CONCLUSIONS

The first chapter by Edgar Morscher was the keynote address of the EARLI SIG 13 conference on "Professionals' Ethos and Education for Responsibility". It provides a philosophically based contribution to a facet of a professional's ethos, in concreto to teacher ethos. Morscher focusses on moral education which is a typical assignment and activity of teachers. He claims that teachers need to know a lot about the language they use when expressing moral norms and values to their pupils because everyday language suffers from lack of clarity and its ambiguities. According to Morscher, this metaethical knowledge is twofold. It refers to (a) the identification and interpretation of prescriptive sentences, i.e., sentences that express moral norms and values (reportive metaethics), and (b) to their unambiguous usage (stipulative metaethics). Analyzing prescriptive sentences based on this metaethical knowledge makes clear that they cannot be true or false in the literal sense of these words. Morscher points to a kind of knowledge (metaethical knowledge) that is currently not taught in teacher education although it would be essential to prepare teachers for the moral nature of their work (see also Sanger, 2008).

Fritz Oser and Horst Biedermann consider the concept of dependency as the primary source of ethos. They point to the professional-client relationship which is characterized by the dependency of the client who cannot cope with a problematic situation or who produces something particular. The authors distinguish between professional morality and professional ethos. While the first refers to a professional's considerations regarding the results of an action the latter refers to a professional's supererogatory attentiveness regarding the individuals he or she is in charge of. With regard to the teaching profession the authors list four essential elements of ethos: (1) the ability to act responsibly in challenging situations, (2) without thinking of one's own profit, (3) supporting learners, and (4) being accurate as regards the contents to be taught. After that, the authors present the discourse model of professional ethos which emphasizes discursive conflict resolution strategies. Oser and Biederman criticise that the discourse model's possible application is restricted to interpersonal conflicts. In many other decision situations of a professional's work, the discourse model is not applicable. Drawing on results of empirical studies about job satisfaction the authors conclude that doing the right thing leads to satisfaction, even in the case of facing negative aspects of professional work. Oser and Biedermann attempt to find a comprehensive model of professional ethos which is applicable to a wide range of typical decision situations teachers encounter in their daily work and which can be evaluated empirically. Jean-Luc Patry claims in his chapter that discourse-ethos is a situation-specific behavior. According to his theory of situation specificity in the social domain, that is when social behavior is at stake, situation specificity is the rule. He further argues drawing on the CAPS theory that in social situations, such as in complex decision situations of a professional, competencies, perceptions, expectations, values and goals, self-regulatory principles and emotions guide our behavior. These cognitive-affective units interrelate with each other. Furthermore, Patry states that in social situations we typically try to achieve several goals simultaneously which cause antinomies and dilemmas. The interrelation of cognitions and emotions and the antinomies and dilemmas in decision situations make each situation unique and "the question whether people act situation specifically in morally relevant situations becomes very complex" (Patry; this volume). Based on the results of an empirical study Patry shows that discursive behavior of teachers is very situation specific. Patry's findings have consequences for the education of professionals (e.g., training based on different situations) and for the assessment of ethos (e.g., assessment based on different situations).

Dimitris Pnevmatikos and Panagiota Christodoulou describe a study about the application of the instructional approach V*a*KE (Values *and* Knowledge Education) in school to integrate moral aspects in teaching socio-scientific issues. Pnevmatikos and Christodoulou claim that the integration of moral aspects in teaching is considered an element of a teacher's professional ethos since each teacher has a double assignment: teaching knowledge and values. According to the authors, the integration of moral aspects in teaching is not realized although it would be highly relevant. Particularly in science moral considerations are significant because scientific and technological innovations and activities, such as Nano-Science and Nano-technology, affect human beings hugely by their benefits but also by their possible negative consequences. V*a*KE is an instructional approach that combines values education with knowledge acquisition employing moral dilemmas to trigger the discussion among the participants. Therefore, moral education can be realized without the detriment of knowledge acquisition. The results of Pnevmatikos and Christoudoulo's study indicate that students reconstructed their initially constructed naïve concepts towards the scientific ones when learning with V*a*KE. The findings show that teachers can use V*a*KE as a possible approach to fulfill the double assignment and hence can act based on a professional ethos.

Johannes Reitinger's contribution deals with theoretical relations between education for responsibility, democratic education, and inquiry learning. He discusses a particular aspect of teacher ethos which refers to the methods of learning a teacher applies in his or her lessons. Based on the ideas of Dewey about education for democracy Reitinger contends that Dewey's central theoretical constructs participation, democratic deliberation, and decision making are also integral elements of inquiry learning. He further states based on Dewey that students must experience active participation and democracy to internalize it and grow up into adults who are themselves able to act responsibly towards themselves, others and the world around them. Bearing in mind the purpose and aim of education in a democratic society, namely to be able to participate and to make democratic and deliberate judgments based on facts, a teacher's decision to use inquiry-based learning as a teaching method can be considered as an ethos-based decision. Reitinger then describes his Theory of Inquiry Learning Arrangements which strongly relates to attributes of education for democracy and responsibility. To empirically assess the main criteria of Inquiry Learning, he delineates the validation procedure of an inventory which easily can be applied in different open learning settings.

For Sarah Forster-Heinzer ethos is closely linked to responsibility which is given if a person is in charge of another person and can be held accountable for his or her decisions. According to Forster-Heinzer a professional should be aware of the scope of responsibility and should anticipate possible consequences. In an empirical investigation with 570 vocational trainers, she found that the trainer's sense of responsibility is influenced by situation and circumstances but also by the trainer's experience of being significant for the apprentice's development. In her conclusion, she points to the relation between the ethos of the institutional and individual level about the sense of a professional's pedagogical responsibility. The society, she claims, can contribute to the establishment of a professional ethos by acknowledging the doing and importance of a profession more explicitly.

Alfred Weinberger reports on a study in which he explored pre-service teachers' mental representations underlying their moral judgments. Moral judgment competence is considered a core element of a professional's ethos. The author sheds light on what is going on in the heads of teachers when they face a morally relevant decision situation. For this, he analyzed moral judgments about a socio-scientific issue in the context of a V*a*KE (Values *and* Knowledge Education)-dilemma discussion. The results of a cognitive-affective process system analysis are shown visually in domain maps which vividly represent the complexity of the interrelations of an individual's encodings, competencies, expectancies and beliefs, goals and values, self-regulatory principles, and affects which are mediated by specific factual knowledge. The main conclusion of this study is that moral judgments are highly situation and person specific. The situation-specificity implies that any model of ethos which is based on decision-making should take into account the peculiarities of the particular situation and person. According to Weinberger the reflection upon one's cognitions (e.g., values) and affects and their interrelation in a morally relevant situation can support the decision-making process.

Yariv Itzkovich and Dorit Alt delve deeper into professionals' ignoble ethos-behavior. They explore pre-service teachers' perceptions of the uncivil behavior of their professors. Interviews with pre-service teachers indicate a broad range of active and passive uncivil behavior. Students' responses to faculty incivility include the termination of the relationship (exit), talking to the professor (voice), the willingness to endure unfavorable conditions (loyalty), and passive negligence or complaining (neglect). The authors suggest several strategies to take precautions against faculty incivility, such as faculty's reflection on and dialogue about ethical decision situations of their own experiences (ethos procedure), open discourses on expected academic behavior, discussion of shared moral values, or the development of an own professional code. Their implications refer to the significance of reflection and discussion on nurturing ethos of professionals.

Karin Heinrichs and Simone Ziegler focus on the relationship between teachers and students as a facet of teacher ethos. They claim that only on the bases of appreciative relationships and a positive social climate effective learning can take place. According to the authors, the nonviolent communication approach of Rosenberg provides the essential guidelines for implementing appreciative relationships. Heinrichs and Ziegler state that ethos becomes not only visible in complex situations but in a wide range of decision situations. Their concept of ethos also highlights the feelings which arise in interpersonal communication and which the agents should be aware of to communicate successfully.

Finally, Brigitte Latzko and Anne-Cathrin Paessler explore ethos by analyzing current concepts found in the literature and by doing a thorough linguistic analysis. Based on these analyses Latzko and Paessler derive three main conclusions which can guide future empirical research and theoretical considerations on teachers' ethos. Firstly, ethos refers to a continually occurring action which typically characterizes teachers' behavior. Secondly, ethos can be nurtured through a guided and supervised reflective practice (e.g., reflection upon typical situations which a professional encounters). Finally, ethos can be understood as a holistic concept. Hence it cannot be operationalized with the help of only one method.

REFERENCES

Baumert, J., & Kunter, M. (2006). Stichwort: Professionelle Kompetenz von Lehrkräften [Keyword: Professional competence of teachers]. *Zeitschrift für Erziehungswissenschaft, 9*(4), 469–520.
Beckenförde, E.-W. (2011). *Vom Ethos der Juristen* [About the ethos in the legal profession]. Berlin: Duncker & Humblot.
Brezinka, W. (1992). *Philosophy of educational knowledge: An introduction to the foundations of science of education, philosophy of education and practical pedagogics.* Dordrecht: Springer.
Carr, D. (2014). Professionalism, profession and professional conduct: Towards a basic logical and ethical geography. In S. Billet, C. Harteis, & H. Gruber (Eds.), *International handbook of research in professional and practice-based learning* (pp. 5–27). Dordrecht: Springer.
Chamberlain, C. (1984). From haunts to character: The meaning of ethos and its relation to ethics. *Helios, 11*, 97–108.
Clarà, M. (2015). What is reflection? Looking for clarity in an ambiguous notion. *Journal of Teacher Education, 66*(3), 261–271.
Dunne, J. (1993). *Back to the rough ground: "Phronesis" and "techne" in modern philosophy and in Aristotle.* Notre Dame, IN: University of Notre Dame Press.
Francis, C. K. (2001). Medical ethos and social responsibility in clinical medicine. *Journal of Urban Health, 78*(1), 29–45.
Frobish, T. S. (2003). An origin of a theory: A comparison of ethos in the Homeric "Illiad" with that found in Aristotle's "Rhetoric". *Rhetoric Review, 22*(1), 16–30.
Geldard, R. (2000). *Remembering Heraclitus.* Herndon, VA: Lindisfarne Books.
Greenwood, E. (1957). Attributes of a profession. *Social Work, 2*(3), 45–55.
Hodson, R., & Sullivan, T. A. (2007). *The social organization of work* (5th ed.). Belmont, CA: Cengage.
Ingersoll, R. M., & Perda, D. (2008). The status of teaching as a profession. In J. H. Ballantine & J. Z. Spade (Eds.), *Schools and society: A sociological approach to education* (3rd ed., pp. 106–118). Thousand Oaks, CA: Sage Publications.
Kennedy, G. (1991). *On rhetoric: A theory of civic discourse.* New York, NY: Oxford University Press.
Kinsella, E. A. (2012). Practitioner reflection and judgment as phronesis. In E. A. Kinsella & A. Pitman (Eds.), *Phronesis as professional knowledge: Professional practice and education: A diversity of voices* (Vol 1, pp. 35–52). Rotterdam, The Netherlands: Sense Publishers.

Loughran, J. (2006). *Developing a pedagogy of teacher education: Understanding teaching and learning about teaching*. New York, NY: Routledge.

McLaughlin, T. (2005). The educative importance of ethos. *British Journal of Educational Studies, 53*(3), 306–325.

Profession. (n.d.). *In Oxford English dictionary*. Retrieved from http://www.oed.com/viewdictionaryentry/Entry/152052

Reale, G., & Catan, J. (1987). *A history of ancient philosophy, 1: From the origins to Socrates*. Albany, NY: SUNY Press.

Reynolds, N. (1993). Ethos as location: New sites for understanding discursive authority. *Rhetoric Review, 11*(2), 325–338.

Sanger, M. (2008). What we need to prepare teachers for the moral nature of their work. *Journal of Curriculum Studies, 40*(2), 169–185.

Senghaas-Knobloch, E. (2008). Care-Arbeit und das Ethos fürsorglicher Praxis unter neuen Markbedingungen am Beispiel der Pflegepraxis [Care-work and the ethos of caring practice of nursing]. *Berliner Journal für Soziologie, 18*(2), 221–243.

Smith, C. R. (2004). Ethos dwells pervasively: A hermeneutic reading of Aristotle on credibility. In M. J. Hyde (Ed.), *The ethos of rhetoric*. Columbia, SC: University of South Carolina Press.

Sobiech, M. J. (2014). *The ethos of conspiracy argument: "Character" as persuader in conspiracy rhetoric* (Unpublished dissertation). University of Louisville, Louisville, KT.

Tenorth, H.-E. (2006). Professionalität im Lehrerberuf: Ratlosigkeit der Theorie, gelingende Praxis [Professionalism in the teaching occupation]. *Zeitschrift für Erziehungswissenschaft, 9*(4), 580–597.

Warnick, Q. (2011). *What we talk about when we talk about talking: Ethos at work in an online community* (Doctoral. Dissertation). Iowa State University, Ames, IA.

Worman, N. (2002). *The cast of character: Style in Greek literature*. Austin, TX: University of Texas Press.

Zulick, M. D. (2004). The ethos of invention: The dialogue of ethics and aesthetics in Kenneth Burke and Mikhail Bakhtin. In M. J. Hyde (Ed.), *The ethos of rhetoric* (pp. 20–33). Columbia, SC: University of South Carolina Press.

Alfred Weinberger
Department of Research and Development
Private University of Education of the Diocese of Linz
Austria

Horst Biedermann
Universtiy of Teacher Education of St. Gallen
Switzerland

Jean-Luc Patry
Department of Education
University of Salzburg
Salzburg, Austria

Sieglinde Weyringer
Department of Education
University of Salzburg
Salzburg, Austria

EDGAR MORSCHER

2. METAETHICS AND MORAL EDUCATION[1]

I dedicate this text and in particular the little manifesto at its end to those philosophy teachers who are my former students.

INTRODUCTION

In what follows I will try to show by means of examples how crucial metaethical knowledge is for teachers of moral norms and values.

It is more or less common usage today to understand by 'prescriptive ethics' the prescriptive (i.e., the normative and evaluative) assessment of morality. Prescriptive ethics itself, on the other hand, is the subject matter of metaethics, which reflects on its language and methods. Not the only, but by far the most important parts of the language of prescriptive ethics are its prescriptive *sentences*, and these sentences express moral norms and values.

When we say, in short, that the main task of metaethics is the analysis of moral language, we have to take into account that, like any kind of linguistic analysis, also the metaethical task of analyzing the language of morals is *twofold*: on the *one hand* it concerns the expressions of moral norms and values in everyday language where we have to find out how to identify, understand and interpret them. This task is of a *hermeneutical* character and must be performed by what I will call "*reportive* metaethics". On the *other hand* there is a further, even much more important task of metaethics which is of a *stipulative* nature – and I therefore will call this part of metaethics "*stipulative* metaethics". (The terminology that I am using thereby comes from the theory of definitions where we distinguish between reportive and stipulative definitions.)

The study of prescriptive moral sentences of everyday language brings soon to light that this area of everyday language suffers seriously from what in other areas may be an advantage of everyday language: from its lack of clarity, its vagueness, and its ambiguities. Ethical issues are in fact much too important for us and our society to leave open and unclear what our answers to them really mean. In prescriptive ethics we want to criticize certain normative and evaluative claims, we want to argue in a rational way for or against certain prescriptive positions. An indispensable means and prerequisite for being able to do that is to have a clear and precise language at our disposal in which we can express the prescriptive claims in an unambiguous way and in which the meaning of sentences expressing these claims are independent of the situation and the context in which they are uttered. This is necessary for the same reason as for the language of scientific discourse because most of the participants of such a discourse are usually not present, which is why in general we do not know their facial expression and gesturing and the circumstances of their utterance of a sentence. Unfortunately, the trend of the current logic and philosophy of language goes in fact in the opposite direction by taking into account more and more the context and situation of the utterance of a sentence. However, by focusing on this important hermeneutical goal, the much more important task of regulating our language for the purpose of a scientific and rational discourse is inexcusably neglected. It is the task of *"stipulative metaethics"* to prepare such an unambiguous prescriptive language out of our everyday language by "regimenting" it and thereby develop, for prescriptive purposes, a "regimented" language as Willard Van Orman Quine (1960) calls it.[2]

Having said all this by way of introduction, it should be clear that the rest of my talk will be divided into two main parts as follows:

- Part I: Reportive Metaethics (Hermeneutics).
- Part II: Stipulative Metaethics (Regimentation).

PART I: REPORTIVE METAETHICS (HERMENEUTICS)

How to Distinguish Prescriptive from Descriptive Speech

One of the first things a moral educator should know is how moral norms and values are expressed in the language of her or his pupils, i.e., in everyday language. Since in everyday language one and the same linguistic expression or sentence (such as, e.g., 'Nobody smokes in this room') can be used in a merely descriptive or in a prescriptive way, the first – hermeneutic – question will be: how can we find out whether a linguistic expression is used in a prescriptive or in a merely descriptive intention? The mere linguistic form of an expression or a sentence alone is obviously not decisive for the way it is used in a certain context. We must therefore not remain on a mere syntactic or semantic level when we look for a distinction between prescriptive and descriptive discourse in everyday language. This distinction concerns, in fact, the complete *speech act* in question and is therefore of a pragmatic nature. John Searle, one of the representatives of modern speech act theory, has proposed what he called the *direction of fit* as a criterion for distinguishing between prescriptive and descriptive speech acts (Searle, 1975; cf. Morscher, 2016a). Let me explain this criterion briefly.

If what we say ("our language") and what is the case ("the reality") do not match each other, we have two options: we can either change what we say in such a way that it fits what is the case, or we can change what is the case in such a way that it fits what we say. In the *first* case our speech act is *descriptive*, characterized by the *language-to-reality direction of fit*; and in the *second* case, our speech act is *prescriptive*, characterized by the *reality-to-language direction of fit*.

By way of example, let us assume that a member of the security staff of our university enters this room, interrupts my talk and utters the following words: 'Nobody smokes in this room'. From his stern look and a specific undertone in his voice, you can conclude that the sentence expresses a prohibition and is therefore prescriptive. Using Searle's criterion, you have to ask: What will the speaker do in case somebody *is* really smoking in this room right now? Will he change his words and say instead of '*Nobody*' now '*Somebody* smokes in this room'? Obviously, this would not be his reaction, he rather will take away your cigarette, and by doing this, he changes the reality to make it fitting to his words. This shows that the sentence was used in a prescriptive way according to Searle's criterion.

Exactly the same sentence, however, can also be used in a purely descriptive way. Let us now assume that another member of our security staff has *not* the task to *proclaim* one of the rules of this house but to *control* whether these rules are observed, and he asks me whether this is the case. My answer will be 'Nobody smokes in this room'. When I now find out that I have overlooked someone of you who is smoking, I will change my words and say: Excuse me, in fact someone *is* smoking here, I have just overlooked him when I said 'nobody'. I have changed my words to make them fit to the reality, and this shows that my words were used in a purely descriptive way according to Searle's criterion.

This should give you a rough idea of Searle's *direction of fit* criterion for distinguishing prescriptive from descriptive speech in everyday language and communication. This way of distinguishing between prescriptive and descriptive speech has the benefit that as a by-product it establishes why *descriptive* speech is *cognitive* in the following sense: performing it is – under normal circumstances – combined with the intention that it corresponds to reality, and it, in fact, *does* correspond or *fail* to correspond to reality, i.e., it is true or false. In *prescriptive* speech, however, we do not even *intend* that our utterance corresponds to reality, but we rather perform it under the supposition that it does *not* correspond to reality and hope and intend that due to our utterance the reality will be changed in a way that it will then fit the uttered sentence.

It is this informal reflection where the ground lies for what we call 'metaethical non-cognitivism': the main function of a prescriptive sentence is – as the term says – to *pre*scribe and *not* to *de*scribe, and its primary goal, therefore, is not to be true; in fact it *can neither* be true *nor* false in the original and literal sense of these words.

How to Tell Different Kinds of Prescriptive Speech from One Another

Being able to distinguish between prescriptive and descriptive discourse is not enough, however. In everyday language, it is very often undoubtedly clear that a speech act is of a prescriptive nature, but at the same time, it is pretty unclear *what kind* of prescription is intended by it. Even in the philosophical jargon an action is very often simply called *correct* and you do not know whether it is meant to be obligatory or merely permissible, which makes quite a difference. A second hermeneutic task is, therefore, to find out how to distinguish between different prescriptive categories in natural language.

The importance of this task emerges from the fact that not even Kant's ethics is exempted from a confusion of prescriptive categories. When Kant experts say that Kant's Categorical Imperative provides a criterion for determining whether an act is correct or not, it is sometimes far from being clear what is meant: some of these experts thereby use the word 'correct' in the sense of 'permissible' and others in the sense of 'obligatory' depending on which of Kant's formulations of the Categorical Imperative they base their interpretation. As you know Kant has sometimes formulated his Categorical Imperative *with* and sometimes *without* the little word 'only':

> *Act* – or: Act *only* according to that maxim of which you can will that it should become a universal law.[3]

Those who take the 'only' in this formulation to be essential, interpret the categorical imperative in such a way that it demarcates the forbidden acts from all other acts, which are *correct*, and this means in this case: *permissible*, including those acts which are morally irrelevant.

Those experts, however, who take the 'only' as inessential, interpret the categorical imperative in such a way that it demarcates exclusively among the *morally relevant* acts those which are *correct*, and that means in this case: *obligatory*.

Both interpretations provide us with a coherent understanding of Kant's categorical imperative within two different frameworks. Without clearing up the difference between the two frameworks. However, Kant's Categorical Imperative ends up in a complete confusion and theoretical catastrophe.

If confusions of this kind appear already in the language of experts, it is even more difficult if not hopeless to try to develop criteria for distinguishing different prescriptive categories within the framework of everyday language. A real solution to this problem seems to be possible only via certain regulations within a regimented language. Let us therefore now switch to the second part: Stipulative Metaethics.

PART II: STIPULATIVE METAETHICS (REGIMENTATION)

Since everyday language is full of irregularities and chance, those who take prescriptive ethics to be a rational and critical or even a theoretical enterprise must develop their own standards for a well-ordered and systematic prescriptive language to be used. Moreover, the same holds for teachers of moral values and norms in their moral education. Such a language which avoids ambiguities and displays its logical structure was called – as already mentioned – a *"regimented language"* by Quine (1960).

How to Differentiate between the Prescriptive and Descriptive Speech within a Regimented Language

The *direction of fit* criterion can be of help in telling prescriptive from descriptive speech in everyday communication. It is, however, far from being theoretically satisfactory. Within a natural language, it will never be possible to draw a *sharp* demarcation between prescriptive and descriptive speech. This is only possible for a language with a clear formal structure, i.e., for a regimented language, or a formalized (or symbolic) language evolving from it. The results of a theoretical investigation carried out for a regimented or symbolic language can then be transferred, even if only approximately, to the corresponding investigation of our speech and communication in everyday language.

In a regimented prescriptive language, we must not leave the expression of prescriptivity to the circumstances of an utterance such as gestures or intonation which usually are only present in the moment of the utterance. We must rather express the prescriptive components in a regimented prescriptive language verbally and explicitly by making certain elements of the vocabulary of the language available for this purpose.

In a regimented prescriptive language, it must be clear from the beginning whether an expression of the language is purely prescriptive or not. To fulfill this requirement the primitive prescriptive expressions of the language must be specified by enumeration, and the formation rules (i.e., the rules which tell us how to construe complex expressions, in particular sentences) must be specified in a purely syntactic way. This allows us to distinguish exactly in a merely syntactic way different kinds of sentences of our regimented prescriptive language, such as purely prescriptive ones, mixed ones, and purely descriptive ones. The requirement to deal with these distinctions on a merely syntactic level – in clear opposition to everyday language – is specific for any kind of regimented language, and it should be fulfilled at least approximately.

Here the question may arise: why not – instead of differentiating – *reducing* the prescriptive to the descriptive speech as metaethical naturalism does and thereby getting rid at one blow of all the problems of how to confirm or disconfirm, criticize or justify a prescriptive sentence of ethics. I will come back to this question in the second part of the following section.

How to Differentiate between Prescriptive Categories within a Regimented Language

In a *second* step, the basic prescriptive categories of the regimented language must be specified, and it must be shown how the more complex prescriptive categories can be reduced to them.

Without going into details, it is important to keep in mind that there are several syntactic as well as semantic reasons for using so-called *sentential operators* as our basic prescriptive vocabulary, in particular, the following ones:

1. it is *obligatory* that p [or, alternatively: it ought to be the case that p]
2. it is *permissible* that p
3. it is *forbidden* that p
4. it is *morally indifferent* whether p

The first three of these prescriptive operators are interdefinable, which means that we can pick out arbitrarily one of them as our primitive operator and define the other ones by means of it. Which one we take as primitive is a mere matter of taste, didactics, and psychology.

The mere occurrence of at least one prescriptive operator in a sentence, however, is only necessary but not sufficient for the whole sentence of a regimented language being prescriptive itself. To be prescriptive itself, at least one prescriptive operator must occur "essentially" in it, i.e., without its prescriptive force being neutralized by a prefix such as 'x believes that', 'x says that', or 'according to such and such'. The sentence 'It is forbidden that anyone lies' is prescriptive since the prescriptive operator 'it is forbidden, that' occurs "essentially" in it; but the sentence 'According to one of the ten commands it is forbidden that anyone lies' is purely descriptive although a prescriptive operator and even a whole prescriptive sentence occurs in it, since they do not occur "essentially" in it.

As I already mentioned, the prescriptive operators listed above are interdefinable. Here the question may arise: why not go one step further and reduce the primitive prescriptive operator we have chosen to a purely descriptive operator by a definition such as:

It is forbidden that p: $\leftrightarrow$ the majority of the society disapproves that p
(where ':$\leftrightarrow$' is used as our symbol for definitions and is read as 'if and only if').

Such a definition would allow us to turn prescriptive ethics completely in a purely descriptive and herewith scientific theory.

The famous British moral philosopher G.E. Moore has accused such reductions of committing a *naturalistic fallacy*.[4] Although I do not follow Moore's argument for his condemning the naturalistic fallacy, I accept its spirit in the following way:

Reducing the prescriptive speech to descriptive speech and thereby committing a naturalistic fallacy of the type Moore had in mind, amounts to refraining altogether from prescriptive speech. We would only continue to use prescriptive words but without any prescriptive "force" or meaning. By reducing prescriptive to descriptive speech, we turn its genuinely reality-to-language direction of fit into a language-to-reality direction. In important areas of human life such as, e.g., law and morality, however, we cannot do without genuinely prescriptive speech. If we reduce prescriptive speech to descriptive speech, we can give up from the beginning our efforts to distinguish them on the grammatical level.

How to Enrich a Regimented Prescriptive Language

In a language appropriate for the expression of moral norms and values it is certainly not enough to have prescriptive operators. In addition also some important descriptive operators beyond those of elementary logic must be available, such as:

1. *x acts* in such a way that *p* [or, alternatively: *x sees to it* that *p*]
2. *x believes* that *p*
3. it is *possible* that *p*

Let me give you an example in order to show how important it is to use a regimented language of this kind in ethics and moral education.

The concept of a human right is an important prescriptive category of ethics. The Swedish logician Stig Kanger (2001) has shown that we can distinguish in a systematic way 26 different types of human rights and that they all appear already in the U.N. Declaration of Human Rights (Kanger, 2001, pp. 120–185; Morscher, 2004). Article 3 of the declaration guarantees the "*right to life*". Even this common term for *the* basic human right allows within Kanger's framework to choose between several opposite interpretations such as "you *must not kill anybody* against his will" and "you *must keep alive everybody* with all possible medical means". No wonder that in ideological and political discussions the term 'right to life' is, due to its ambiguity, very often misused, and even today high courts of justice often have to decide in concrete cases how to interpret it as in the case of the French coma patient Vincent Lambert (a case widely discussed in 2015).

Let me also present another example: One of the focuses of this conference is education for *responsibility*. Education for responsibility does not, of course, include teaching about the concept of responsibility and its analysis. Those who are responsible for the education for responsibility, however, should be pretty clear about what is meant by 'responsibility'. By Searle's criterion, you can find out easily that the word 'responsible' is used in everyday language sometimes in a purely descriptive and sometimes in a prescriptive way. When you talk about education for responsibility, however, it is clearly used in a prescriptive sense. Responsibility in this sense is obviously a kind of obligation. Analyzed in the framework of a regimented prescriptive language it is rather complex as Stig Kanger has shown. According to his analysis, we can define it in the following way:

x is *responsible* for the state of affairs that *p*: ↔
x is *blameworthy* for the state of affairs that *p*

or

x is *praiseworthy* for the state of affairs that *p*

The definition of being blameworthy and of being praiseworthy, however, requires in addition to the prescriptive notion of obligation also several other important operators as Kanger's exemplary analysis brings to light:

x is *blameworthy* for the state of affairs that *p*: ↔

1. it is obligatory that *it is not the case that p*,
2. *x* acts in such a way that *p*,
3. it is possible that *x* does not act in such a way that *p*,
4. it is possible that *x* believes that it is obligatory that *it is not the case that p*,
5. it is possible that *x* believes that *x* acts in such a way that *p*, and
6. it is possible that *x* believes that it is possible that it is not the case that *x* acts in such a way that *p*.

In addition to the prescriptive operator for obligation, this analysis requires an operator for acting, an epistemic operator for believing and an alethic modal operator for possibility.

The definition of 'praiseworthy' differs from that of 'blameworthy' only insofar that the underlined negation in clause (1) and clause (4) must be omitted.

x is *praiseworthy* for the state of affairs that *p*: ↔

1. it is obligatory that *p*,
2. *x* acts in such a way that *p*,
3. it is possible that *x* does not act in such a way that *p*,
4. it is possible that *x* believes that it is obligatory that *p*,
5. it is possible that *x* believes that *x* acts in such a way that *p*, and
6. it is possible that *x* believes that it is possible that it is not the case that *x* acts in such a way that *p*.

Here you have an example of a relatively simple normative concept whose analysis turns out to be already quite complicated and demanding.

AFTERTHOUGHTS ON MORAL EDUCATION

What are the conclusions that we can draw from these metaethical considerations for moral education?

For me, as a confirmed non-cognitivist, prescriptive sentences in general and the prescriptive sentences of ethics, in particular, cannot be true or false in the original and literal sense of these words. Although these sentences cannot be true or false, there is, nevertheless, a logic for these sentences, and we can, therefore, criticize and justify them in a rational way. There can, therefore, be more or less rationality in prescriptive ethics, but there is no truth and no knowledge in the original and literal sense of these words in prescriptive ethics.

It is therefore merely *metaethics* but *not prescriptive ethics* which in my view – in contrast to the current widespread opinion – is suitable as subject matter to be taught in ethics courses at the university or higher classes of high school. Metaethics, however, seems to be not suitable as a subject matter for pupils under 14 years. What then about moral education for them or for elementary school and even kindergarten for which more and more people plead for moral education?

I am a layman in this area, and most of you are experts. Nevertheless, I dare to present briefly my amateurish view on this question. In what follows I will distinguish between *ethical instruction* in special classes and courses devoted to the teaching of ethics on the one hand and *moral education* in a school or another educational institution on the other hand. Moral education is a multifaceted task. It should – at least primarily – not consist in teaching certain ethical norms and values, but rather in imparting the competence to the pupils and to kids to develop their own moral and ethical views, in fostering the capacity of moral argumentation and criticism, and in making the necessary means for reaching these goals available to them.

One common means is the discussion of great moral examples from history and literature, of moral dilemmas, and of thought experiments. I think that this is an effective and advisable way of practicing moral education, although many of the examples dreamed up by ivory tower philosophers sound quite unrealistic if not silly to me.

The main aim of moral education, however, should consist in conveying to the young people the capacity to feel pity and pleasure for and with other beings, humans as well as animals. There is a modernistic word for it which I personally do not like but which nevertheless fits best what is meant: empathy. This seems to be the basic and most important capacity to be developed in moral education. Moral philosophers have used different metaphors when they refer in an abstract way to this capacity. Richard Hare (1963, p. 113), e.g., requires that, in making moral decisions, we must decide as if we were in the *shoes*, or even more drastically: in the *skin* of those who are affected by the decision. Moreover, John Rawls (1971) uses another metaphor, somehow from the other side, but with the same effect, when he requires judging about moral questions such as justice "under a veil of ignorance", i.e., as if we did not know in whose shoes or skin we are.

The development of empathy of the children and young people is in my view the most important goal of moral education. This, however, is not a task to be fulfilled by *one* teacher in a *special* course called 'Moral Education' and even less in a course on Ethics. It is a task in which the whole staff of teachers and educators of a school or another educational institution must participate.

Saying – as a layman – all this, I am aware that I am arguing against a current trend of my own profession, i.e., philosophy. Many representatives of my profession are happy about the current boom in moral education and in implanting more and more ethic classes on different educational levels because they hope that this development results in the creation of numerous jobs for the graduates of philosophy departments. Having been a member of a philosophy department myself for many years, I am rather skeptic whether a philosophy department of a university is the right place to educate moral educators. Philosophy departments are, in my view, the right places to educate teachers of ethics and in particular metaethics in higher classes of high schools. Philosophy departments are, however, in my view certainly not the places suited to educate moral educators, i.e., people who know how to develop empathy in young people and children. This is a very important task in which all members of the teaching staff of a school or another educational community should participate. This very task, however, does certainly not belong to the field of competence of a philosophy department, nor to its scope and duty.

Let me conclude with a little *manifesto* consisting of three recommendations.

First, there should be no moral instruction in any state-controlled educational institution, from kindergarten up to university! Every staff member of those educational institutions, however, should participate in the *moral education* of the children and young people they have been entrusted with, by being living examples themselves and by presenting appropriate examples from their various fields of expertise, be it history, literature, biology, whatsoever, even mathematics or physics.

Second, teaching *courses in ethics* is not advisable to young persons under an age of about 14. The main purpose of such courses is to convey the ability to assess different views of morality and prescriptive ethics critically and to develop one's own position within prescriptive ethics rationally. The methods of metaethics are indispensable in reaching this goal. Therefore, prescriptive ethics itself is not the subject matter, but merely the illustrative material to be dealt with in ethics classes; their real subject matter must be metaethics. At the forest, the methods of metaethics should be demonstrated *via* their application to concrete cases. (But please no "Trolley" or other silly examples, nor one of the great global problems such as the important but for didactic purposes too complex problem of refugees!) These should be developed explicitly and systematically only *after* the introduction of metaethical methods by way of example.

As for the *third* and last recommendation, addressed particularly to philosophy teachers of Austrian high schools: Please do not forget the main objective of philosophy classes at Austrian high schools. Their origin, tradition, and destination are completely different from the ones in other countries such as Germany. The subject matter of Austrian high school philosophy has always been described by the title "philosophical *propaedeutics*", and its main topic has been "*logical* propaedeutics" (cf. Morscher, 2016b). And so should it remain.

NOTES

[1] The lecture style of this text has been preserved. I would like to thank my friends Peter Simons and Guillaume Fréchette for improvements.

[2] Quine, 1960, pp. 157–190: Chapter V. Regimentation. From a regimented language it is only a small and marginal step to a formal or symbolic prescriptive language by using certain symbols as abbreviations of words. Since this additional step is merely marginal and not essential for the metaethical enterprise, I will not bother you with it.

[3] An example for the version with 'only' can be found in *Grundlegung zur Metaphysik der Sitten* (*Grounding for the Metaphysics of Morals*) BA 52, and three versiones without 'only' in BA 81 f.

[4] For a detailed reconstruction of Moore's argument see Morscher (2012a, pp. 69–76).

REFERENCES

Hare, R. M. (1963). *Freedom and reason.* Oxford: Clarendon.
Kanger, S. (2001). *Collected papers of Stig Kanger with essays on his life and work* (Vol. I, G. Holmström-Hintikka, S. Lindström, & R. Sliwinski, Eds.). Dordrecht: Reidel.
Morscher, E. (Ed.). (2004). *Was heißt es, ein Recht auf etwas zu haben? Stig und Helle Kangers Analyse der Menschenrechte* [What does it mean to have a right on something? Stig and Helle Kangers analysis of human rights]. Sankt Augustin: Academia Verlag.
Morscher, E. (2012a). *Normenlogik: Grundlagen – Systeme – Anwendungen* [Logic of norms: Fundamentals – systems – applications]. Paderborn: Mentis.
Morscher, E. (2012b). *Angewandte Ethik: Grundlagen – Probleme – Teilgebiete* [Applied ethics. Fundamentals – problems – branches]. Sankt Augustin: Academia Verlag.
Morscher, E. (2016a). The descriptive-normative dichotomy and the so called naturalistic fallacy. *Analyse & Kritik, 38*(2), 317–337.
Morscher, E. (2016b). Plädoyer für eine logische Propädeutik. In J. Mittelstraß (Ed.), *Paul Lorenzen und die konstruktive Philosophie* [Paul Lorenzen and the constructive philosophy] (pp. 121–132). Münster: Mentis.
Quine, W. V. O. (1960). *Word and object.* Cambridge, MA: MIT Press.
Rawls, J. (1971). *A theory of justice.* Cambridge, MA: Belknap Press.
Searle, J. R. (1975). A taxonomy of illocutionary acts. In K. Gunderson (Ed.), *Language, mind, and knowledge* (pp. 344–369). Minneapolis, MN: University of Minnesota Press.
Searle, J. R. (1979). *Expression and meaning: Studies in the theory of speech acts.* Cambridge: Cambridge University Press.

Edgar Morscher
Department of Philosophy
Faculty of Cultural & Social Sciences
University of Salzburg
Salzburg, Austria

FRITZ OSER AND HORST BIEDERMANN

3. THE PROFESSIONAL ETHOS OF TEACHERS

Is Only a Procedural Discourse Approach a Suitable Model?

DEPENDENCY AS THE MAIN SOURCE OF ETHOS

Why is reflecting on the necessity of the development of a professional ethos a major concern in both teacher education and everyday classroom teaching, and why is it not enough if teachers are persons of moral integrity? The concept of professional ethics is closely associated with the concept of dependency. Patients depend on medical specialists, children depend on professional instructors and someone who stimulates their learning, and, more broadly speaking, anyone who is not able to cope with a difficult situation or to produce something particular himself or herself depends on the skills and the specialized knowledge of the one who is in charge of such cases. Thus, professional ethics in a general sense means that dependent individuals can trust in specialists in a certain domain. These specialists are expected to do their best, to be available, to be accountable for their actions, to be a member of a controlling professional community, and to be qualified, i.e., to hold a certificate for the services they offer (see Höffe, 1977). This dependency is not absolute, however. Rather, it is situational and demand-specific. Teachers, for instance, are not completely responsible for a child, but their expertise is needed if teaching-learning processes are to be fostered. Furthermore, they should react appropriately to learning problems, learned helplessness, or exam anxiety, and they are supposed to counsel adolescents in their career decisions. Although students sometimes do not understand what their teachers are doing and why they are acting in an incomprehensible way, they still depend on them.

What is at stake in such situations can be illustrated by the following example: Two students did very well on a test. When handing back the examination sheets, the teacher comments on the first student's performance by saying "Excellent, as always", while the second student receives the feedback "You had a good day yesterday". Both students depend on this feedback. The teacher is kind to both of them (moral integrity), but there is nevertheless a decisive difference. In the first case, the teacher refers to internal and stable resources whereas in the latter case external and instable factors are adduced to explain the student's achievement. This is a typical situation that evidently exemplifies a lack of ethos. A highly developed professional ethos, by contrast, would have manifested itself in feedback that relates the performance of both students equally to internal and external as well as stable and instable factors.

Thus, although the teacher may be a person of moral integrity, the example indicates that something else is at stake. It is a situation in a specific setting in which only professionals can do the right or the good thing. Professional ethos therefore always involves a professional action and someone who depends on this action.

IF THE EXPERTS ARE WRONG

In an analysis of a classroom video from a vocational school, a group of educational experts judged the observed teacher's behavior to be utmost dysfunctional, the instruction to be pedagogically poor, and the subject of the lesson to be boring and not clearly defined. They deemed the teacher to be unqualified from a professional point of view, and they even suggested dismissing him because he seemed to be unable to reach his eighteen-year-old students and not to know how to stimulate their thinking processes and how to motivate them. Moreover, the teacher was sitting instead of standing. After posing a question, he did not wait for an answer but immediately answered himself. He asked the students for their opinion, but he never encouraged them to reflect on whether their contribution had been right or wrong. In view of this critical overall judgment, our research group was convinced to have identified an unequivocal and incontestable example of bad teaching.

For gaining additional data on this case, we had questioned the students about the quality of their teacher, first by means of an anonymous questionnaire and thereafter in an open discussion. Much to our surprise, the students expressed their enthusiasm about this teacher. According to their reports, the teacher never teases them, and he is never cynical. In exams, he never poses questions that had not been dealt with in class. He is very helpful and supports the students in finding a job. If they have a problem, they can even call him at night. These favorable and approving statements amounted to the following conclusion: "Don't say anything negative against him! He is our best teacher."

The example illustrates the complexity of evaluating the quality of teaching very clearly: the focus was on the behavior of one particular teacher, but the rating resulted in two completely different pictures. This raises the question as to which rating is accurate or, with a different accentuation, as to which rating is more important. In any case, it is necessary to consider both opinions seriously. At first sight, the students' view seems to be more important than the experts' judgment because they are the direct "subjects" of their teacher's actions. They assess the quality of his teaching in terms of how well he is able to initiate and support their learning, and regarding the extent to which he cares about them. But is it that simple? It seems that two contrasting "worlds" of complexity are involved: one is focused on the teaching as such (and pays only little attention to the students and their individual conditions) whereas the other refers to purpose and life (giving only little consideration to the teacher's knowledge of effective teaching).[1] From a descriptive point of view, both "worlds" or "syndromes of beliefs" are valuable, but from a normative perspective, they are both deemed deficient. Even though it may seem obvious to suggest that the two "worlds" should be integrated into one comprehensive picture, it is not that simple to conjoin them.

Taking this example as a paradigm, we can infer a two-profile model of professional ethos. On the one hand, there is a teacher's everyday teaching practice with its daily routines. On the other hand, there is something like a special ethical sensitivity that leads to a particular type of caring behavior. These aspects are distinct and should be kept apart.

SOME HELPFUL DISTINCTIONS

Professional Ethos and Professional Morality

Although teacher educators rarely distinguish between the concept of professional ethos and the concept of professional morality, we propose drawing the following distinction: professional ethos refers to a supererogatory attentiveness to the individuals one is in charge of and to their development whereas professional morality consists in an indispensable consideration of the results of a professional action. The former emphasizes core aspects like care, concern, and support in general. The latter rests on accountability and responsibility for the "production" of a particular outcome or for an immediate result of an action. Thus, a teacher's professional ethos manifests itself in caring about the development and the growth of a student while professional morality focuses on student learning and gives special weight to properly imparting the contents of the subject to be dealt with.

Discourse Morality and Social Responsibility

A second distinction should be drawn between discourse morality and social responsibility. The first concept refers to situations in which a student has been seriously offended or unjustly treated. In such situations, a teacher is required to do more than just instructing, motivating, and creating a positive atmosphere. Being aware of the critical situation, a teacher has to organize a round-table discussion in the course of which all the parties involved try to find a mutually acceptable resolution that strives for a balance between justice, care, and truthfulness (see Oser, 1998). Social responsibility, by contrast, refers to a general form of professional accountability. In this regard, teachers are supposed to support and encourage their students, to foster their learning processes, and to try to motivate them to help each other and to participate in the class community etc.

Moral and Non-Moral Elements

A third distinction concerns moral and non-moral elements of the discourse approach. Moral elements refer to the traditional issues mentioned above, that is justice, care, and truthfulness, which, however, may collide in certain situations. Being truthful

25

is often incompatible with being caring, and being caring does not necessarily mean being just. Especially in the case of conflicts with or among students, these moral elements take the form of necessary duties *sensu* Kant; but because they frequently contradict each other and clash, they must be balanced in a "realistic discourse" (Oser, 1998). One result of such a discourse is that all participants know about the imperfection of the solution but still accept it. Besides these moral elements, there are teaching-related, non-moral elements. Typical examples are an interruption of the usual flow of the work in class for summoning a round table, giving everybody a voice, interrelating student contributions, or insisting on fairness.

General Morality and a Sui Generis Professional Ethos

In the introduction, we commented on teachers of moral integrity who nevertheless lack a professional ethos. Teachers may be good and conforming citizens who pay taxes, love their children, and are kind to others. In more abstract terms, these characteristics consist in being morally sensitive, acting on a higher moral level, identifying with moral values, and believing in the centrality of these values. Yet all of these characteristics form merely a precondition for ethos. As mentioned above, ethos in teaching pertains to classroom management, the presentation of contents, grading, giving feedback, and to creating a warm classroom climate. Thus, it is possible to lead a highly moral life in general without possessing a professional ethos. Conversely, being not the best moral person in private life does not exclude that a teacher has a high professional ethos. A teacher's professional ethos can thus only be adequately judged if it is considered relative to concrete classroom situations and teaching actions. Furthermore, the general concept of ethos includes "the will to be fair, to be kind, to be honest, and the all-compassing will to show respect for others by having the courage to commit [oneself] to these and other virtues of responsibility and integrity" (Campbell, 2003, p. 29). It is important, however, to keep in mind that these characteristics may be completely different in everyday life and in professional contexts (see also Ziegler, 2016, pp. 117ff.).

CONTRASTS: BAD DEFINITIONS

In the literature, concepts like "ethos", "engagement", "commitment", or "concern" shape the discussion on what an ethical teacher should be like. In most cases, the terminological distinctions and the conceptual deliberations are not precise enough, however. Pusateri (2012), for instance, provides the following definition of ethical teachers:

> Ethical teachers habitually reflect on their teaching effectiveness and actively seek professional development opportunities that increase their mastery and repertoire of teaching pedagogies and methods of assessing student learning. Ethical teachers also view their teaching in the context of a broader program

of study and collaborate with colleagues in ways that promote individual and institutional academic freedom. (Pusateri, 2012, p. 9)

What Pusateri describes is what all teachers normally do – or should do – most of the time, drawing on their professional knowledge. So where does the notion of ethos come in? It seems to be too simple and very easy to state that each action of a teacher can somehow be deemed ethical or relates to ethos without explaining how ethos and a particular action are connected as, for example, Jackson, Boostrom, and Hansen (1993) do. This approach does not get us anywhere. Rather, we must develop a concept that allows distinguishing ethos from general professional skills, work-related motivation, or a professional's daily practice.

A similarly vague and broadly conceived notion of professional ethos forms the conceptual basis of the project "Democratic Ethical Educational Leadership" (DEEL; Gross & Shapiro, 2016). Its basic concept of the ethical character of a teacher includes a wide variety of aspects as the following examples show: a teacher "has a guided inner sense of responsibility to students, faculty, staff, families, the community and social development on a world scale", "leads from an expansive community-building perspective", "dares as democratic leader to shield the community from turbulences", "integrates the concept of democracy, social justice and school reform through scholarship, dialogue and action", "operates from a deep understanding of ethical decision-making in a context of a dynamic, inclusive, democratic vision", "sees [his or her] career as a calling" etc. (Gross & Shapiro, 2016, p. 7, referring to Gross, 2009). In their book, which "flows directly from our mission and the scholarship our New DEEL community has done over the past decade ..." (Gross & Shapiro, 2016, p. 9), Gross and Shapiro (2016) compile instances of these normative posits. We do not consider this compilation of good intentions to be wrong, but in our opinion this approach is somewhat fuzzy from a normative point of view, and it does not provide a suitable basis for a concrete operationalization. Without subscribing to a clearly defined schema of what professional actions should be like, it is easy to claim what teachers ought to do.

Trying to capture the concept in more definite terms, we propose an account that defines a teacher's professional ethos as a specific competence with at least four elements: (1) ability to act responsibly in a difficult situation (not necessarily or only in terms of learning), being accountable, and being caring; (2) supporting, helping, and fostering others in awkward situations without thinking of one's own profit, but rather with the intention of establishing a balance between what is believed to be good or right and what is necessary for creating the conditions for achieving what is believed to be good or right; (3) scaffolding of learners; and (4) being accurate as regards the contents to be taught.

ETHOS – THE REALISTIC-DISCOURSE APPROACH

As mentioned above, adopting a discourse-oriented approach means that discourse is used as an instrument for overcoming an unjust, hurtful, humiliating, degrading, or in whatever way morally problematic situation (see Forster-Heinzer, 2015; Oser, 1994, 1998).[2] For the purpose of illustration, we give an example that we often use for assessing teachers with respect to their discourse-related skills:

> John is 16 years old. His behavior provokes not only the teacher but also his classmates. He is regularly late for school, disrupts the ongoing teaching process and makes negative comments. His reactions to the teacher's instructions are aggressive, and he seldom completes the assignments he has been given. His academic performance is lousy, and his grades are very bad, although in principle he would have the capability to succeed. Because he vents his aggression on his classmates, nobody wants to sit next to him. During the breaks, he behaves like a criminal.
>
> Mr. Brown, John's teacher, has already tried various things: personal conversations after school, special efforts to increase John's motivation in class, involvement of the parents, and diverse forms of punishment. As the end of compulsory education is approaching, John has applied for an apprenticeship as a car mechanic. One evening, the master mechanic Mr. Smith calls Mr. Brown and asks for a reference because apart from John there are many other applicants for the position. What is Mr. Brown to answer?

This problem can only be resolved through what we call a "realistic discourse" in which the duty elements *care, truthfulness,* and *justice* are adequately balanced – and this is exactly what poses the challenge: if Mr. Brown is caring, he cannot tell the truth and is thus not truthful with Mr. Smith; if he tells the truth, he is not caring; and if he recommends John, he causes an unjust or unfair situation for the other applicants. Finding a way to resolve this dilemma requires a discursive process in which all the parties involved are present and directly confronted with each other. All participants are given a voice and make an effort to balance the diverging points of view. Such a process consists of four procedural steps or, as we also call them, decisions (see Figure 1): (1) The first decision has to be made by the teacher and concerns the identification of the type of problem. (2) In a second step, the teacher decides to assume responsibility and organizes a round-table discussion. (3) The third and most difficult step consists in inviting all the parties involved to lay their issues on the table and to verbalize their needs and expectations. By discussing, structuring, and coordinating the individual standpoints, the teacher thereafter tries to mediate between the conflicting perspectives and to arrive at a solution that is acceptable to all participants. This solution is not necessarily the best, but it is the one the parties involved have searched for, developed, and eventually approved in a joint effort. Through actively engaging in this process, they all have taken their share of the overall responsibility. (4) After having reached this mutual consent, the fourth step supposes the participants to commit themselves to the solution and to act accordingly.

Against the background of the theoretical outline of the realistic-discourse approach, the question arises as to what teachers actually do if they are concretely

THE PROFESSIONAL ETHOS OF TEACHERS

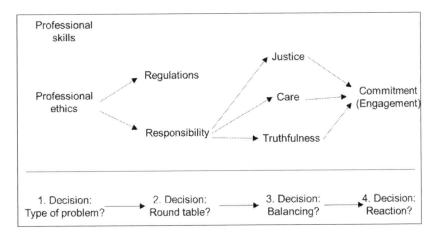

Figure 1. Model of the realistic-discourse approach (Oser, 1998)

faced with such a problem or dilemma. We have empirical evidence that supports the assumption that there are at least five types of reaction (see Oser, 1994, p. 105ff.):

- The first type manifests itself an *avoiding behavior*. Teachers are likely to react in this way if they do not believe that a realistic discourse is possible. They think that there is no need to take action and that there would be no way of sharing the responsibility with those who are immediately involved. Rather, they tend to ignore the implications and possible further consequences of the problem. Even awareness of the risk of violating a moral principle does not lead to a reconsideration of the options so that nothing changes.
- The second type of reaction can be characterized as a *delegating or security-seeking behavior*. The new element here is that awareness of the problem leads to the insight that something must be done to solve it. At the same time, however, the teacher believes that the school board, the state curriculum maker, the supervisor, or some other authority is in a better position to settle the conflict and therefore tries to alert these authorities.
- The third type is *unilateral or "single-handed" decision-making*, in which the teacher is aware of the moral dimension and also willing to take action but reacts intuitively without entering into a discourse.
- The fourth type is called *"incomplete discourse"* because the teacher is aware of what is at stake, tries to find a solution, and thus takes the risk that follows from an active intervention. In an effort to resolve the problematic situation, the teacher talks to the parties involved and helps the students understand why a particular decision has been made.
- The fifth and last type, representing the *complete-discourse approach*, (a) enables the students to have a voice and to express their feelings and thoughts when they

feel victimized by the careless, unjust, or untruthful behavior of someone else; including the teacher; (b) seeks a solution that serves the interests of all parties involved in the best way possible; (c) presupposes an adequate understanding of the problem and the capacity to participate actively in attempts to solve it; and (d) involves decisions that have been developed in a discursive process. This discourse is open, considerate of feelings and needs, and aims to reach a social equilibrium regarding both the participants and the issues discussed.

When this typology is applied for research purposes, the number of teachers who can be assigned to one of the five types depends on the concrete content of the video vignette we are looking at. That is to say, we found an interaction between person and situation with respect to the strategies teachers use in conflict situations (see Patry, this volume). Therefore, this empirically grounded typology of reactions does not describe personal traits but rather a state in the sense of a competence or skill.

Further empirical results indicate that discourse-oriented teachers tend to proceed rather slowly in their efforts to find a solution. In other words, this means that discourse-oriented teachers usually do not achieve immediate success (or, conversely, do not make hasty or impetuous decisions) in such dilemma situations. All the same, everybody knows about their trustworthiness and the willingness to strive for a morally satisfying solution if a critical incident occurs (see Oser, 1998). The slow-moving nature of the mediation process is a consequence of the necessary steps teachers have to take when they act in a discourse-oriented way. The first and most important step, which needs to be taken straight away though, consists in judging a situation to be serious: someone suffers unjustly, and this has to be stopped (see the stop-and-change model proposed by Oser, 2015). For initiating the problem-solving process, the teacher interrupts the daily routines and arranges a round-table discussion whose participants can be a group of two, four or more persons, a whole class, a school, etc. All the parties concerned are emphatically and in a normatively unconditioned way invited to participate actively in the discourse, always presupposing (as a fundamental "trust-in-advance belief") that everyone is in principle able to balance justice, care, and truthfulness. The most difficult task is thereafter to ensure that all individuals at the round table get the feeling of being part of the discourse group and have a voice. The final step consists in accepting a solution even if it is not the best one (procedural morality). Another research result revealed that student ratings of aspects like interpersonal respect, commitment, teaching skills, justice, truthfulness, and general wellbeing are higher for discourse-oriented teachers than for teachers who are not discourse-oriented.[3]

The realistic-discourse model has established itself in the context of teacher education and has been introduced and imparted in training programmes. Intervention studies with video clips led to a highly significant increase in the participating teachers' discourse orientation after three months of training (see Zutavern, 2001).

LIMITS OF THE DISCOURSE MODEL

The realistic-discourse model applies to serious situations in which a student who is in the charge of a teacher (or of another person in general) is unjustly treated and severely hurt in his or her bodily or cognitive-emotional integrity. The aim of the model consists in providing effective guidelines for stopping negative behavior and inducing change. In this context, ethos amounts to the commitment to striving for a "positive" solution.

Recalling the two paradigmatic situations presented above (the bad versus highly rated teacher in the first example, and John and his teacher Mr. Brown in the second example), it becomes clear that their basic structure is not the same. The first example is about care and concern in general. Such situations do not necessarily require the arrangement of a round-table discussion. The second example, by contrast, is situation-specific in the sense that the resolution of the conflict necessitates a discursive approach. If we are interested in investigating such situations empirically, what should be measured in the first case? One option might be that students are asked to rate their teacher's work by means of scales and rating items that cover aspects like helpfulness, support, encouragement, help in overcoming loneliness and coping with identity issues, intervention when a student is excluded from the peer group or class community, establishment of positive relationships, etc. As regards the second case, measurements could be based on the presentation of conflicts or tensions and asking teachers in what way the problem could be solved. This approach would shed some light on how they react holistically when they are required to search for a practicable solution to an authentic conflict situation that allows returning to the usual classroom routines and activities. Thus, in the first case measurement is competence-oriented and in the second case performance-oriented.

The limits of the second, i.e., the discourse-oriented approach are a consequence of the fact that without the occurrence of emergency situations nothing can be said about a teacher's ethos. That is to say that the richness of the concept can solely be grasped in exceptional situations in which the question as to what should be done is crucial and the related efforts become manifest. In brief, this means that the dimensions of a teachers' professional ethos are always tied to the actual problem. The extent of professional ethos is therefore contingent on the courage a teacher needs to intervene actively in critical situations. As for the first approach, we undeniably have to take further pertinent dimensions into account. Ethos relates not only to frictions between persons in a given system but also includes aspects like general professional anxiety, profession-related feelings of helplessness, inner doubts, insecurities, demotivation, fear of joblessness, lacking self-acceptance, etc.

Despite their methodological differences, both approaches are grounded in the following premise: there is always a person who is determined to change a problematic situation for the better. The ensuing actions rest on the commitment to resolve a conflict and can be justified by responsibility claims that, in turn, are related to specificities of the profession. In her book *The challenge to care in schools*,

Noddings (1992) refers to earlier work and summarizes her thoughts as follows: "I described the state of consciousness of the carer (or 'one-caring') as characterized by engrossment and displacement. By engrossment I mean an open, nonselective receptivity for the cared-for" (Noddings, 1992, p. 15). A decade later, she writes:

> An ethic of care does not eschew logic and reasoning. When we care, we must employ reasoning to decide what to do and how best to do it. We strive for competence because we want to do our best for those we care. But reason is not what motivates us. It is feeling with and for the other what motivates us in natural caring. In ethical caring, this feeling is subdued, and so it must be augmented by a feeling for our own ethical selves. (Noddings, 2002, p. 14)

Summing up our deliberations on the two examples and the implications for empirical research, we can conclude that the concept of professional ethos in both types of situation hinges on a person who takes appropriate action (usually under critical circumstances), on accountability and care but also on the willingness to support, help, encourage, and guide others in difficult situations without thinking of one's own profit. Moreover, the concept includes the effort to attain a balance between what is believed to be good and the necessary measures to create the conditions for what is believed to be good. The two research approaches set forth above (first approach: scales, rating of ethos-specific items; second approach: contextually situated performance testing) provide a gateway to accessing and capturing the concept of professional ethos empirically. This implies that the discourse approach provides only one means of understanding and measuring ethos.

For the purpose of a conceptual comparison, we now proceed to present further concepts of ethos that have been proposed and discussed in the literature.

EIGHT COMMON CONCEPTS OF ETHOS

A review of the literature on ethos that builds on the Aristotelian concept of ethos[4] leads to the identification of eight different conceptions and corresponding research streams. Two of them have already been introduced above, namely the general-care approach, which associates ethos with concern, commitment, and caring behavior (Noddings, 1992; Veugelers, 2011), and the realistic-discourse model (Forster-Heinzer, 2015; Oser, 1998; Zutavern, 2001). Both conceptions regard ethos as a complementary facet of a teacher's professional competence in general. In addition to what we teach and to what we know about teaching, ethos is something that can be acquired and developed through social engagement, which presumes a different set of skills.

Besides, there are further concepts of ethos that we briefly outline (the references are selected and therefore only examples):

- *Ethos as an essential part of the "moral life in schools"* (Jackson et al., 1993). This concept rests on the assumption that it does not make sense to distinguish between two groups of teachers, characterized by the presence or absence of ethos. Instead, there is only one professional community in which the ethical dimension is always fully embedded and invariably forms an integral part of it. The reason for this basic assumption is "that all judgments of a person's conduct are ultimately moral in the sense of being based on a conception what ought to be. They imply a standard of goodness or its opposite against which a comparison has been made. Teachers communicate those comparative judgments by words and deeds in terms that leave no doubt of the worthiness or unworthiness of what the student has done" (Jackson et al., 1993, p. 11). According to this concept, each single choice of teaching methods, each feedback, each selection of contents, and each way of presenting these contents etc. includes a responsibility issue that calls for moral sensitivity to what professionals ought to do when they perform their duties.

- *Moral identity and sensibility as indications of ethos* (e.g., Blasi, 1984; Edelstein, Nunner-Winkler, & Noam, 1993; Jackson et al., 1993; Krettenauer & Hertz, 2015; Lapsly & Stey, 2014; Tirri, 2008). In this conception, the self and morality are supposed to form an integral whole and thus regarded as a unity. An implication of this assumption is that striving for one's own goals and striving to advance the goals of others are reconciled (Walker & Frimer, 2006). This concept is purely theoretical, however, because it has not been applied to a specific profession – the teaching profession for instance – yet. What needs to be shown is that certain conditions for professional growth can foster the development of a professional moral self. One possible approach could build on the presumption that moral sensitivity, unlike moral identity, establishes a link to external situations. Hence it is conceivable that moral identity or its effects manifest themselves in sensible reactions to ethically problematic situations, which would provide a starting point for empirical explorations.

- *Moral judgments and value judgments as an expression of ethos* (e.g., Bauer & Prenzel, 2016; Biedermann & Oser, 2016; Coklar, 2012; Harder, 2014). This concept is mostly used in large-scale models that focus on several dimensions of one particular aspect of a teacher's ethos and relate them to different actions. An operationalization of such models could include, among others, the following scales: moral accountability; moral-related professional motivation; courage needed to realize moral decisions (Hamburger, Baumert, & Schmitt, 2015); intentions to take action that rest on moral considerations; coping with moral shortcomings and inadequacies. All these scales must of course specifically relate to teaching as a profession (or to some other profession).

- *Ethos as a systemic concept that classifies social structures as just or unjust and thus holds them responsible for injustice* (e.g., Berliner, 2009; Durkheim, 1925/1961; Heid, 1991, 2017; Nucci & Powers, 2014). Three elements are essential to this concept: (a) a sense of obligation (Nisan, 1987),

(b) a common norm system manifested in shared values (Kohlberg, 1984; Luterbacher & Oser, 2013; Power, 1979; Wehrlin, 2009), and (c) a positive social climate (e.g., Hascher & Hagenauer, 2011).
- *Leadership as an outer manifestation of ethos* (Leightwood & Louis, 2012; Sergiovanni, 1992; Starratt, 2004). This concept refers to the idea of moral role models (Colby & Damon, 1992). Katzenmeyer and Moller (2011) define this kind of leadership by listing the following characteristics: "teachers lead within and beyond the classroom; identify and contribute to a community of teacher learners and leaders; influence others toward educational practice; and accept responsibility for achieving the outcomes of their leadership" (Katzenmeyer & Moller, 2011, p. 6; see also the research group associated with Walker, 2000).
- *Ethos as a type of code-oriented behavior* (Strike & Soltis, 1985). A prototypical example of such a code is – besides the Hippocratic Oath taken by physicians – the code of the National Education Association in the United States that stipulates, for instance, that teachers should "not deliberately suppress or distort subject matter relevant to the student's progress" (cited in Strike & Soltis, 1985, p. 7). Adhering to such codes means to understand the teaching process as an act of transforming generalizable and universally acknowledged norms into concrete actions in the classroom. One vital prerequisite for doing so is the acceptance of the United Nations' Convention on the Rights of the Child from 1989 (ratified by Germany in 1992; see Krappmann & Petry, 2016).

Most of the other conceptions that are discussed in the literature as well, conceiving ethos as a guiding attitude, a manner of teaching (Fenstermacher, 1992), or as a vision (Campbell, 2003), can be associated with one of the approaches listed above. Very frequently cited older and classical concepts of ethos are those developed by Sergiovanni (1992), Goodlad, Soder, and Sirotnik (1990) or Oser, Dick, and Patry (1992). According to Goodlad (1990), apart from well-developed content-related knowledge and teaching skills "full recognition of teaching in schools as a profession depends on teachers, individually and collectively, demonstrating the awareness of and commitment to the burdens of judgment that go with a moral enterprise" (p. 30). It is possible to assign this approach to the first model that sees ethos as an exceptional professional competence in addition to the general teaching skills. It is worth mentioning, however, that this view has not yet found its way into in teacher training programs, at least not in a systematic way.

In conclusion, we can state that all conceptions – irrespective of their varying theoretical assumptions and perspectives – emphasize the traditional call of duty that requires teachers to do the necessary good for the students and thus to show virtue. In adopting this stance, the conceptions implicitly share the belief that ethos helps generate happiness in the sense of Aristotle (1968), which leads us to the subject of the next section.

HAPPINESS RESULTING FROM PROFESSIONAL ETHOS: A POISONED GIFT?

Professional satisfaction (Landert, 2014) is one of the most clear-cut dimensions of the development of teaching quality. As a central hypothesis, we assume that the most positive effect in this regard can be ascribed to a teacher's ethos. The meta-analysis by Gkolia, Belias, and Koustelios (2014) on job satisfaction in the teaching profession identified three important aspects: first, job satisfaction is always treated as a dependent variable; second, a high extent of professional self-efficacy correlates positively with satisfaction; and third, "[a] promising direction for future research is to test through empirical research whether teachers who are satisfied with their job and have high self-efficacy have a better impact on students' performance" (Gkolia et al., 2014, p. 333). This is the positive side of the story. It should be kept in mind, however, that issues like burnout, disengagement, and demotivation in the teaching profession and thus the opposite of job satisfaction are also intensely treated in the literature and regarded as a matter of grave concern. So, if the above hypothesis is right, how can we bring ethos and professional satisfaction together? And is having a professional ethos also a relevant factor in overcoming the negative aspects of the teaching profession?

Making reference to Aristotle (1968), a first distinction can be drawn between happiness and satisfaction. It seems to us that the notion of satisfaction is more adequate for describing and analyzing the professional field than the notion of happiness. First of all, being happy is something that is not associated with a concrete action whereas being satisfied results from evaluating a completed task and deeming oneself and one's performance to be something important, which implies a relation to a purpose. Second, we believe that doing the right thing (see again Aristotle, 1968) leads to satisfaction, even if a teacher feels tired and exhausted after school. In our opinion, satisfaction is more important than happiness and also more important than being successful in merely functional respects. Satisfaction is grounded in knowing that we have done everything possible in order to fulfill our duties.

Furthermore, satisfaction is not something one can strive for. Teachers can strive for good teaching, for being a caring, helpful, supportive, and concerned mentor – but they cannot strive for satisfaction as such. Satisfaction (like sovereignty) is only a by-product of their actions, though an important one. The attainment of professional satisfaction is highly probable if teachers possess a well-developed ethos. This connection between ethos and satisfaction can also be explored with the instruments of empirical research. It is possible, for instance, to measure the extent of satisfaction – understood as a result of the work and the tasks that have been accomplished in and beyond the classroom – retrospectively by means of regression analyses. In this approach, satisfaction acts as an indirect measure of teaching quality. At the same time, this implies that we should recall what philosophers point out: "virtue – without being identical to or a cause for it – is meaningful with respect to happiness. All the same, neither is virtue happiness nor does virtue generate happiness" (Höffe, 2007, p. 176, translated by Oser).

In summary, ethos that is discernible in actions like those described above leads to satisfaction, especially under conditions of tension. In his popular book on "authentic happiness", Seligman (2002) suggests that we should not strive for satisfaction. Rather, we should try to realize what he calls "signature strengths". Taking this perspective, a teacher may conclude at the end of the week that the work included routine very much and was somehow boring but still think something along the following lines: "I supported one student in a very effective way. I kept another from taking drugs again. And, not least, I discovered a new form of student participation. This is positive, and that's why I feel satisfied." Teachers of this type possess a professional ethos that becomes manifest in what they do and in what they deem important. Thus, the concept of professional ethos consists in the ability to notice what is beneficial to the wellbeing of every individual student attended to and to act accordingly in one's everyday professional practice.

NOTES

[1] Educational psychology often distinguishes between three dimensions of teaching: (a) content, (b) teaching process, and (c) student learning. This, however, is exactly not what we mean. Many good pedagogues care about student learning, but they do not care about the students themselves. This is a considerable difference.

[2] We refer neither to Habermas' idealized model of practical discourse nor to his concept of the ideal speech situation in which reason ("Vernunft") is called for, the highest moral level is at stake, and the better argument is always acknowledged (see Habermas, 1985, 1991; Apel, 1988). Instead, we opt for a concept that locates the parties involved at lower level of moral judgment. In our conception, the participants express their feelings of injustice, and the better argument is often rejected or may be adopted only in a long-term discursive process.

[3] In certain cases, this finding also applies to teachers with an avoidance behavior, presumably because students at a certain age prefer teachers who do not interfere in their personal affairs and problems.

[4] Aristotle (1968) discusses two meanings of "ethos": (1) habit, convention, or custom; (2) knowledge of the necessary good in a concrete situation.

REFERENCES

Apel, K.-O. (1988). *Diskurs und Verantwortung: Das Problem des Übergangs zur postkonventionellen Moral*. [Discourse and responsibility. The problem of the transition to postconventional morality]. Frankfurt: Suhrkamp.

Aristotle. (1968). *Hauptwerke* [Main works] (W. Nestle, Trans. & Intro.). Stuttgart: Kröner.

Bauer, J., & Prenzel, M. (2016, January). *Erfassung von Lehrerethos in Large-Scale-Studien: Befunde zu Erziehungszielen Lehramtsstudierender* [Evaluation of teacher ethos in large scale studies: Educational goals of pre-service teachers]. Paper presented at the Symposium "Ethos of teachers: A core-competence of professional teachers?", Otto-Friedrich-University Bamberg, Bamberg, Germany.

Beck, K. (2016). Individuelle Moral und Beruf: eine Integrationsaufgabe für die Ordnungsethik. In G. Minnameier (Ed.), *Ethik und Beruf* [Ethics and occupation] (pp. 41–54). Bielefeld: Bertelsmann.

Berliner, D. C. (2009). The incompatibility of high-stakes testing and the development of skills for the 21st century. In R. Marzanno (Ed.), *On excellence in teaching*. Bloomington, IN: Solution Tree Press.

Biedermann, H., & Oser, F. (2016, April). *Do teachers know what students are doing? Teachers' professional information and communication technology responsibility*. Paper presented at the annual meeting of the American Educational Research Association (AERA), Washington, DC.

Blasi, A. (1984). Moral identity: Its role in moral functioning. In W. M. Kurtines & J. L. Gewirtz (Eds.), *Morality, moral behavior, and moral development* (pp. 129–139). New York, NY: Wiley.

Campbell, E. (2003). *The ethical teacher*. Maidenhead, PA: Open University Press.

Çoklar, A. N. (2012). ICT Ethical Leadership Scale (ICTELS): A study of reliability and validity on Turkish preservice teachers. *International Journal of Human Sciences, 9*(1), 82–101.

Colby, A., & Damon, W. (1992). *Some do care: Contemporary lives of moral commitment*. New York, NY: The Free Press.

Durkheim, E. (1925/1961). *Moral education*. New York, NY: The Free Press.

Edelstein, W., Nunner-Winkler, G., & Noam, G. (1993). *Moral und Person* [Morality and individual]. Frankfurt: Suhrkamp.

Fenstermacher, G. D. (1992). The concepts of method and manner in teaching. In F. Oser, A. Dick, & J.-L. Patry (Eds.), *Effective and responsible teaching: The new synthesis* (pp. 95–108). San Francisco, CA: Jossey-Bass.

Forster-Heinzer, S. (2015). *Against all odds: An empirical study about the situative pedagogical ethos of vocational trainers*. Rotterdam, The Netherlands: Sense Publishers.

Gkolia, A., Belias, D., & Koustelios, A. (2014). Teacher's job satisfaction and self-efficacy: A review. *European Scientific Journal, 10*(22), 321–342.

Goodlad, J. I. (1990). The occupation of teaching in schools. In J. I. Goodlad., R. Soder, & K. A. Sirotnik, (Eds.), *The moral dimensions of teaching* (pp. 3–34). San Francisco, CA: Jossey-Bass.

Goodlad, J. I., Soder, R., & Sirotnik, A. (Eds.). (1990). *The moral dimensions of teaching*. San Francisco, CA: Jossey-Bass.

Gross, S. J. (2009). (Re)constructing a movement for social justice in our profession. In A. H. Normore (Ed.), *Leadership for social justice: Promoting equity and excellence through inquiry and reflective practice* (pp. 257–266). Charlotte, NC: Information Age.

Gross, S. J., & Shapiro, J. P. (2016). *Democratic ethical educational leadership*. New York, NY: Routledge.

Habermas, J. (1985). Moral und Sittlichkeit: Hegels Kantkritik im Lichte der Diskursethik [Morality and ethical life: The critics of Hegel on Kant in light of the discourse ethics]. *Merkur, 39*(12), 1041–1052.

Habermas, J. (1991). *Erläuterungen zur Diskursethik* [Explanations to the discourse ethics]. Frankfurt: Suhrkamp.

Hamburger, A., Baumert, A., & Schmitt, M. (2015). Anger as driving factor of moral courage in comparison with guilt and global mood: A multimethod approach. *European Journal of Social Psychology, 45,* 39–51.

Harder, P. (2014). *Werthaltungen und Ethos von Lehrern* [Values and ethos of teachers]. Bamberg: University of Bamberg Press.

Hascher, T., & Hagenauer, G. (2011). Schulisches Wohlbefinden im Jugendalter: Verläufe und Einflussfaktoren. In A. Ittel, H. Merkens, & L. Stecher (Eds.), *Jahrbuch Jugendforschung 2010* [Yearbook on research in adolescents 2010] (pp. 15–45). Wiesbaden: Springer VS.

Heid, H. (1991). Problematik einer Erziehung zur Verantwortungsbereitschaft [The difficulty of education for responsibility]. *Neue Sammlung, 31*(3), 459–481.

Heid, H. (2017). *Gerechtigkeit* [Justice]. Forschungsgruppe Berlin. (Unpublished manuscript)

Höffe, O. (1977). Stichwort Ethos. In O. Höffe (Ed.), *Lexikon der ethik* [Encyclopedia on ethics] (pp. 19–20). München: Beck.

Höffe, O. (2007). *Lebenskunst und Moral: Oder macht Tugend glücklich?* [The art of living and morality: Or, makes virtue happy?]. München: Beck.

Jackson, P. W., Boostrom, R. E., & Hansen, D. T. (1993). *The moral live of schools*. San Francisco, CA: Jossey-Bass.

Katzenmeyer, M., & Moller, G. (2011). Understanding teacher leadership. In E. B. Hilty (Ed.), *Teacher leadership: The "new" foundations of teacher education* (pp. 3–21). New York, NY: Peter Lang.

Kohlberg, L. (1984). *The psychology of moral development* (Essays on Moral Development, Vol. 2). San Francisco, CA: Harper & Row.

Krappmann, L. (2016). Kinderrechte, Demokratie und Schule: Ein Manifest. In L. Krappmann & C. Petry (Eds.), *Worauf Kinder und Jugendliche ein Recht haben* [The rights of children and adolscents] (pp. 17–65). Schwalbach: Debus.

Krettenauer, T., & Hertz, S. (2015). What develops in moral identities? A critical review. *Human Development, 58*, 137–153.
Landert, C. (2014). *Die Berufszufriedenheit der Deutschschweizer Lehrerinnen und Lehrer: Bericht zur vierten Studie des Dachverbandes Lehrerinnen und Lehrer Schweiz (LCH)* [Job satisfaction of German-Swiss teachers]. Zürich: Landert Brägger Partner.
Lapsly, D. K., & Stey, P. C. (2014). Moral self-identity as the aim of education. In L. D. Narvaez & T. Krettenauer (Eds.), *Handbook of moral and character education* (pp. 84–100). New York, NY: Routledge.
Leightwood, K., & Louis, K. S. (2012). *Linking leadership to student learning*. San Francisco, CA: Jossey-Bass.
Luterbacher, M., & Oser, F. (2013). *"Together is better!": Evaluation eines Just-Community-Programms auf der Sekundarstufe I* (Forschungsbericht Nr. 37) [Evaluation of a just community project]. Luzern: Pädagogische Hochschule Zentralschweiz, Hochschule Luzern.
Nisan, M. (1987). Sense of obligation as a motivational factor in school. In V. Last (Ed.), *Psychological work in school*. Jerusalem: Magnes Press.
Noddings, N. (1992). *The challenge to care in schools: An alternative approach to education*. New York, NY: Teachers College Press.
Noddings, N. (2002). *Educating moral people: A caring alternative to character education*. New York, NY: Teachers College Press.
Nucci, L., & Powers, D. (2014). Social cognitive domain theory and moral education. In L. Nucci, D. Narvaez, & T. Krettenauer (Eds.), *Handbook of moral and character education* (2nd ed., pp. 121–139). New York, NY: Routledge.
Oser, F. (1994). Moral perspectives in teaching. *Review of Research in Education, 20*(1), 57–128.
Oser, F. (1998). *Ethos – die Vermenschlichung des Erfolgs: Zur Psychologie der Berufsmoral von Lehrpersonen* [Ethos – the humanization of success: On the psychology of the professional ethics of teachers]. Opladen: Leske+Budrich.
Oser, F. (2015). Moral change is not a birthday journey: The stop-and-change model of moral education. In B. Zisek, D. Garz, & E. Nowak (Eds.), *Kohlberg revisited: Moral development and citizenship education* (pp. 169–186). Rotterdam, The Netherlands: Sense Publishers.
Oser, F., Dick, A., & Patry, J.-L. (Eds.). (1992). *Effective and responsible teaching: The new synthesis*. San Francisco, CA: Jossey-Bass.
Power, F. C. (1979). *The moral atmosphere of a just community high school: A four-year longitudinal study* (Doctoral dissertation). Harvard Graduate School of Education, Cambridge, MA.
Pusateri, T. P. (2012). Teaching ethically: Ongoing improvement, collaboration and academic freedom. In R. E. Landrum & M. A. McCarty (Eds.), *Teaching ethically: Challenges and opportunities* (pp. 9–20). Washington, DC: APA.
Seligman, M. (2002). *Authentic happiness*. New York, NY: Atria.
Sergiovanni, D. J. (1992). *Moral leadership*. San Francisco, CA: Jossey-Bass.
Starratt, R. J. (2004). *Ethical leadership*. San Francisco, CA: Jossey-Bass.
Strike, K. A., & Soltis, J. F. (1985). *The ethics of teaching*. New York, NY: Teachers College Press.
Tirri, K. (Ed.). (2008). *Educating moral sensibilities in urban schools*. Rotterdam, The Netherlands: Sense Publishers.
Tirri, K. (2008). Introduction. In K. Tirri (Ed.), *Educating moral sensibilities in urban schools* (pp. ix–xv). Rotterdam, The Netherlands: Sense Publishers.
Veugelers, W. (2011). *Education and humanism*. Rotterdam, The Netherlands: Sense Publishers.
Walker, L. (2000). Choosing biases, using power and practising resistance: Moral development in a world without certainty. *Human Development, 43*, 135–156.
Walker, L. J., & Frimer, J. A. (2006). *Moral personality of brave and caring exemplars*. Vancouver: University of British Columbia.
Wehrlin, J. (2009). *Shared cooperation: On the amount and the meaning of shared cooperation norms of teachers in primary school* (Unpublished dissertation). University of Fribourg, Fribourg.
Ziegler, B. (2016). Berufswahl und Berufsmoral. In G. Minnameier (Ed.), *Ethik und Beruf* [Ethics and occupation] (pp. 109–132). Bielefeld: Bertelsmann.

Zutavern, M. (2001). *Professionelles Ethos von Lehrerinnen und lehrern: Berufsmoralisches Denken, Wissen und Handeln zum Schutz und zur Förderung von Schülerinnen und Schülern* [Professional ethos of teachers: Professional moral thinking, knowledge and action for the protection and promotion of pupils] (Unpublished dissertation). University of Fribourg, Fribourg.

Fritz Oser
University of Fribourg
Fribourg, Switzerland

Horst Biedermann
Universtiy of Teacher Education of St. Gallen
St. Gallen, Switzerland

JEAN-LUC PATRY

4. SITUATION SPECIFICITY OF DISCOURSE

INTRODUCTION

Hartshorne and May (1928, 1929; Hartshorne, May, & Shuttleworth, 1930) showed for honesty that "the most striking thing about the conduct of school children is the amount of inconsistency exhibited" (Hartshorne & May, 1930, p. 755); this result of empirical research refuted their original hypothesis that by "virtue of past experiences, or heredity, or both, the individual may be more or less permanently predisposed to make an honest or dishonest response in situations involving this type of conduct" (May & Hartshorne, 1926, p. 147), and however critical one might evaluate this research methodologically or disagree on philosophical grounds with its outcomes (e.g., Croom, 2014; Mower, 2013; Slingerland, 2011), one can hardly contest the empirical evidence that moral behavior is situation specific (Doris, 1998). However, situation specificity does not mean situationism, i.e., the concept, that behavior is purely (or mainly) dependent on the situations (see, for instance, Mischel, 2004). The question to be addressed in this chapter is what situation specificity means for discourse in education, namely dealing with problems in the interaction with the partners based on equal participation and shared responsibility.

As will be argued below in the third section (Elements of a theory of situation-specific discursive ethos), there are good reasons to assume that situation specificity holds for discursive behavior as well. In this chapter, the application of the theory of situation specificity on discursive behavior is discussed. Elements of a theory of situation specificity and elements of the theory of discursivity in teachers' ethos are presented and related to each other, leading to a study addressing situation specificity in teachers' ethos and finally to the discussion of the role of situation specificity (and its theory) in teachers' ethos.

SITUATION SPECIFICITY AND ITS THEORY

Situation specificity can roughly be defined as a person behaving differently in different situations. Its opposite is cross-situational consistency of behavior. One can also say: The more one can predict someone's behavior in a specific situation when one knows his or behavior in another situation, the more there is consistency of this behavior across these two situations. With regard to the definition of *behavior*, I follow Shwayder's (1965) reasoning, according to which behavior *parameters*[1] need to be addressed (which do not represent the full behavior!), and that behavior might be situation specific concerning one parameter, cross-situationally consistent concerning another. Whether a behavior parameter is the same or similar in two situations depends on the underlying theory, which, accordingly, needs to be stated.

The concepts of *situation* and *situation specificity* require more elaborate specifications which will be addressed in the next section. Then the elements of the theory of situation specificity and the situation specificity of discourse are discussed.

Definition of Situation

As Heraclitus said: You could not step twice into the same river. This means that the conditions in which people behave – or in terms of the present chapter: situations – will always differ in some regards. However, it is our daily experience that some situations are more similar to each other than others (e.g., similar: two lecture-style teaching situations; two group work situations; as compared to pairs with much less similarity: lecture-style teaching vs. group work in class). However, the judgment of similarity depends on the underlying theory; for instance, lecture-style teaching with eight-years-olds and with adults might be quite different, as might be group work with these two groups of students. We know from research and everyday experience that teaching eight-years-olds differs from adult education, whether with lecture-style teaching or group work (for instance, the teaching method VaKE – see the contribution of Weinberger in this volume – works with elementary school children only when adapted to the children's competences, Demetri, 2015); this knowledge about difference is a theory. Hence, our estimation of whether situations are similar or different (and in the latter case, how large is the difference) depends on the underlying theory.

Further, we have only a limited information processing capacity (e.g., Miller, 1956), and this applies undoubtedly to the discrimination between situations as well, which hence is limited as well. One cannot assume that someone behaves reliably differently in separate situations, however different these situations might be theoretically if the person cannot discriminate between them. Hence it makes only sense to address situation specificity if the subjects differentiate between the situations.

Finally, we assume that people choose the criteria according to which to discriminate between situations depending on what is important to them (cf. Patry, 2011b). In the above example, it might be the age of the students, but in other cases, other issues can become important, such as the topic, teaching goals, etc. One can see, hence, that there is not *the* difference between situations, but that whether situations differ or not, and in what regard, depends on the theory used in the particular case – and this theory might differ from case to case (or from study to study).

As Thonhauser (2007) has emphasized, there is the risk of circularity when one defines situations and situation differences in the context of the study of situation specificity. An argument is circular if a variable (here: the situation) is defined in function of another variable and then the latter variable is explained by the former one. Often, situation differences are defined as conditions that yield behavioral differences, and then behavioral differences are "accounted for" by the situation differences. For instance, Pervin's (1978) classical definition is as follows:

> A situation is defined by *who* is involved, including the possibility that the individual is alone, *where* the action is taking place, and the nature of the *action* or activities occurring. The situation is defined by the organization of these various components so that it takes on a gestalt quality, and if one of the components changes we consider the situation to have changed. (Pervin, 1978, pp. 79–80; italics in original)

This is at least partly circular with respect to situation specificity because situation is *defined* (among others) by the behavior (or action), but in the study of situation specificity, situation differences should *explain* why the behavior changes.

A fully circular definition can be found in Frederiksen, Jensen, Beaton, and Bloxom (1973): "A situation is a set of circumstances that is likely to influence the behavior of at least some individuals, and that is likely to recur repeatedly in the same form" (p. 22). Behavior must be situation specific if situation is defined this way. In the same vein, Price and Bouffard (1974) developed a situation taxonomy by asking students to rate their behavior in specific contexts: Again, behavior variance determines what must be regarded as situation. How, then, can situation specificity be analyzed since by definition behavior is situation specific? Such a circular definition must be avoided through using appropriate theories and research designs (Patry, 2007; Patry, 2011a, p. 3). Similarly, although less strict, Bienengräber (2011, pp. 32–33) requires that although situation and action are closely related, they must be clearly distinguished and separated in the definition.

For the present purpose, my generic definition is based on Pervin's (1978, pp. 79–80) definition with the exception of the reference to action:

> A situation is a set of elements of the environment which the protagonist can perceive and discriminate, such as the persons that are involved (including the possibility that the person is alone), the place and the elements that are present, etc. The situation is defined by the organization of these various components so that it takes on a gestalt quality, and if one of the relevant components changes we consider the situation to have changed.

With Bienengräber (2011, pp. 45–47), it might be added that *these changes of relevant components can be a consequence of the protagonist's own behavior.*

This definition is so general that it cannot be used for research purposes. Rather, in a particular research study, the components, their relationships, and what is considered as "relevant" need to be specified. This must be done through theories. For the analysis of situation specificity, then, the following issues must be addressed:

1. *A theory of the situation.* Any taxonomy of situations that is not purely based on bbehavior variability has an underlying theory about the components of the situation that might affect the protagonists.
2. *A theory of situation specificity.* This theory is necessary to explain behavior differences (or consistency) based on differences in situative components. Insofar the study addresses situation specificity, it tests hypotheses derived from this theory.
3. *A theory of the protagonist.* This theory identifies the characteristics of the protagonist. This can be a general theory that refers to many people, or a theory specific for a given person (idiographic theory in the sense of Groeben & Westmeyer, 1975, pp. 115–119) on an individual person. This theory might address, for instance, what is perceived by the protagonist and which components of the situation are relevant and which are not and why.
4. For the scientific argumentation with respect to situation specificity, the following conditions must be satisfied:
5. To avoid circularity the theory of situation (1) must be independent of the part of the theory of situation specificity (2), which should explain the behavior parameter and that should be tested, i.e., the part of the theory of situation specificity addressed by the hypothesis.
6. To permit an explanation, the theory of situation specificity (2) must overlap with the theory of situation (1) (except for (1)) but add a part that leads to an explanation of the behavior.
7. The theory of the protagonist (3) establishes the link between the theory of the situation (1), the theory of situation specificity (2), and the behavior parameter. This theory might address, for instance, what components of the situation are perceived by the protagonist and which are seen as relevant (and in what regard and why). It might be mentioned here that this theory of the protagonist is crucial to avoid that a concept of moral behavior – or of discursive action – be characterized as purely situationist, which was rightly criticized, e.g., by Slingerland (2011), Mower (2013), and Croom (2014).

Beck (1996, pp. 92–94; see also Bienengräber, 2011, particularly pp. 70–195) proposed a system of six so-called basic elements that constitute situations: time (which refers, among others, to the time frame within which the protagonist directs the intentional attention on a state of affair); space (again, special features directing the protagonist's attention); perceived constellation of objects; the protagonist's concepts (how the objects are integrated in his or her cognitive structures); actualized roles (expectations that the protagonist perceives); and values (attitudes, claims, etc.). In all of these basic elements, the protagonist's interpretation (in the above terms, a theory of the protagonist (3) is constitutive for the theory of situation (1) but is not addressed independently, rather there is an explicit relationship, as well as with behavior (6).

While situation specificity is not an explicit topic in Beck's system (and hence there is no explicit theory of situation specificity) used by Bienengräber, the latter alludes to it in at least two ways: (i) with respect to teaching activities, which means preparing opportunities to enable students' learning yet that differ in function of the circumstances (situations); and (ii) with respect to curricular goals, that students should acquire dispositions, which means that they should behave appropriately (e.g., solve problems) in different situations; the underlying principle is that they should learn for life (with its diversity of situations) and not (only) for school (which actually means dealing with a variety of situation, although the heterogeneity might be less than in life). Whether Bienengräber's (2011) theory of situation is circular concerning these issues of situation specificity (4) is difficult to detect because he does not explicate his theory of situation specificity.

This concept is based on a theory of action that includes perception, attention, concept formation, role theory, and subjective values. While such a concept makes sense from a social learning theory conception (e.g., Mischel, 1973), as I do, it is not self-evident. And someone based on a different theoretical framework (e.g., purely behavioristic, constructivist, psychoanalytical, symbolic interactionist, or systemic) might conceive a taxonomy on entirely different grounds. Hence there is no "universal taxonomy of situations", and it is essential to state the theoretical underpinning.

Situation Specificity

The definition of situation specificity presented above at the beginning of section 2 (different behaviors in different situations) was very superficial. For research purposes, a much more precise definition is required. It turns out that there are

Table 1. *Types of consistency or situation specificity (see text)*

	Relative consistency or situation specificity	Absolute consistency or situation specificity		Coherence
		Groups	Individual	
Definition	Rank orders of the subjects' parameter values are similar (consistency) or different (situation specificity) in the different situations	Means of the subjects' parameter values are approximately equal (consistency) or different (situation specificity) in the different situations	Mean of the subject's parameter values over repeated measures in situation 1 is similar (consistency) or different (situation specificity) to the mean of the same parameter values across situation 2, etc.	Behavior patterns across situations are similar for similar subject populations but different for different subject populations.

(Continued)

Table 1. (Continued)

	Relative consistency or situation specificity	Absolute consistency or situation specificity		Coherence
		Groups	Individual	
Statistical test	Correlation, regression analysis, etc.	t-Test, ANOVA, etc.; possibly Chi-square etc.	Single-case analyses (ARIMA; ANOVA, if no serial dependency)	ANOVA and others
Statistical parameter	Correlation and the like; if high: consistency, i.e., no situation specificity	Effect size; if high: situation specificity, i.e., no consistency	Effect size; if high: situation specificity, i.e., no consistency	Interaction Person by Situation; high variance accounted for means high coherence
Variance accounted for	r^2: variance accounted for by subjects	E.g., Eta^2: variance accounted for by treatment or situation	E.g., Eta^2: variance accounted for by treatment or situation	Variance accounted for by the interaction Person by Situation
Subjects	Same	Same or similar	Only one	Same
Assessment instrument	Same or different (presumably addressing the same behavior or trait)	Same	Same	Same
Required scale level (D2.8)	At least ordinal	Nominal possible	Nominal possible	Usually interval
Examples for situation specificity (coherence); horizontal axis: situations (time for individual); vertical axis: parameter value; each line is one subject			Sit. S_1 Sit. S_2	Persons: type 1: straight lines type 2: dashed lines

different types of situation specificity, as shown in Table 1 (similar, yet not so detailed tables have been provided, among others, by Krahé, 1992, pp. 13–15, and Magnusson, 1982, p. 32):

- Relative situation specificity: comparing *rank orders* (e.g., using correlations);
- Absolute situation specificity of a group of people: *comparing means* (e.g., through t-test);
- Absolute individual situation specificity: comparing one person's behavior in similar and different situations (e.g., comparing two time series, one for each situation);
- Coherence: looking at behavioral patterns of different groups of people in different situations (e.g., using variance accounted for by the person-situation interaction in a repeated-measurement Analysis of Variance; Endler, Hunt, & Rosenstein, 1962).

It is not possible here to discuss these different types. It suffices to emphasize that the decision which definition to choose depends, again, on theoretical grounds: For some research questions, relative consistency is appropriate, for others, the absolute one or coherence is more appropriate. One must also mention that it is quite possible that when comparing the behavior of the same person in two situations, one can find all combinations of high vs. low absolute consistency and high vs. low relative consistency, i.e., it is quite possible that people have high relative but low absolute consistency, or vice versa.

In the 1970ies and 1980ies, there was an intense debate about situation specificity in social behavior, triggered by Mischel's (1968) review. In this debate, none of the issues discussed above concerning theory were taken into consideration: Because some studies (among them, prominently, the Hartshorne et al. studies mentioned above) did not yield cross-situational consistency. Some authors like Bem and Allen (1974) and Epstein (1979, 1980) insinuated that for instance Mischel defended a purely situationist position, pretending that all behavior was situation specific, to which these authors fervently opposed – among others based on their intuitions (Bem & Allen, 1974, p. 510), which can be considered an implicit theory of (lack of) situation specificity. The argumentations presented above concerning the definition of situations as well as the definition of situation specificity show that a more differentiated approach is necessary. For instance, within this debate, situation concepts were used in quite undifferentiated ways, and situation specificity was discussed uniquely in terms of relative consistency, with no theoretical justification for doing this.

Theory of Situation Specificity

Despite the lack of differentiation in the discussion of situation specificity in the consistency debate, but also since then – as far as such a discussion has taken place –

one can draw some general conclusions about situation specificity of behavior (see Patry, 1991):

1. In the *social domain*, i.e., when social behavior is at stake, situation specificity is the rule. For this, there are exceptions under well-defined, theoretically justified conditions (see for instance Price & Blashfield, 1975; Price & Bouffard, 1974), which include cross-situational consistency due to biases in the assessments (Patry, 2011a).
2. In the *cognitive domain*, that is when cognitive abilities, intelligence, achievement, knowledge, and the like are at stake, cross-situational consistency is the rule, provided that in the two situations of interest the same ability is asked for and the protagonists aim at doing their best concerning this ability. However, consistency seems to be lower than usually assumed. One can mention the problems in transfer (Detterman, 1993; Salomon & Perkins, 1989) or the problems of situated cognition (Brown et al., 1989; Cognition and Technology Group at Vanderbilt, 1990; Greeno & The Middle School Mathematics Through Applications Project Group, 1998; cf. also Lave, 1988), and inert knowledge (Renkl, 1996; Whitehead, 1967). Inert knowledge refers to knowledge the subjects have learned but which they do not apply in new situations although this would be appropriate.
3. One can distinguish roughly two types of research questions (Mischel & Peake, 1983):
   Question 1 deals with *interpersonal variance* and situational variance is interpreted as measurement error ("measurement noise that obscure(s) a clear view of the person," Shoda, 2007, p. 327). This is the case for instance in differential psychology and many studies in educational psychology. This is not to deny the importance of this type of questions, instead to draw the attention to the feature of situation specificity as a source of error. This error might be more or less random (which would have an impact on reliability), but possibly it is systematic (with consequences on validity).
   Question 2 deals with *intra*personal variance. Among others, one tries to account for the measurement error of question 1. The biases mentioned above can be due to situation specificity (e.g., when comparing different assessment methods, such as questionnaires compared to observations), and a theory of situation specificity might contribute to reducing biases (Patry, 2011a).
4. To account for situation specificity, a theory is required. However, only rudimental concepts of such a theory have been provided in the scientific literature so far.

Mischel and Shoda (1995) proposed such a theory, namely a cognitive-affective processing system (CAPS) to be used as basic framework for a theory of situation specificity. It consists of six cognitive-affective units (CAUs – one must mention that in other publications some of the original CAUs were combined so that fewer units are addressed) which in combination account for the behavior: competencies (what am I able to do?); perception (how do I categorize the environment as perceived); expectations (what are the consequences of my behavior?); goals and values (what is important to me? What do I want to achieve?); self-regulatory principles (how do I control my behavior? For instance: What are the moral principles that I use when deciding what to do?); and emotions (what do I feel, what are my affects?). The different CAUs are interdependent, and each can be analyzed more deeply using additional theories (see Patry, 2013, for details). In different situations, different CAUs might be present or absent, and in the former case, they might be activated differently. If CAPS is used to account for behavior, the situation definition must not include the CAUs (or include them differently than in CAPS) to avoid the circularity problem discussed above.

The ethos addresses one CAU in particular: the goals and values. It is possible that in a given situation several goals or values are activated. In social situations, we typically try to achieve several goals simultaneously. There may well be antinomies between such goals, that is, it is not possible to achieve all goals fully, rather there is a tradeoff between the realization of the goals or the realization of one goal might even exclude the realization of another one (for details, see Patry, 2012); in the latter case one speaks of dilemmas, and research in moral development following Kohlberg's (1984) tradition is very much based on such dilemmas. One can assume that a given person will deal differently with such antinomies in different situations, thus behaving situation specifically.

ELEMENTS OF A THEORY OF SITUATION-SPECIFIC DISCOURSIVE ETHOS

In the present context, ethos means a professional's decisions in morally relevant situations taking into account both moral values as well as instrumental rationality. For a situation to be morally relevant, two issues must be taken into account:

- When confronted with a situation, the protagonist has to take a decision how to act. He or she has several options, one of which might be not to do anything.
- In a morally relevant situation, each of these options involves moral values, but choosing one option will break some moral values which are satisfied when choosing another option. In other words, there is an antinomy (in the sense discussed above) between the different options concerning the moral values to be put into effect.

The decision of the protagonist and its justification are the *behavior parameters* in the sense of Shwayder (1965; see above). As to the definition of the *situation*, one can refer to its normative features. According to the non-naturalistic non-cognitivist meta-ethical position (see Morscher, this volume), it is important to distinguish how (and why) professionals *should* decide in relevant situations from how (and why) they actually *do* decide. How and why they should decide is an issue of norms that require ethical justification, which is considered independent of what is actually the case. Indeed, whether something should be done is not dependent on what someone does. There are many reasons for this distinction, some of which have been addressed by Morscher. What someone decides in actual situations to do, and how he or she justifies it, is the topic of descriptive statements, i.e., of statements that describe phenomena. We know many instances of people doing something that from an ethical standpoint cannot be approved. The justification of norms cannot be based on what someone, or a group of people, thinks is appropriate, but requires a justification logic of its own (see, for instance, Frankena, 1973), which is a question of philosophy. It might well be that people use justifications that, from a philosophical point of view, are considered appropriate, yet this is not necessarily the case, and often philosophers would not agree with the protagonists' decisions and justifications.

The normative features used to define the situation, then, can be the moral values that are at stake from an ethical standpoint. It is not what the protagonist should do, but it is what he or she might *consider* when taking the decision. It is possible that the protagonist does not regard one of the normative values addressed by the situation, or that he or she considers a value that has not been taken into account from an ethical point of view. This shows that the features used to define the situation and those crucial for the behavior and its *situation specificity* address similar issues (namely values) but are independent in that the situation is defined on ethical grounds (*prescriptive* perspective) while the protagonists decide on their actions based on their subjective judgments (*descriptive* perspective). For instance, from an *ethical* standpoint, tax evasion is a moral issue and entirely different from buying an object for the lowest price, but from a *business* standpoint, one might regard both situations as similar, namely as optimizing tasks (one issue being not getting caught) with no moral relevance.

According to the ethos theory by Oser et al. (1991), from an ethical point of view, the moral issues of the situation are *justice* (in the tradition, among others, of Kohlberg, 1984), *care* (e.g., Gilligan, 1982), and *truthfulness* (Habermas, 1984), and these issues are in antinomy with each other.

In such a situation, according to this theory, the protagonist's decision-making follows three steps:

- Responsibility: Do I want or think I need to intervene? If the protagonist decides that he or she does not need or does not want to take responsibility, one can speak of *avoiding to intervene*.
- In the case he or she wants to intervene, he or she is confronted with different claims related to the antinomic issues mentioned above. To deal with such antinomies, this intervention can be (i) *delegation* to other people; (ii) *single-handed* (unilateral) *decision-making* of different qualities; or (iii) *discourse* of different qualities.
- Commitment: How much time and energy do I want to invest in solving the problem using the strategy addressed in the second step?

The different types of actions are as follows:

Avoiding to intervene. The protagonist decides that there is no need to intervene, or that he or she does not want to get involved in the situation. For instance, he or she might think that the problem is not severe enough to require an action from his or her side so that not intervening is justified from his standpoint, or that he or she might get into trouble if he or she gets involved although he or she should, etc.

Delegation. The protagonist decides not to take direct action him- or herself, but to make sure that someone else takes care of the problem. For instance, the protagonist thinks he or she is not able to handle the problem but someone else is, and it is part of the protagonist's responsibility to hand over the action to this other person – and he or she possibly takes action to establish the contact, etc.

Single-handed decision-making. The protagonist decides by his or her own how to proceed. When doing so, he or she might or might not consider different issues, such as the perspectives of the people involved in the situation, questions of justice, care, and truthfulness, his or her personal interest, etc., and he or she might ask different people about their opinion. However, in the end, the decision is taken by him- or herself.

Discourse. The protagonist not only asks the other people concerned by the situation about their opinion but involves them in the decision-making and asks them to take responsibility. He or she might consider some of the other people, or all of them (participation), and assume that they are able and willing to decide not only for their own end but consider the needs of other people as well (presupposition of the other's responsibility taking).

Some possible reasons for the decision a protagonist takes were alluded to when describing the types of actions. Considering the CAPS, the justifications for a decision can be addressed more in detail:

Competence. If the protagonist considers him- or herself not competent to address the problem, he or she will *avoid* to intervene or *delegate* to someone whom he or she considers to be more competent. From a normative standpoint, this can be appropriate: It can be irresponsible to act inappropriately due to lack of knowledge while specialists (for instance, the school psychologist) know what to do. On the other hand, does the protagonist know about principles and techniques of discoursivity? Is he or she able to apply them? If not, one must not be surprised if he or she does not act discoursively.

Perception. A protagonist might perceive different yet apparently similar situations (i.e., situations which are similar from a normative standpoint) entirely differently; how they perceive them can depend on the other CAUs, for instance, previous experiences with similar situations and expectations and values related with it. Further questions are: Does the professional recognize a given situation as morally relevant? Which characteristics (parameters) of the situation are relevant from the perspective of the professional? As repeatedly mentioned above, these are not necessarily those that are considered relevant from a normative point of view.

Expectations. What does the protagonist assume the consequences of his or her action might be? Intervening in a complex situation like one that is morally relevant might yield a multitude of consequences, which are difficult, if not impossible, to anticipate, and the anticipation pattern will be different for different protagonists. When considering the consequences, the protagonist might or might not address side-effects of his or her actions. For instance, the protagonist can ask: What are the consequences of discoursive and non-discoursive behaviors, respectively, in the given situation?

Values and goals. What are the consequences that the protagonist wants to achieve in this situation? Among them are moral goals, such as to support an individual (care) or to establish equal opportunities for all or at least some of the people concerned by the situation (justice). However, there are also personal goals like minimizing effort or personal risks (negative side-effects already addressed in the expectations above). It must be mentioned that addressing values and goals refer automatically to norms since they need to be justified; however, this automatism is often only implicit in that the protagonists often do not reflect on these justifications.

Self-regulatory principles. A protagonist can have his or her actions guided by moral principles like justice, care, or truthfulness regardless of the consequences (deontic principles; this distinguishes this CAU from the more teleological values and goals). And he or she can differentiate with respect to justice (e.g., everyone gets the same, or everyone gets what he or she needs, etc.), care (who will be cared for?), or truthfulness (e.g., do I hide something that I believe to be true, or do I tell something that I know is not true?), etc. Other self-regulatory principles, like emotion control or modifying the perception to reduce some problems (e.g., internal justification of obviously inappropriate actions), can also be possible.

Emotions. Antinomies like in morally relevant situations are likely to trigger emotions like anxiousness or fear, particularly if one does not feel competent to deal with it. Other emotions like love for some of the persons or curiosity might arise in the same or different situations.

As alluded to in some of the descriptions, the different CAUs are inter-related. For instance, how most of the other CAUs are actualized has a strong impact on how the situation is perceived. Moreover, there is a high relationship between expectations and goals and values: I am particularly interested in the likelihood (expectation) that a consequence arises which is essential to me. It is not possible to analyze here all these relationships (for an example from the moral domain, see Weinberger & Patry, 2012).

Within and between many of the CAUs there are antinomies; this is particularly evident for goals and values (or in the case of deontic principles, of self-regulation) which are a constitutive part of the (normative) conception of the situations. Further, the different CAUs can be actualized completely differently in different situations, therefore leading to different (situation-specific) behavior. Hence, it might well be that a protagonist decides in some situations to act discoursively while in others he or she decides to decide single-handedly, but still act in full responsibility and in a moral way, while another protagonist decides just the other way round and still be judged as morally adequate when the way he or she actualizes the different CAUs testify responsible decision-making.

Overall, then, the question whether people act situation specifically in morally relevant situations becomes very complex. There is not one single answer like "In situations of type x, competent people are more discursive than in situations of type y" (which would address absolute situation specificity according to the definition above), or "Those who act more discursively in situations of type u than other protagonists also act more discursively in situations of type v" (relative consistency). What decisions individual protagonists take, and how they justify it, might differ from situation to situation, and the approaches may differ from protagonist to protagonist. This is exactly what is addressed by the concept of *coherence* as discussed above in the section on situation specificity: The variance accounted for by the interaction between persons and situations is likely to be the highest.

PROCEDURES

The analysis to be reported here has been presented in more details by Klaghofer and Patry (1995). A questionnaire had been constructed according to the principles first used by Endler, Hunt, and Rosenstein (1962): ten situations were described, and the teachers were given five possible solutions, each representing one of the reaction possibilities of the model (avoiding; delegation; single-handed decision-making; incomplete discourse; and complete discourse; the expert rating yielded an interrater agreement of 95%). A situation from the questionnaire is shown in Table 2. The teacher is asked what he or she would do in this situation, and the possible reactions are also given in Table 2; the type of reaction is indicated in italics (not visible for the respondents).

The situations were conceived using the situation definition above: All of them address, from a normative point of view, the issues of care, justice, and truthfulness. They stem from the experiences that we had made at that time and were conceived to address different types of relationship (parents-teachers; authorities-teachers; students-teachers; students-students; teachers-teachers), but since these fields are not directly related to our theory of ethos, they cannot be used as a theory for distinguishing situations.

The subjects were experienced teachers (teachers who were mentors for pre-service teachers) of different types (primary and secondary I schools) who had volunteered to participate in an intervention study. This study had four groups with different treatments. One addressed ethos issues ($N = 26$), as discussed above, one was a similar course, yet dealing with didactical topics ($N = 19$), the third was a combined course where the didactical and ethos topics were related to each other ($N = 17$), and the fourth was a control group, partly realized as a delayed treatment control group ($N = 27$). The intervention lasted ten weekly sessions of three hours each.

Table 2. Situation 6 of the questionnaire with the proposed items (from Oser et al., 1991, p. 492); in italics: ethos type

---

Peter, a twelve-year-old, is the oldest in his class, yet also the smallest. So, he is often teased. In the math lesson, you (the teacher) discuss linear measures, and you are aware that the time is becoming short. Just as you are about to finish, there is again a teasing remark about Peter, and the class begins to giggle.
How do you judge the following reactions and the corresponding reflections in this situation?

1. I address the problem directly and explain to the students that it disturbs me if someone is treated in a depreciatory way. I make clear that the value of a human does not depend on his or her height. I ask the teaser to explain what they object to Peter.

    disagree   1   2   3   4   agree   *Incomplete discourse*

2. It is important to me to make clear that I don't accept such a behavior in my class. It is degrading and unfair concerning Peter. Thus, I severely reprimand the teasers and then turn to my lesson.

    disagree   1   2   3   4   agree   *Single-handed decision*

3. I tell the students that such a behavior hurts the human dignity. However, prejudices of children of that age are not due to conscious badness. Thus I try not to show up the teasers in turn. I organize a talk with Peter and the teasers, even if I risk that the class considers me to be weak.

    disagree   1   2   3   4   agree   *Full discourse*

4. Since it did not happen for the first time, I must think how to solve the problem once and for all. Thus, as soon as I can, I talk with the school psychologist who can give me advice what to do.

    disagree   1   2   3   4   agree   *Delegation*

5. I will ignore the event demonstratively. Learning theory tells us that a behavior will disappear if it is ignored consequently. An intervention would worsen the situation since it would demonstrate Peters need for assistance. As a teacher's darling he would even be less accepted by his peers.

    disagree   1   2   3   4   agree   *Avoiding*

There were three assessment times: a pre-test before the intervention, a post-test a few days or weeks after the intervention, and a follow-up about one year later. Each assessment was with all ten situations and all five reaction types.

RESULTS

In the present chapter, I will only present the results relevant to the issue of situation specificity of the answers to the questionnaire; other results are presented elsewhere (Oser et al., 1991). First, the results for the pre-test for the four course types combined are shown (see Figure 1); this is appropriate because here all subjects have the same experience, namely none. For the purpose of clarity, a line diagram is chosen, although the data are not of a time series. Further, the situations are ordered from low to high full discourse. As one can see, the picture is quite complex. Apparently, there must be differences between the situations. The full discourse option is the least likely one in one situation (situation 9) but the most likely one in another situation (situation 5), while partial discourse is the most likely in situation 9 and the second least likely in situation 7.

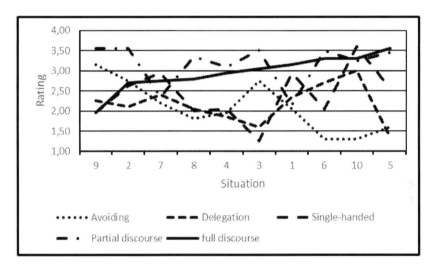

Figure 1. Situation specificity of discursive behavior

With respect to coherence, i.e., the interaction between person and situation which is addressed here, the question is whether the pattern is different for different subjects who are combined in this figure. The method used was ANOVA with the estimation of the amount of variance the different factors account for, according to the method used by Endler et al. (1962) in the Person-Situation-Interaction Analyses. An ANOVA with the following factors was used:

- Courses (4; between subjects);
- Time (3, repeated measures);
- Situations (10, repeated measures);
- Types of reaction (5, repeated measures).

The results of the ANOVA are given in Table 3. For the present purpose, only the variances accounted for (last column) are of importance and will be discussed. In the upper half, there is the course factor in which persons are combined, which is a between-subjects factor. In the lower part, the persons are taken as a factor by itself;

Table 3. Results of the ANOVA

Effect	SSQ	Variance	F	p	%
Course (C)	29.40	9.80	2.14	.11	.37
Time (T)	.02	.01	.01	.99	.00
Situation (S)	104.27	11.59	16.25	.00**	1.32
Type or reaction (R)	1551.99	388.00	166.77	.00**	19.64
C * T	6.79	1.13	1.53	.18	.09
C * S	15.12	.56	.79	.77	.19
C * R	29.00	2.42	1.04	.42	.37
T * S*	9.96	.55	1.72	.03*	.13
T * R	8.77	1.10	2.07	.04*	.11
S * R	1487.64	41.32	39.38	.00**	18.82
C * T * S	22.75	.42	1.31	.07+	.29
C * T * R	11.55	.48	.91	.59	.15
C * S * R	112.77	1.04	.99	.50	1.43
T * S * R	41.36	.57	1.48	.01**	.52
C * T * S * R	77.95	.36	.93	.77	.99
Person (P)	206.01	4.58			2.61
P * S	288.70	.71			3.65
P * T	66.47	.74			.84
P * R	418.81	2.33			5.30
P * S * T	261.26	.32			3.31
P * S * R	1700.11	1.05			21.51
P * T * R	191.09	.53			2.42
P * S * T * R	1261.56	.39			15.96

hence the course factor cannot be accounted for because it is confounded with the person factor, and estimating significance does not make sense.

For the present purpose, the most crucial factor combination is the interaction person by situation by reaction. With more than 21%, this interaction accounts for most variance. This is quite a high percentage, given the many factors that must be taken into account. This pattern is stable over time since the time factor is not involved in this interaction. Apparently, different people behave differently in different situations, and this is true for different behaviors (types of reactions) in a different amount. This is exactly what is meant with "coherence".

If time is taken into account (last row), 16% of percentage accounted for can be added. The time influence is different for different people and for different reaction types in different situations; this makes sense since different people experience different courses (visible in the post and follow-up assessments).

The situation also has an influence generally on all people, as seen by the interaction "situation by type" with almost 19% variance accounted for. This indicates that for all subjects the situations have specific characteristics which lead the teachers to prefer certain response types, with different response types in different situations.

Finally, it is clear that the teachers prefer certain response types over others in general. Particularly avoidance gets low values (with the remarkable exception of situation 9), i.e., teachers tend in almost all situations to take responsibility, while discursive approaches tend to have high values.

DISCUSSION

Since the teachers' ethos is addressed in terms of the CAPS, it is a construct which refers to cognition. The results show that situation specificity concerning ethos applies to these cognitions as well as to the behavior, as assessed, for instance, by the Hartshorne and May studies (1928, 1929; Hartshorne et al., 1930). It is obvious that a simple concept of ethos based on general tendencies (in the sense of ethos traits) is not appropriate. It is also visible that while a purely normative concept how one should act in different situations is conceivable in principle, it might not meet the reality because the weights of the different arguments will be different for different persons. A purely normative concept as a prescription for teachers would not be appropriate for another reason: such an approach would take away the teachers' responsibility. The latter is normatively necessary, however, because the situations that teachers encounter are more complex than in the questionnaire. One can assume that each teacher responding to the questionnaire will have his or her interpretation of the respective situations and focus differently on different features (see the CAU "perception"), with consequences on the actualization of the other CAUs as well.

With the present approach, it is not possible to get into more details than about coherence (person-situation interaction). The decisions of the individual protagonists in the respective situations cannot be accounted for, because it would require much more information than is usually available; for instance, we would have to analyze in detail how the protagonists argue for specific situations, as we are doing, in other contexts, in our project "pedagogical tact" (see Gastager & Patry, in preparation) where we ask the protagonists what they think in the situations they encounter, using the method of cued recall.

The answer to the question whether ethos and morality need to be accounted for by situations or traits, hence, cannot be either one or the other, as the discussions (Croom, 2014; Doris, 1998; Mowrer, 2013; Slingerland, 2011; and many more) seem to assume. If the CAPS approach is meaningful for this type of behavior as it is for other behaviors, it is possible to analyze the ethos, but there is no simple answer. Further studies of the topic are essential, but apparently, it would be necessary to consider both, person characteristics like those addressed in the CAPS as well as situational characteristics. As discussed in the section on the definition of situations and on the risk of its circularity concerning situation specificity, then, it is essential that an appropriate theory of situations be used. The approach presented above, namely using the normative features of the situation, is one possibility. However, this concept has been used here to define the set of situations to be used (namely dilemma situations), but it has not been used to address the differences between the situations.

Teaching is situation specific (e.g., Patry, 2000) but theories about teaching are not (Patry, 1989). To deal appropriately with teaching, the scientific community needs to overcome this contrast, i.e., we need to develop appropriate theories that can account for intrapersonal variance in teaching. This can only be achieved if the circularity in the argumentation can be overcome, i.e., if we have not only theories of situation specificity, but also related theories of situation and theories of the protagonist as presented above. It also means that we cannot make general statements (statements that can be claimed to be viable across situations) about teaching without taking the situations – with appropriate definitions – into account. This also holds for dealing with values in education: Teachers do not need to act similarly in all morally relevant situations. Instead, they should act appropriately – but what does this mean if we do not have a theory about such situations and what it means to act appropriately? Most teachers do this intuitively, but if research in education should be able to help them in that – and this is a task of research in education –, we need theories that address this issue explicitly. The present chapter is an attempt to clarify some aspects that are relevant in this regard.

NOTE

[1] A parameter is a quantifiable variable whose value contributes information to the state of a phenomenon of interest (e.g., skin resistance as indicator for anxiety) for a specific population (e.g., a person).

REFERENCES

Beck, K. (1996). Die "Situation" als Bezugspunkt didaktischer Argumentation. Ein Beitrag zur Begriffspräzisierung. In W. Seyd & R. Witt (Ed.), *Situation Handlung Persönlichkeit: Kategorien wirtschaftspädagogischen Denkens: Festschrift für Lothar Reetz* [Situation action personality: Categories of thinking in business education: Festschrift for Lothar Reetz] (pp. 87–98). Hamburg: Feldhaus.

Bem, D. J., & Allen, A. (1974). Predicting some of the people some of the time: The search for cross-situational consistencies in behavior. *Psychological Review, 81*, 506–520. doi:10.1037/h0037130

Bienengräber, T. (2011). *Eine Theorie der Situation: Mit Beispielen für ihre Konkretisierung im Bereich der kaufmännischen Berufsbildung* [A theory of the situation: With examples to concretise it in the context of business education]. Frankfurt: Lang.

Brown, J. S., Collins, A., & Duguid, P. (1989). Situated cognition and the culture of learning. *Educational Researcher, 18*(1), 32–42. doi:10.3102/0013189X018001032

Cognition and Technology Group at Vanderbilt. (1990). Anchored instruction and its relationship to situated cognition. *Educational Researcher, 19*(6), 2–10.

Croom, A. (2014). Vindicating virtue: A critical analysis of the situationist challenge against Aristotelian moral psychology. *Integrative Psychological and Behavioral Science, 48*, 18–47.

Demetri, A. (2015). *Kombination moralischer Werterziehung mit konstruktivistischem Wissenserwerb in der Grundschule: Das Unterrichtsmodell VaKE in der Grundschule* [Combining moral values education with constructivist knowledge acquisition in elementary school] (Dissertation at the Faculty of Cultural and Social Sciences). University of Salzburg, Salzburg.

Detterman, D. K. (1993). The case for the prosecution: Transfer as an epiphenomenon. In D. K. Detterman & R. J. Sternberg (Eds.), *Transfer on trial: Intelligence, cognition, and instruction* (pp. 1–24). Norwood, NJ: Ablex.

Doris, J. M. (1998). Persons, situations, and virtue ethics. *Noûs, 32*, 504–530.

Endler, N. S., Hunt, J., & Rosenstein, A. J. (1962). An S-R inventory of anxiousness. *Psychological Monographs: General and Applied, 76*(17), 1–33. doi:10.1037/h0093817

Epstein, S. (1979). The stability of behavior: I. On predicting most of the people much of the time. *Journal of Personality and Social Psychology, 37*, 1097–1126.

Epstein, S. (1980). The stability of behavior: Implications for psychological research. *American Psychologist, 35*, 790–806. doi:10.1037//0003-066X.35.9.790

Frankena, W. K. (1973). *Ethics* (2nd ed.). Englewood Cliffs, NJ: Prentice-Hall.

Frederiksen, N., Jensen, O., Beaton, A. E., & Bloxom, B. (1973). *Prediction of organizational behavior*. New York, NY: Pergamon.

Gastager, A., & Patry, J.-L. (Eds.). (in preparation). *Die Aktualität des pädagogischen Takts* [The actuality of pedagogical tact] (working title). Graz: Leykam.

Gilligan, C. (1982). *In a different voice*. Cambridge, MA: Harvard University Press.

Greeno, J. A., & The Middle School Mathematics Through Applications Project Group. (1998). The situativity of knowing, learning, and research. *American Psychologist, 53*, 5–26. doi:10.1037//0003-066X.53.1.5

Groeben, N., & Westmeyer, H. (1975). *Kriterien psychologischer Forschung* [Criteria of psychological research]. München: Juventa.

Habermas, J. (1984). *Vorstudien und Ergänzungen zur Theorie des kommunikativen Handelns* [Primary study and supplement to the theory of communicative action]. Frankfurt am Main: Suhrkamp.

Hartshorne, H., & May, M. A. (Eds.). (1928). *Studies in the nature of character, Vol. 1: Studies in deceit*. New York, NY: Macmillan.

Hartshorne, H., & May, M. A. (Eds.). (1929). *Studies in the nature of character, Vol. 2: Studies in service and self-control*. New York, NY: Macmillan.

Hartshorne, H., & May, M. A. (1930). A summary of the work of the character education inquiry. *Religious Education: The official journal of the Religious Education Association, 25*, 754–762. Retrieved from http://dx.doi.org/10.1080/0034408300250810

Hartshorne, H., May, M. A., & Shuttleworth, F. K. (Eds.). (1930). *Studies in the nature of character, Vol. 3: Studies in the organization of character*. New York, NY: Macmillan.

Klaghofer, R., & Patry, J.-L. (1995, August 26–31). *Person-situation-interaction in ethical conceptions of teachers*. Paper presented at the 6th European Conference for Research on Learning and Instruction of EARLI, Nijmegen.

Kohlberg, L. (1984). *Essays on moral development, Vol. 2: The psychology of moral development*. San Francisco, CA: Harper & Row.

Krahé, B. (1992). *Personality and social psychology: Towards a synthesis*. London: Sage Publications.

Lave, J. (1988). *Cognition in practice*. New York, NY: Cambridge University Press.

Magnusson, D. (1982). Interaktionale Modelle des Verhaltens. In H.-W. Hoefert (Ed.), *Person und Situation: Interaktionspsychologische Untersuchungen* [Person and situation: Interaction psychological studies] (pp. 28–43). Göttingen: Hogrefe.

May, M. A., & Hartshorne, H. (1926). First steps toward a scale for measuring attitudes. *The Journal of Educational Psychology, 17*, 145–162.

Miller, G. A. (1956). The magical number seven plus or minus two: Some limits on our capacity for processing information. *Psychological Review, 63*, 81–97. (Reprinted in 1994, *Psychological Review, 101*, 343–352.)

Mischel, W. (1968). *Personality and assessment*. New York, NY: Wiley.

Mischel, W. (1973). Toward a cognitive social learning reconceptualization of personality. *Psychological Review, 80*, 252–283.

Mischel, W. (2004). Toward an integrative science of the person. *Annual Review of Psychology, 55*, 1–22.

Mischel, W., & Peake, P. K. (1983). Some facets of consistency: Replies to Epstein, Funder, and Bem. *Psychological Review, 90*, 394–402. doi:10.1037//0033-295X.90.4.394

Mischel, W., & Shoda, Y. (1995). A cognitive-affective system theory of personality: Reconceptualizing situations, dispositions, dynamics, and invariance in personality structure. *Psychological Review, 102*, 246–268.
Mower, D. S. (2013). Situationism and confucian virtue ethics. *Ethic Theory and Moral Practice, 16*, 113–137. Doi:10.1007/s10677-011-9312-9
Oser, F., Patry, J.-L., Zutavern, M., Reichenbach, R., Klaghofer, R., Althof, W., & Rothbucher, H. (1991). *Der Prozess der Verantwortung: Berufsethische Entscheidung von Lehrerinnen und Lehrern* [The process of responsibility: Professional ethical decisions of teachers]. Freiburg: Pädagogisches Institut der Universität.
Patry, J.-L. (1989, March). *Teaching is situation specific but theory is not: Towards a higher impact of research on practice*. Paper presented in the AERA Annual Meeting, San Francisco, CA. Retrieved from http://eric.ed.gov/ERICWebPortal/search/detailmini.jsp?_nfpb=true&_&ERICExtSearch_SearchValue_0=ED311017&ERICExtSearch_SearchType_0=no&accno=ED311017
Patry, J.-L. (1991). *Transsituationale Konsistenz des Verhaltens und Handelns in der Erziehung* [Cros-situational consistency of behavior and action in the education]. Bern: Lang.
Patry, J.-L. (1999). Teachers' ethics. In J.-L. Patry & J. Lehtovaara (Eds.), *European perspectives on teacher ethics* (pp. 11–33). Tampere: Reports from the Department of Teacher Education in Tampere University.
Patry, J.-L. (2000). Kaktus und Salat: Zur Situationsspezifität in der Erziehung. In J.-L. Patry & F. Riffert (Eds.), *Situationsspezifität in pädagogischen Handlungsfeldern* [Situation specificity in educational action fields] (pp. 13–52). Innsbruck: StudienVerlag.
Patry, J.-L. (2007). Lehrerinnen und Lehrer handeln situationsspezifisch: Oder sie sollten: Eine Antwort auf Thonhausers Frage "Tun sie das?" [Teachers act situation specifically: Or they should: An answer to Thonhauser's question "do they do that?"]. *Salzburger Beiträge zur Erziehungswissenschaft, 11* (1–2), 61–70.
Patry, J.-L. (2011a). Methodological consequences of situation specificity: Biases in assessments. *Frontiers in Psychology: Quantitative Psychology and Measurement, 2*(18). Retrieved from http://www.frontiersin.org/quantitative_psychology_and_measurement/10.3389/fpsyg.2011.00018/abstract
Patry, J.-L. (2011b). Subjektive Theorien und Handeln. In A. Gastager, J.-L. Patry, & K. Gollackner (Eds.), *Subjektive Theorien über das eigene Tun in sozialen Handlungsfeldern* [Subjective theories about one's own actions in social action fields] (pp. 27–41). Innsbruck: StudienVerlag.
Patry, J.-L. (2012). Antinomien in der Erziehung. In C. Nerowski, T. Hascher, M. Lunkenbein & D. Sauer (Eds.), *Professionalität im Umgang mit Spannungsfeldern der Pädagogik* [Professionality when dealing with tension fields in education] (pp. 177–187). Bad Heilbrunn: Klinkhardt.
Patry, J.-L. (2013). Beyond multiple methods: Critical multiplism on all levels. *International Journal of Multiple Research Approaches, 7*, 50–65.
Pervin, L. A. (1978). Definitions, measurements, and classifications of stimuli, situations, and environments. *Human Ecology, 6*, 71–105.
Price, R. H., & Blashfield, R. K. (1975). Explorations in the taxonomy of behavior settings: Analyses of dimensions and classifications of settings. *American Journal of Community Psychology, 3*, 335–351. doi:10.1007/BF00880776
Price, R. H., & Bouffard, D. L. (1974). Behavioral appropriateness and situational constraints as dimensions of social behavior. *Journal of Personality and Social Psychology, 30*, 579–586. doi:10.1037/h0037037
Renkl, A. (1996). Träges Wissen: Wenn Erlerntes nicht genutzt wird [Inert knowledge: When not using what was learnt]. *Psychologische Rundschau, 47*, 78–92.
Salomon, G., & Perkins, D. N. (1989). Rocky roads to transfer: Rethinking mechanisms of a neglected phenomenon. *Educational Psychologist, 24*, 113–142. doi:10.1207/s15326985ep2402_1
Shoda, Y. (2007). From humunculus to a system: Toward a science of the person. In Y. Shoda, D. Cervone, & G. Downey (Eds.), *Persons in context: Building a science of the individual* (pp. 327–331). New York, NY: Guilford.
Shoda, Y., Cervone, D., & Downey, G. (Eds.). (2007). *Persons in context. Building a science of the individual*. New York, NY: Guilford.

Shwayder, D.S. (1965). *Stratification of behavior: A system of definitions propounded and defended*. London: Routledge & Kegan Paul.
Slingerland, E. (2011). The situationist critique and early Confucian virtue ethics. *Ethics, 121*, 390–419.
Thonhauser, J. (2007). "Lehrer/innen handeln situationsspezifisch:" Tun sie das? ["Teachers act situation specifically": Do they do that?]. *Salzburger Beiträge zur Erziehungswissenschaft, 11*, 47–60.
Weinberger, A., & Patry, J.-L. (2012, November). *A cognitive affective processing system analysis of moral arguments in a VaKE (Values and Knowledge Education)-dilemma discussion*. Paper presented at the 38th Annual Conference of the Association for Moral Education, San Antonio, TX.
Whitehead, A. N. (1967). *The aims of education and other essays*. New York, NY: Macmillan.

Jean-Luc Patry
Department of Education
University of Salzburg
Salzburg, Austria

DIMITRIS PNEVMATIKOS AND PANAGIOTA CHRISTODOULOU

5. PROMOTING CONCEPTUAL CHANGE THROUGH VALUES *AND* KNOWLEDGE EDUCATION (V*A*KE)

INTRODUCTION

Current official educational policy papers in the field of science education underline the importance of the preparation of students to be competent in making responsible decisions for real, technological, social and environmental problems which they will encounter as citizens (Bybee & McCrae, 2011; Goodrum & Rennie, 2007). For instance, OECD and EU-Commission official documents emphasize the need for scientific literacy that integrates aspects of citizen education. According to the OECD definition, "scientific literacy is the ability to engage with science-related issues, and with the ideas of science, as a reflective citizen" (OECD, 2015, p. 20). At the same time, the EU-Commission report on science education places considerable attention on "promoting Responsible Research and Innovation and enhancing public understanding of scientific findings and the capabilities to discuss their benefits and consequences" (EU-Commission, 2015, p. 24).

The discussion of the pros and cons of the scientific findings demands a reflection beyond the financial aspects of the products and based on the value system. This reflection is necessary because the benefits and consequences might differ between people and time. For instance, the benefits for an in-group might be harmful to an outgroup, or an advantage might direct, but the adverse consequences might be seen in the future. Hence, scientific humanism, namely the ability to sensitize students in the ethical dimension of science apart from the scientific methods and epistemological aspects of knowledge, is outlined as the cornerstone in science and technology curricula (Pnevmatikos et al., 2016).

Therefore, Science Education is considered as an attempt to link scientific knowledge and inquiry skills with the sociocultural frames to develop better decision-makers (Zeidler, Berkowitz, & Bennett, 2011; Sammel, 2014). Nevertheless, little attention has been given to the link between the scientific knowledge and the sociocultural frames; scholars in the field investigated in many deep aspects related to the knowledge acquisition, leaving outside from their investigation how scientific knowledge is related to sociocultural aspects, and how teachers should deal with these two aspects in their everyday teaching practice. In particular, research findings indicate that teachers omit moral and citizenship education because (a) they are unaware of methods, goals or topics for its implementation, (b) they fear that values education might interfere with the value systems of parents, administration or other stakeholders by avoiding its integration eventually, and (c) they are reluctant to integrate aspects in their teaching that goes beyond the knowledge acquisition due to the pressure from the curriculum, exams and students' evaluation (Gruber, 2009; Patry, Reichman, & Linortner, 2017; Willemse, ten Dam, Geijsel, van Wessum & Volman, 2015). Hence, despite the compulsory character of citizenship education in many curricula around the EU countries (Euridyce, 2012), it depends upon teachers' professional ethos whether they will integrate moral aspects in their teaching practices after all. This chapter presents an attempt to integrate a science and technology topic with the sociocultural aspects related to it in two sixth grade classes.

Knowledge Acquisition in Science

According to constructivist theorists, knowledge is constructed either based on the everyday experiences of acting on objects and drawing inferences from observations (physical knowledge), through the learners' constructive processes as a result of reflective mental actions on objects (logico-mathematical knowledge), or through communication with other people in the case of the conventional arbitrary knowledge (DeVries, 2000). Scientific knowledge introduces characteristics that are not evident in the everyday experience of the action-reaction processes, it is beyond the individuals' ideas and is mainly a logico-mathematical knowledge. By the time students are engaged in systematic instruction, they have already constructed concepts for explaining various phenomena (i.e., physical knowledge) which usually are incompatible with the scientific view of the same phenomena (logico-mathematical knowledge). Therefore, an issue arises from the incompatibility of learner's prior knowledge and the scientific view in interpreting phenomena in everyday life. Framework theories claim that the scientific knowledge could not be acquired through the simple enrichment of the initial conceptual structures that have been constructed on the everyday experience, but various forms of conceptual reconstruction (most of the times a radical reconstruction) should take place in order the individual construct the scientific knowledge and the new qualitative different structures emerge (Vosniadou, 2007). Particularly, in the framework theory approach of conceptual change (Vosniadou, 2013) naïve physics is considered as generative skeletal structures, which provide the learners with the possibility to formulate explanations and predictions to unfamiliar problems forming a framework theory in order to explain various phenomena. However, when students try to incorporate the scientific information into their prior knowledge synthetic models are created, providing the learner with illusionary coherence and explanatory power (Vosniadou, 2013). As a result, conceptual change can be slow, gradual and cannot happen overnight (Vosniadou & Skopeliti, 2014).

Research also focuses on examining teaching practices that will facilitate the acquisition of scientific concepts. At an instructional level conceptual change can be facilitated through approaches such as (i) inquiry-based teaching – namely the educational strategy in which students follow methods and practices similar to those of professional scientists in order to construct knowledge (Pedaste et al., 2015), (ii) the design and development of a teaching-learning sequence (TLS) – namely a short topic-oriented curriculum (Méheut & Psillos, 2004; Psillos & Kariotoglou, 2016), (iii) models and multiple representations (e.g., Jonassen & Easter, 2013) (iv) the direct teaching of procedural and epistemological knowledge (e.g. Zoupidis, Pnevmatikos, Spyrtou & Kariotoglou, 2016) as well as through (v) experimentation with physical and virtual manipulatives (e.g., Olympiou & Zacharia, 2012). Nevertheless, focusing on these aspects of the acquisition of conceptual knowledge, scholars omitted to think about how they might sensitize students to the ethical dimension of scientific and technological activities.

Integrated Values in Knowledge Education

Values *and* Knowledge Education (V*a*KE) is considered a method promoting scientific humanism as well as science as human endeavor not only in the field of education (Patry, Weinberger, Weyringer, & Nussbaumer, 2013) but also in the field of lifelong learning (e.g., Patry et al., 2017; Pnevmatikos et al., 2016). V*a*KE is an instructional approach combining constructivist knowledge acquisition with constructivist values education, employing moral dilemmas in order to trigger the discussion among participants (Patry et al., 2013). Participants in a V*a*KE unit are anticipated (a) to acquire content knowledge on the subject matter under consideration, (b) to relate their arguments to the underlying values and (c) to adopt a more global and sustainable perspective towards socio-cultural and socio-scientific issues. V*a*KE can be implemented in every subject matter. Inquiry-based learning is employed while participants search for information, while participants' learning characteristics are considered for both knowledge and values acquisition. However, there is limited evidence regarding the effectiveness of the method in promoting conceptual change. Still, V*a*KE shares many common links with instruction for conceptual change. Firstly, V*a*KE and instruction for conceptual change can address a specific subject matter in a micro (e.g., during a specific session) and medium level (e.g., during a single topic sequence). Secondly, they share in common the integration of inquiry through activities such as collecting and analyzing data, discussing ideas and drawing conclusions by developing evidence-based explanations. Additionally, the level of participants' autonomy during inquiry is crucial for both V*a*KE and instruction for conceptual change, since students have the impetus for fulfilling their learning needs. Also, learners' characteristics are considered while designing V*a*KE and instruction that promotes conceptual understanding (cf. Pnevmatikos & Christodoulou, in preparation for more details regarding the common links between V*a*KE and conceptual change). Nevertheless, the effective teaching of certain concepts demands changes not only in the content of the previous knowledge (i.e., belief revision) but also in the structure of the concepts; that is conceptual change.

Although V*a*KE can be implemented in every subject matter, it is evident that in the cases where the acquisition of conceptual knowledge is required, additional teaching approaches should be incorporated into teaching to promote conceptual change (e.g., multiple representations and models, experimentation with physical and virtual manipulatives, etc.).

The Current Study

Although there is enough experimental evidence regarding the effectiveness of V*a*KE in promoting both knowledge acquisition and values education (e.g., Keast & Marango, 2015; Patry & Weinberger, 2004; Pnevmatikos & Christodoulou, 2015; Weinberger, 2006), there is not much evidence if V*a*KE is an efficient method to promote conceptual change. Particularly, it is not known what adaptations are necessary to be done to, when this is necessary, facilitate beyond the knowledge acquisition, the promotion of conceptual change in the structure of concepts. Therefore, the aim of the current study was to investigate whether V*a*KE might be an effective approach to promote, beyond the ethical dimension of science, conceptual change too. In particular, the research question of the study was to examine whether V*a*KE could promote conceptual understanding, after being modified according to the principles of science teaching and conceptual change theory. We hypothesized that V*a*KE would be effective in promoting conceptual change after the modifications made in order to be in line with science education principles and instruction for conceptual change.

For the implementation of the current research, the field of Nanoscience and Nanotechnology (N-ST) was employed. On the one hand, the societal and ethical issues arising from the invasion and the extensive use of N-ST products in everyday life render the education regarding N-ST issues as essential for the development of nano-literate students and future citizens (Laherto, 2010). On the other hand, N-ST is a field inaccessible to direct experience which could easily lead students in constructing misconceptions. Students are most likely to transfer their experiences from the macroscale to the nanoscale, which nonetheless is inappropriate since nano-sized objects present different properties than in the macro-scale.

METHOD

Participants

Forty-four Greek sixth graders (23 female, $M = 11.49$ years, $SD = .29$ years) from two classes participated in the V*a*KE unit concerning N-ST. Students that participated in the study were coming from two primary education schools in a rural area of Western Macedonia, in northern Greece. Most of the participants attended the school are coming from low to middle-class families.

Materials

To examine conceptual understanding a questionnaire with generative questions was constructed. Generative questions aim at examining whether students have fully comprehended the scientific view and their ability to use these scientific facts in the generative concepts (Vosniadou, 2002; Vosniadou, Skopeliti, & Ikospentaki, 2005). Generative questions also enable the researchers to infer for the conceptual structure of the given concepts. All means of measures were coded to secure anonymity among participants. The questions of the generative questionnaire were open-ended addressing students' concepts and misconceptions regarding (i) size-dependent property of gold to change colour (3 items, e.g., *"If we cut bulk gold into smaller pieces which are we still able to see with our eyes, what is going to be their colour? Why is that?"*), (ii) size-dependent property of hydrophobicity (3 items, e.g., *"If I spill a drop of water on a cabbage leaf, and a lettuce leaf, the shape of the water droplet will be the same? Why?"*), and (iii) the concept of size (7 items, e.g., *"John says that there is a special filter which can clean water even from bacteria. Is this possible? What kind of filter is that? How is this happening?"*) and the concept of size-dependent property of hydrophobicity in the application of nano-coatings (3 items, e.g., *"I apply a coating on a wall and a special coating on the iron railings of the porch. However, the weather is windy, and dust makes them dirty again. I take a wet piece of cloth to clean them. Which one of the two surfaces will clean the best, the wall or the iron railings? Why?"*).

Students' answers were classified as correct/scientific (3 points) if they were in accordance with the scientific view, as initial/intuitive (1 point) if they were in accordance with a naïve theory of physics, and as an alternative (2 points) if they were in accordance with synthetic models (Skopeliti, 2011). Those questions which were left unanswered or provided with irrelevant answers were classified as irrelevant (0 points). Synthetic models are supposed to be in the middle of the process of conceptual change as individuals have partially changed their initial naive theory, and therefore the coding used here is considered as an interval scale. Criteria were established, and two coders coded the data. The first coder had knowledge in both fields of nanotechnology and conceptual change while the second coder was a cognitive psychologist. For the interrater agreement Krippendorff's alpha coefficient, namely Kalpha (Krippendorff, 1970) was applied. Kalpha coefficient can be used regardless the number of observers, levels of measurement, sample sizes, and the presence of missing data (Hayes & Krippendorff, 2007). The interrater agreement for all items and measurements was high (.82 and 1.0) while after discussion a full agreement was reached. A satisfactory reliability was found between the items in each category of items: (i) size-dependent property of gold to change colour (3 items, Cronbach's alpha = .71), (ii) size-dependent property of hydrophobicity (3 items, Cronbach's alpha = .77), and (iii) the concept of size (7 items, Cronbach's alpha = .63) and the concept of size-dependent property of hydrophobicity in the application of nano-coatings (3 items, Cronbach's alpha = .65).

Design & Procedure

VaKE theorists propose eleven steps in a prototypical VaKE unit (Patry, Weyringer, & Weinberger, 2007; Patry et al., 2013), which were nevertheless adopted in the current study in order for conceptual change to be promoted. Table 1 presents the steps of VaKE as modified in the present study, the formation of the class as well as the concept introduced in each intervention of the TLS.

Table 1. Modified steps of the VaKE procedure, class formation, and concepts introduced during the interventions

	Steps in VaKE	Class formation in VaKE	Concepts related to N-ST
1st intervention	Introducing the dilemma	Class	Size and scale
	First decision	Class	
	1st dilemma discussion	Class	
	Missing information	Class	
	Looking for evidence	Group	
	Exchange information	Class	
2nd intervention	Looking for evidence	Group	Size-dependent property of hydrophobicity
	Exchange information	Class	
3rd intervention	Looking for evidence	Group	Size-dependent property of absorption
	Exchange information	Class	
	2nd dilemma discussion	Class	
	Synthesis of results	Class	
	General synthesis	Group	
	Generalization	Class	

A pre-, post- and follow-up measurement of students' conceptual knowledge took place after a three months interval. The intervention lasted three weeks, and the concepts of *size and scale* and size-*dependent properties of hydrophobicity & absorption* were introduced. The TLS was designed according to the theoretical assumptions of science education and conceptual change theory, which are described in detail elsewhere (cf. Pnevmatikos & Christodoulou, in preparation). During the first intervention, a moral dilemma was designed to address the topic related to N-ST and the following moral issues that arise from the use of the nanoproducts. More details regarding the design and development of the TLS, the preparation of the dilemma and the implementation of the TLS are presented thoroughly elsewhere (cf. Christodoulou & Pnevmatikos, 2016; Pnevmatikos &

Christodoulou, in preparation). Additionally, the concept of size and scale was introduced, during the second intervention, the size-dependent property of hydrophobicity along with the lotus effect was introduced while during the third intervention the size-dependent property of absorption was presented. Each intervention lasted 90 minutes. At an instructional level, multiple representations and models were employed in order to introduce the concept of size as well as the concept of size-dependent properties. Additionally, students performed and designed real-life experiment regarding the size-dependent property of hydrophobicity while at the same time employed the control of variables strategy (cf. Pnevmatikos & Christodoulou, in preparation).

RESULTS

A 4 (dimension: concepts) x 3 (measures: pre, post and follow up) repeated measures analyses of variances ANOVA was conducted in order to examine whether the designed TLS integrating values in the conceptual understanding and change. Mauchly's test indicated that the assumption of sphericity had been violated, $p < .001$. Therefore, degrees of freedom were corrected using Greenhouse-Geiser (1959) estimates of sphericity. The within-subjects factors were dimension and time. Results revealed a significant both main effects of dimension, $F_{(2.759, 220.757)} = 20.108$, $p < 0.1$, $\eta_p^2 = .201$, and of time, $F_{(2,160)} = 30.629$, $p < 0.1$, $\eta_p^2 = .277$. Moreover, a significant interaction of dimension with time was obtained, $F_{(5.234, 418.718)} = 35.739$, $p < 0.1$, $\eta_p^2 = .309$ (see Table 2). Paired sample t-tests were performed for each of the four knowledge dimensions in order to examine the comparisons among different time measurements.

With respect to the dimension size-dependent property of gold a significant difference was revealed between pre and post measurement with a medium effect size, $t_{(43)} = 3.676$, $p < 0.1$, $d = 0.605$ as well as between pre and follow-up measurement, $t_{(43)} = 4.743$, $p < 0.1$, $d = 0.793$, where a medium effect size was also revealed. As expected, post and follow-up measurement did not reveal any significant difference, $t_{(43)} = -0.154$, $p = $ n.s. Students performed better after the intervention, and they kept their understanding for the size-dependent property long after the intervention. Regarding the dimension of hydrophobicity significant differences were revealed between pre and post measurement with a large effect size, $t_{(43)} = 6.128$, $p < 0.1$, $d = 1.040$, and between pre and follow-up measurement, again with a large effect $t_{(43)} = 5.966$, $p < 0.1$, $d = 0.977$. No difference was revealed between post and follow-up measurement $t_{(43)} = 1.045$, $p = $ n.s. Students performed better after the intervention, and they kept their understanding for the hydrophobicity long after the intervention. Concerning the dimension size concept between pre and post measurement, $t_{(43)} = 4.759$, $p < 0.1$, $d = 0.728$ as well as pre and follow-up measurement $t_{(43)} = 9.193$, $p < 0.1$, $d = 1.717$ were found significant differences in mean scores with a medium and a large effect size respectively. There was not found a significant difference between post and follow-up measurement $t_{(43)} = 2.758$,

p = n.s.). Students performed better after the intervention, and they kept their understanding for the size long after the intervention.

Finally, for the dimension of hydrophobicity application of the nano-coatings, significant differences were found only between the pre and follow-up measurement, $t_{(43)} = 1.827$, $p < 0.1$, $d = 0.275$ with a small effect size. There were not found significant differences between pre and post measurement, $t_{(43)} = -1.120$, p =n.s, as well as between post and follow-up measurement, $t_{(43)} = -0.350$, p = n.s.. Students performed better for the dimension of hydrophobicity application of the nano-coatings after the intervention, but their achievement appears to have large standard deviation. This was eliminated in the follow-up measure and regardless the lower difference in the means long after the intervention; the difference was found to reach a significant level.

Table 2. *Mean scores and standard deviations of students conceptual understanding of the four knowledge dimensions and different time measurements*

Dimension of knowledge	Time measurements					
	Pre-measurement		Post-measurement		Follow up measurement	
	M	SD	M	SD	M	SD
Size dependent property of gold	1.01	0.18	1.29	0.52	1.35	0.42
Hydrophobicity	0.92	0.23	1.60	0.61	1.44	0.54
Size concept	1.11	0.36	1.59	0.48	1.75	0.36
Hydrophobicity application of the nano-coatings	1.14	0.38	1.24	0.52	1.22	0.38

DISCUSSION

The aim of the current study was to investigate whether using V*a*KE as a basis for teaching science could promote besides the ethical dimension of science, conceptual change as well. Repeated measures ANOVA was conducted with dimension and time as the within-subjects factor. The main effect was revealed with respect to time and dimension, which means that students among the three different time measurements constructed new knowledge on N-ST regarding the four dimensions introduced.

The low mean scores in the pre-measurement indicate that students had already constructed naïve conceptions before instruction on N-ST in order to provide explanations for real-life problems. The post-measurement suggests that although students reached a better understanding of the introduced concepts, and thus they performed better in the generative questionnaire, they did not achieve full conceptual understanding meeting the requirements for conceptual change. This finding is in agreement with the framework theory suggesting that the conceptual change could be reached only through the enrichment of the previous conceptual structure, but, beyond the content, demands changes in many other levels such as the ontological, the representational and the epistemological level (Vosniadou & Skopeliti, 2014).

In addition, the fact that no significant difference was found between the pre and post measurements regarding the dimension *hydrophobicity application of the nano-coatings* implies that students faced difficulties in transferring knowledge from the context of hydrophobicity of the lotus effect to a similar context, namely nano-coatings. This can be due to the misconceptions students formed, which can inhibit the transfer of knowledge (Federer, Nehm, Opfer, & Pearl, 2014).

Further analysis based on different qualitative measurements is needed to examine whether students create alternative conceptions and the presuppositions that they support them. At the same time, transferring of knowledge can be particularly challenging in the case students cannot identify similarities between the "source" and the "target" context (Lucariello et al., 2016; Singh, 2008). This is generated due to the fact that knowledge is encoded in memory with the context in which it was acquired. Furthermore, the ability to transfer knowledge can be improved through expertise (Singh, 2008).

Finally, the mean scores of the follow-up measurements revealed that students retained their previously acquired knowledge in high levels – something which is in line with previous research findings (e.g., Lombardi, Sinatra, & Nussbaum, 2013; Loyens, Jones, Mikkers, & van Gog, 2015; Zoupidis et al., 2016).

The current study provided evidence indicating that VaKE, when adapted appropriately, can promote conceptual understanding. Since the designed TLS provided many opportunities for students to engage, it could be assumed according to previous findings that students were motivated to be involved in the learning challenges (Loukomies et al., 2013). Nevertheless, crucial for the achievement of conceptual understanding, are the adjustments made in the typical VaKE unit with respect to the theory and instruction for conceptual change. The adjustments focused on three important aspects that facilitate conceptual change. First, the topic of the models and how these facilitate the production and acquisition of the scientific knowledge were introduced. Particularly, modeling and multiple representations were integrated into the TLS since according to previous findings (Duit, Treagust, & Widodo, 2013; Jonassen & Easter, 2013) conceptual change can be facilitated due to their importance in the development of metaconceptual awareness, metacognitive skills and intentional learning (Vosniadou, 2010). Therefore, ontological, epistemological and representational changes can be promoted, and conceptual understanding can be achieved. Second, students employed at the beginning of the intervention to the control variable strategy through an experiment and then were asked to design an experiment on their one implementing once again the control variable strategy. Zoupidis et al. (2016) documented that direct teaching of procedural knowledge facilitates conceptual understanding. Third, students performed real experiments with physical manipulatives in the class as it is known that they promote conceptual understanding (Zacharia & Olympiou, 2011).

The current study showed that V*a*KE could be an effective teaching method to integrate values and citizenship education to the science education, and particularly to reach phenomena that need radical reconstruction of the initially constructed naive concepts towards the scientific ones. Thus, the current study challenges the reluctance of teachers to go beyond the scientific knowledge and to integrate topics strongly related to the decisions in real life considering the pros and cons of decisions in the problem-solving. The integration of moral aspects in teaching practices is upon the teachers' professional ethos.

At this point, it is crucial to mention the limitations of the study. The knowledge dimensions introduced were more with respect to the restricted duration of the TLS. Future research should devote more time for each concept in order for students to have the opportunity to become involved in the related activities and integrate the scientific information properly. Also, explicit instruction of epistemological knowledge should be taken into consideration for future implementations through the instruction of the nature of models. Finally, it would be important to design a study where the modified V*a*KE for conceptual change would be compared with a control group participating either in the typical V*a*KE unit (Patry et al., 2013) or in the inquiry-based teaching which is a challenging approach promoting conceptual change (Duit, Treagust, & Widodo, 2013).

REFERENCES

Bybee, R., & McCrae, B. (2011). Scientific literacy, and student attitudes: Perspectives from PISA 2006 science. *International Journal of Science Education, 33*(1), 7–26. doi:10.1080/09500693.2010.518644

Christodoulou, P., & Pnevmatikos, D. (2016, October 3–4). *Promoting conceptual change with values and knowledge education*. Electronic proceedings of the 3rd international conference education across borders, Bitola.

DeVries, R. (2000). Vygotsky, Piaget, and education: A reciprocal assimilation of theories and educational practices. *New Ideas in Psychology, 18*(2), 187–213.

Duit, R., Treagust, F., & Widodo, A. (2013). Teaching science for conceptual change: Theory and practice. In S. Vosniadou (Ed.), *International handbook of research on conceptual change* (2nd ed., pp. 487–503). New York, NY: Routledge.

EU-Commission. (2015). *Science education for responsible citizenship*. Luxembourg: EU Commission. Retrieved from http://ec.europa.eu/research/swafs/pdf/pub_science_education/KI-NA-26-893-EN-N.pdf

Euridyce. (2012). *Citizenship in Europe*. Brussels: European Commission.

Federer, M. R., Nehm, R. H., Opfer, J. E., & Pearl, D. (2015). Using a constructed-response instrument to explore the effects of item position and item features on the assessment of students' written scientific explanations. *Research in Science Education, 45*(4), 527–553.

Goodrum, D., & Rennie, L. (2007). *Australian school science education national action plan 2008–2012*. Canberra: Department of Education, Science and Training, Common wealth of Australia.

Gruber, M. (2009). Barriers to value education in schools: What teacher think. *Newsletter from EARLI SIG 13 Moral and Democratic Education, 4*, 26–30. Retrieved from http://vhost0309.web04.level27.be/resources/sigs/Sig%2013/Newsletters%20SIG%2013/Newsletter_5_SIG13.pdf

Hayes, A. F., & Krippendorff, K. (2007). Answering the call for a standard reliability measure for coding data. *Communication methods and measures, 1*(1), 77–89.

Jonassen, D., & Eatser, M. A. (2013). Model building for conceptual change. In S. Vosniadou (Ed.), *International handbook of research on conceptual change* (pp. 580–600). New York, NY: Routledge.

Keast, S., & Marango, K. (2015). Values and Knowledge Education (VaKE) in teacher education: Benefits for pre-service teachers when using dilemma stories. *Procedia – Social and Behavioral Sciences, 167*, 198–203.

Krippendorff, K. (1970). Estimating the reliability, systematic error and random error of interval data. *Educational and Psychological Measurement, 30*, 61–70.

Laherto, A. (2010). An analysis of the educational significance of nanoscience and nanotechnology in scientific and technological literacy. *Science Education International, 21*(3), 160–175.

Lombardi, D., Sinatra, G. M., & Nussbaum, E. M. (2013). Plausibility reappraisals and shifts in middle school students' climate change conceptions. *Learning and Instruction, 27*, 50–62.

Loukomies, A., Pnevmatikos, D., Lavonen, J., Spyrtou, A., Byman, R., Kariotoglou, P., & Juuti, K. (2013). Promoting students' interest and motivation towards science learning: The role of personal need and motivation orientations. *Research in Science Education, 43*, 2517–2539. doi:10.1007/s11165-013-9370-1

Loyens, S. M., Jones, S. H., Mikkers, J., & van Gog, T. (2015). Problem-based learning as a facilitator of conceptual change. *Learning and Instruction, 38*, 34–42.

Lucariello, J. M., Nastasi, B. K., Anderman, E. M., Dwyer, C., Ormiston, H., & Skiba, R. (2016). Science supports education: The behavioral research base for psychology's top 20 principles for enhancing Teaching and Learning. *Mind, Brain, and Education, 10*(1), 55–67.

Méheut, M., & Psillos, D. (2004). Teaching–learning sequences: Aims and tools for science education research. *International Journal of Science Education, 26*(5), 515–535.

OECD. (2016). *PISA 2015 assessment and analytical framework: Science, reading, mathematics and financial literacy*. Paris: OECD Publishing. Retrieved from http://dx.doi.org/10.1787/9789264255425-en

Olympiou, G., & Zacharia, Z. C. (2012). Blending physical and virtual manipulatives: An effort to improve students' conceptual understanding through science laboratory experimentation. *Science Education, 96*(1), 21–47.

Patry, J.-L., Reichmann, R., & Linortner, L. (2017). Values and Knowledge Education (VaKE) for lifelong learning in applied fields: Principles and general issues. In H. E. Vidergor & O. Sela (Eds.), *Innovative teaching strategies and methods promoting lifelong learning in higher education: From theory to practice* (pp. 187–213). New York, NY: Nova Sciences.

Patry, J.-L., & Weinberger, A. (2004). Kombination von konstruktivistischer Werterziehung und Wissenserwerb [Combination of constructivist values education and knowledge acquisition]. *Salzburger Beiträge zur Erziehungswissenschaft, 8*(2), 35–50.

Patry, J.-L., Weinberger, A., Weyringer, S., & Nussbaumer, M. (2013). Combining values and knowledge education. In B. J. Irby, G. Brown, R. Lara-Alecio, & S. Jackson (Eds.), *The handbook of educational theories* (pp. 565–579). Charlotte, NC: IAP- Information Age Publishing.

Patry, J.-L., Weyringer, S., & Weinberger, A. (2007). Combining values and knowledge education. In D. N. Aspin & J. D. Chapman (Eds.), *Values education and lifelong learning* (pp. 160–179). Dordrecht: Springer.

Pedaste, M., Mäeots, M., Siiman, L. A., De Jong, T., Van Riesen, S. A., Kamp, E. T., Manoli, C. C., Zacharia, C. Z., & Tsourlidaki, E. (2015). Phases of inquiry-based learning: Definitions and the inquiry cycle. *Educational Research Review, 14*, 47–61.

Pnevmatikos, D., & Christodoulou, P. (2015, August). *Nurturing in-service teachers' reflective thinking on values education using VaKE*. Paper presented at the 16th European Conference for Research on Learning and Instruction, Limassol.

Pnevmatikos, D., & Christodoulou, P. (in preparation). *The international handbook of mathematics teacher education*. Leiden, The Netherlands: Brill | Sense.

Pnevmatikos, D., Patry, J.-L., Weinberger, A., Linortner, L., Weyringer, S., Maron, R., & Gordon-Shaag, A. (2016). Combining values and knowledge education for lifelong transformative learning. In E. Panitsides & J. Talbot (Eds.), *Lifelong learning: Concepts, benefits, and challenges* (pp. 109–134). New York, NY: Nova Science.

Psillos, D., & Kariotoglou, P. (2016). Theoretical issues related to designing and developing teaching-learning sequences. In D. Psillos & P. Kariotoglou (Eds.), *Iterative design of teaching-learning sequences* (pp. 11–34). Dordrecht: Springer.

Sammel, A. J. (2014). Science as a human endeavour: Outlining scientific literacy and rethinking why we teach science. *Creative Education, 5*, 849–857.

Singh, C. (2008). Assessing student expertise in introductory physics with isomorphic problems. II. Effect of some potential factors on problem solving and transfer. *Physical Review Special Topics-Physics Education Research, 4*(1), 1–10. doi:10.1103/PhysRevSTPER.4.010105

Skopeliti, I. (2011). *The problem of conceptual change in the field of science education: Methodological and theoritical issues* (Unpublished doctoral dissertation). National and Kapodistrian University of Athens (UOA), Department of Philosophy and History of Science, Athens.

Vosniadou, S. (2002). Mental models in conceptual development. In L. Magnani & N. J. Nersessian (Eds.), *Model-based reasoning* (pp. 353–368). New York, NY: Springer.

Vosniadou, S. (2007). The cognitive-situative divide and the problem of conceptual change. *Educational Psychologist, 42*(1), 55–66.

Vosniadou, S. (2010). Instructional considerations in the use of external representations. In L. Verschaffel, E. De Corte, T. de Jong, & J. Elen (Eds.), *Use of representations in reasoning and problem solving* (pp. 36–54). New York, NY: Routledge.

Vosniadou, S. (2013). Conceptual change in learning and instruction: The framework theory approach. In S. Vosniadou (Ed.), *International handbook of research on conceptual change* (2nd ed., pp. 11–30). New York, NY: Routledge.

Vosniadou, S., & Skopeliti, I. (2014). Conceptual change from the framework theory side of the fence. *Science & Education, 23*(7), 1427–1445.

Vosniadou, S., Skopeliti, I., & Ikospentaki, K. (2004). Modes of knowing and ways of reasoning in elementary astronomy. *Cognitive Development, 19*(2), 203–222.

Weinberger, A. (2006). *Kombination von Werterziehung und Wissenserwerb: Evaluation des konstruktivistischen Unterrichtsmodells VaKE (Values and Knowledge Education) in der Sekundarstufe I.* Hamburg: Kovac.

Willemse, T. M., ten Dam, G., Geijsel, F., van Wessum, L., & Volman, M. (2015). Fostering teachers' professional development for citizenship education. *Teaching and Teacher Education, 49*, 118–127.

Zacharia, Z. C., & Olympiou, G. (2011). Physical versus virtual manipulative experimentation in physics learning. *Learning and Instruction, 21*(3), 317–331.

Zeidler, D. L., Berkowitz, M. W., & Bennett, K. (2014). Thinking (scientifically) responsibly: The cultivation of character in a global science education community. In M. P. Mueller, D. J. Tippins, & A. J. Stewart (Eds.), *Assessing schools for generation R (responsibility)* (pp. 83–99). Dordrecht: Springer.

Zoupidis, A., Pnevmatikos, D., Spyrtou, A., & Kariotoglou, P. (2016). The impact of procedural and epistemological knowledge on conceptual understanding: The case of density and floating–sinking phenomena. *Instructional Science, 44*(4), 315–334. doi:10.1007/s11251-016-9375-z

Dimitris Pnevmatikos
Department of Primary Education
University of Western Macedonia
Kozani, Greece

Panagiota Christodoulou
Department of Primary Education
University of Western Macedonia
Kozani, Greece

JOHANNES REITINGER

6. DEMOCRACY, RESPONSIBILITY, AND INQUIRY IN EDUCATION

Relationship and Empirical Accessibility Using the Criteria of Inquiry Learning Inventory (CILI)

INTRODUCTION AND STUDY OUTLINE

Based on John Dewey's far-reaching works (e.g., "Studies in Logical Theory", 1903; "Democracy and Education", 1916; "How We Think", 1933) democracy, responsibility, education, and inquiry are said to have a significant linkage with a high degree of practical relevance. In Dewey's sight, democracy is more than about being loyal, critical, and eager to learn; beyond that, it is linked to participation and is accompanied by responsibility. It embodies a "disposition to consider in advance the probable consequences of any projected step and deliberately to accept them" (Dewey, 1916, p. 24). Oser, Dick, and Patry (1992, p. 12) associate fairness, accountability, and careful decision-making with responsibility. According to Roth (2007) responsibility embraces a shift "from the moral commitment to learn about the other, the world and ourselves to a willingness to participate in and to pursue democratic deliberation in education" (p. 119). These arguments suggest a relationship between the pivotal theoretical constructs of this chapter, since participation, democratic deliberation, and decision-making are also inherent elements of inquiry learning arrangements (Reitinger, 2013, p. 25f; cf. Dewey, 2016, p. 115).

In this chapter, principles of democratic education are discussed, accompanied by an outline of ideas concerning its nexus with education for responsibility as well as their realization in practice. In a further step, a contemporary approach of inquiry-based education is introduced: the Theory of Inquiry Learning Arrangement (TILA; Reitinger, 2013, pp. 186–189; cf. Reitinger, Haberfellner, & Keplinger, 2016; cf. Patry, 2016). Thereby, the focus lies on a description of a set of criteria that define inquiry learning according to TILA. Further, the question is regarded, whether endeavors in democratic education for responsibility principally support the evolvement of the criteria of inquiry learning. Although it is theoretically plausible they do, an empirical verification will depend on appropriate measurement. It has to be emphasized that the research interest of the study at hand is not explicitly located in the empirical investigation of the relationship between democratic education for responsibility and inquiry learning, but rather in the introduction and advancement of an inventory able to measure the evolvement of criteria of inquiry learning. In concreto, the Criteria of Inquiry Learning Inventory (CILI; Reitinger, 2016) is recommended, introduced, and further developed (testing of a second-order model). The considerations close with an invitation to use CILI to pursue empirical investigations of the relationship between democratic education for responsibility and inquiry learning.

LIVED DEMOCRACY WITHIN LEARNING ARRANGEMENTS

According to Saether (2012), the ultimate aim of democratic education is "that the individual acts morally and democratically in social settings, not only as an immediate result of educational innovations in the short run but also in the long run" (p. 188). To achieve this aim, democratic educational efforts follow a range of principles that are theoretically or/and empirically reasonable.

Principles of Democratic Education for Responsibility

Democratic education understood as "an education that democratizes learning itself" (Gould, 2003, p. 244), begins with involvement. Hence, discourse and collaborate decision-making concerning content and method of learning are fundamental principles teachers and learners pursue in democratic educational arrangements.

Decades ago, Dewey (1916) already argued that students must experience active participation and democracy in order to internalize it and grow up into adults who are themselves able to act responsibly towards themselves, others, and the world around them (cf. Garrison, Neubert, & Reich, 2016, p. 75; Alt & Reingold, 2012, p. 2). In this concern, Dewey (1916) analyses:

> A society which makes provision for participation in its good of all its members on equal terms and which secures flexible readjustment of its institutions through interaction of the different forms of associated life is in so far democratic. Such a society must have a type of education that gives individuals a personal interest in social relationships and control, and the habits of mind that secure social changes. (p. 115)

Parallels to Dewey's deliberations can be found in contemporary literature. According to Saether (2012), democratic education should be related to participation, responsibility, autonomous thinking, tolerance, empathy, trust, justice, and the dignity of a human being (p. 182). From Ressissi's (2012) point of view, democratic education for responsibility and the improvement of democracy itself can be fostered "by constant practicing of children and youth as problem solvers, and thus – preparing them for their future role as democratic decision makers, concerning their very interests and problems" (p. 79). In reference to Lester and Onore (1990), Alt (2012) also highlights cooperation and problem solving through compromise as necessary essences of a democratic society (p. 124). Benner's (2008, pp. 102, 112) reflections on democratic togetherness accentuate the importance of participation, interaction, and communication that seal traditional gaps between specific groups (cf. Dewey, 1916, p. 136). Waghid (2014) emphasized the principle of equality of students' and teachers' voices (p. 33).

Democratic Education in Practice

Activities for a democratic educational practice that supports its participants to develop a "sense of responsibility" (Töremen, 2011, p. 273) are diverse. Nevertheless, a review of the practice-oriented literature (e.g., Dewey, 1903; European Democratic Education Community, 2016; Knoester, 2012; Kohlberg, Wasserman, & Richardson, 1978; Ressissi, 2012) reveal some common characteristics:

- An understanding of democracy as both a goal and method of education.
- Government boards with representatives of all partners of a learning institution.
- Confrontation with moral conflicts.
- Student involvement in responsible decision-making.
- Strong parent participation.
- Usage of summative assessments and portfolios for the visualization of individual achievement.
- Arranging experiences with opportunities to solve personally relevant problems.

Although the taken review of democratic principles in education is anything but sufficient, a coherency with the construct of inquiry learning is identifiable, whereby we come across the content of the following section.

DEMOCRATIC EDUCATION FOR RESPONSIBILITY AND INQUIRY LEARNING – CORRESPONDENCE AND EMPIRICAL ACCESSIBILITY

Dewey (1916) states that "education is not an affair of 'telling' or being told, but an active, constructive process" (p. 46). Associating this process with inquiry – understood as the experimental method (Dewey, 1932/1985, pp. 151, 329) – he designed a model that describes inquiry learning in five steps: (a) suggestion, (b) rational examination of the problem to identify its constitution, (c) formation of hypotheses, (d) reasoning to allow logical implications, and (e) testing by observation or experimentation (Dewey, 1903, 1933, pp. 72–78; cf. Aulls & Shore, 2008, p. 155). Dewey associated the experimental method with responsible, reflective thinking (cf. Reitinger, 2014) and described it as the "method of democracy" (Dewey, 1932/1985, p. 329).

Considering this as well as some of the above-mentioned principles of democratic education (e.g., participation, autonomous thinking, problem-solving) according to Alt (2012), Ressissi (2012), Saether (2012), and Waghid (2014), the inherent nexus with inquiry learning becomes visible. In the next section, this correspondence will be worked out more explicitly by adducing a concrete theoretical approach; the Theory of Inquiry Learning Arrangements (TILA; Reitinger, 2013, pp. 186–189).

THE THEORY OF INQUIRY LEARNING ARRANGEMENTS (TILA)

Inquiry learning has been developed, evaluated, and implemented in various educational contexts (e.g., elementary education, education at schools, teacher education) by means of various concepts and approaches (e.g., Ansari, 2009; Aulls & Shore, 2007; Dewey, 1903, 1933; Littleton, Scanlon, & Sharples, 2012; Roters, Schneider, Koch-Priewe, Thiele, & Wildt, 2009). The Theory of Inquiry Learning Arrangements (TILA) according to Reitinger (2013, pp. 186–189) represents another attempt of that kind. This theory specifies the concept of self-determined inquiry learning according to the precepts of a critical multiplism (Patry, 2013, 2016, pp. 172–175), which, in short, means that TILA is underpinned by multiple theoretical systematics (Campbell, 1988) and accompanied by a critical research using multiple methods (Patry, 2013, pp. 51–52). The multiple theoretical systematics of TILA refers mainly to Self-Determination Theory (SDT; Ryan & Deci, 2004), the early roots of inquiry learning coined by Dewey (1903, 1933), Constructivism (Reich, 2010; Patry, 2014), and the German scholarly debate of the issue of *Bildung* (cf. Benner, 2008; Gudjons, Teske, & Winkel, 1999).

Criteria of Inquiry Learning According to TILA

One of TILA's frame constructs – and probably the most essential theoretical key idea of the approach – is the so-called definitional frame construct (Reitinger, 2013, pp. 20–45). It encompasses a set of criteria that describes what inquiry learning is. In Table 1 these criteria are listed, accompanied by their pivotal indicators. (For more details concerning the theoretical connection of these criteria with TILA, see Reitinger, Haberfellner, & Keplinger, 2016.)

According to TILA, the evolvement of these criteria within educational arrangements indicates inquiry learning. However, the criteria should not be

Table 1. The criteria of inquiry learning (Reitinger, 2013, pp. 20–45)

Criterion	Indicators	Characteristic
Discovery interest	Expressing interest in the content of learning.	Inquiry-related conditions
Method affirmation	Expressing interest in the method of learning.	
Experience-based hypothesizing	Making suppositions concerning personally relevant contexts; thinking about possible solutions.	Inquiry-related action domains
Authentic exploration	Being encouraged to explore and discover; gaining exciting new insights by oneself.	
Critical discourse	Having opportunities to tell and reflect ideas; participating in interesting and meaningful conversations.	
Conclusion-based transfer	Being encouraged to do more with gained insights; having ideas about meaningful applications of learned contexts.	

understood as absolute attributes. They are of a continual nature and can emerge from a very low to a maximum extent. "That is to say, the higher the number of criteria met and the more fully the evolvement, the more intensive the Inquiry Learning process" (Reitinger, Haberfellner, & Keplinger, 2016, p. 4).

TILA and Its Nexus with Education for Responsibility

In a democratic society, it is essential that individuals learn to fulfill their responsibilities. According to Töremen (2011), this learning process needs realms of experience that offer free choices as well as educators who are aware of their own responsibilities, adopting "a more humanistic control ideology instead of a custodial one" (p. 274; cf. Ryan & Deci, 2004; Hoy, 2001). In the criteria of inquiry learning mentioned above, people's right of choice represents a source of responsibility. Further, the criteria typify authentic and personally relevant actions and interactions, considering one's psychological and emotional needs. Experiences of this kind are also essential to develop a sense of responsibility for behavior (Töremen, 2011, p. 273). Not least, responsibility is an inherent element of inquiry learning arrangements according to TILA itself as responsible acting when facing a problem alone or with others is a denominator of successful learning (cf. Reitinger, 2013, pp. 26, 35, 51, 57).

RESEARCH INTEREST

By reflecting the aforementioned characteristics of democratic education for responsibility and recognizing its nexus with criteria of inquiry learning according to TILA (inquiry-related action domains; experience-based hypothesizing, authentic exploration, critical discourse, and conclusion-based transfer), the hypothesis arises that endeavors of democratic education for responsibility may concurrently support the evolvement of criteria of inquiry learning. To ascertain this theoretically plausible thesis, empirical investigations will be necessary.

However, the objective of the study at hand is not the realization of such an investigation but rather the discussion and further advancement of an inventory that could be used for investigation due to its potential to measure the evolvement of criteria of inquiry learning. The following chapter will deal with this intention.

SCALE DEVELOPMENT

To measure the evolvement of criteria of inquiry learning within various learning arrangements (e.g., approaches of democratic education) the Criteria of Inquiry Learning Inventory (CILI; Reitinger, 2016) may be helpful. This post-interventional, retrospective scale, applicable especially in tertiary education, quantifies four out of six criteria of inquiry learning. These criteria are the inquiry-related action-domains (see Table 1), namely a) experience-based hypothesizing (*exhy*), b) authentic exploration (*auex*), c) critical discourse (*crdi*), and d) conclusion-based transfer (*cotr*).

Recapitulation of Previous Scale Development Endeavor

Reitinger (2016) developed CILI according to the directives of Classical Test Theory (CTT; DeVellis, 2011). As shown as follows, the theoretically underpinned four-factor-model according to the operationalized four criteria of inquiry learning (*exhy, auex, crdi, cotr*) could be confirmed. The testing of a potential existence of a second-order overall construct representing inquiry learning (*inle*) as a whole has not been performed up to now, though such a construct is theoretically assumable. The testing of it will be the subsequent aim of the treatise at hand.

Table 2. The Criteria of Inquiry Learning Inventory (CILI; Reitinger, 2016, p. 56)

Code	Item	R^2	Related partial construct	Std. regression weights
(a)	This Learning activity encouraged me to discover open questions.	.379	*auex*	.616
(b)	Many situations occurred where I was able to tell my ideas.	.295	*crdi*	.543
(c)	This learning activity led me to suppositions about possible solutions.	.451	*exhy*	.671
(d)	I gained exciting insights into the matter through exploration.	.244	*auex*	.494
(e)	I definitely want to do more with the insights I have gained during this learning activity.	.493	*cotr*	.702
(f)	I remember many interesting conversations during this learning activity.	.576	*crdi*	.759
(g)	At this learning activity, many suppositions came to my mind.	.414	*exhy*	.643
(h)	During this learning activity, I found out new insights by myself.	.360	*auex*	.600
(i)	I have many ideas about meaningful things I can do with the new insights.	.647	*cotr*	.804
(j)	This learning activity was full of meaningful discussions.	.611	*crdi*	.781
(k)	I thought about possible solutions.	.545	*exhy*	.738
(l)	This learning activity gave me ideas for interesting further activity.	.602	*cotr*	.776

The 12 CILI-Items are anchored on a 7-fold scale ranging from 1 (not true at all) over 4 (somewhat true) to 7 (very true).

Instruction and items of CILI. CILI consists of 12 items. Each construct (exhy, auex, crdi, cotr) described further up is indicated by three items respectively (see Table 2). For the application of CILI, the following instruction should be used:

Please rate the statements below about the experienced *X*, termed hereafter as learning activity!

X means the considered specific learning activity. When applying CILI, it should be replaced by concrete terms (e.g., workshop, tutorial, course, V*a*KE project [Weinberger, Patry, & Weyringer, 2008], chemistry lesson, inclusive learning arrangement, democratic learning experience [cf. Waghid, 2014, pp. 83–87; Dewey, 1916], pedagogic seminar, cooking class, lecture, internship).

Review of already performed analyses of CILI. In the course of the initial publication of CILI, Reitinger (2016) traced scale development endeavors, performed in the course of two studies with different samples. The first study (N = 302; student teachers from tertiary educational institutions) was used to find a set of suitable items through item tests, Exploratory Factor Analysis (EFA), tests of internal consistency, and tests of partial construct correlations (pp. 45–49). Within the second study (N = 544; also student teachers from tertiary educational institutions), tests of internal consistency, normal distributions, and partial construct correlations, as well as First-order Confirmatory Factor Analysis (First-order CFA) were performed (pp. 49–54) to obtain a standardized set of 12 items. The result of the CFA confirms the presumed four-factor model (exhy, auex, crdi, cotr) with the parameters SRMR = .038 (threshold: < .050; Byrne, 2010, p. 77), CFI = .955 (threshold: > .950; Schreiber, Stage, King, Nora, & Barlow, 2006, p. 330), and RMSEA = .063 (threshold: < .070; Steiger, 2007), as well as an acceptable Chi-Square-Test (χ^2) for Goodness-of-Fit. (For more details see Reitinger, 2016, pp. 49–54.)

The 12 items of CILI are shown in Table 2 together with their squared multiple correlations (R^2) as well as their standardized regression weights relating to the associated partial construct.

Current Intention

As mentioned above, CILI has not yet been examined about a potential second-order main construct. Notwithstanding, the theoretical background represented by TILA, highly significant covariances, and considerable correlations between the partial constructs (see Table 3) are giving good reasons to do this.

Hence, this chapter intends to enlighten this context by testing the following hypothesis:

H: The four partial constructs of CILI (a) experience-based hypothesizing (*exhy*), (b) authentic exploration (*auex*), (c) critical discourse (*crdi*), and (d) conclusion-based transfer (*cotr*), representing four criteria of inquiry learning according to TILA, are sheltered by a statistically verifiable main construct theorized within TILA as inquiry learning (*inle*).

Table 3. Covariances (unstandardized estimates) and correlations (standardized estimates) between the partial constructs

Path	Covariances (unstd.)	S.E.	C.R.	p	Correlations (std.)
exhy ẞà auex	1.160	.118	9.812	< .001	.908
auex ẞà crdi	1.277	.130	9.854	< .001	.876
crdi ẞà cotr	.933	.108	8.629	< .001	.560
auex ẞà cotr	1.249	.124	10.085	< .001	.897
exhy ẞà crdi	.884	.105	8.460	< .001	.578
exhy ẞà cotr	1.100	.108	10.158	< .001	.753

Method

To investigate H, it has to be tested, whether the main construct inquiry learning (*inle*) loads well into the underlying partial constructs. Therefore, authors of statistics literature (e.g., Byrne, 2010; Weber, 2017, pp. 134–136; Chen, Sousa, & West, 2005) recommend performing a Second-order Confirmatory Factor Analysis (Second-order CFA). The concrete objectives of a Second-order CFA are (a) the estimation of regression weights and factor loadings of a main construct on several partial constructs as well as (b) the calculation of various Goodness-of-Fit parameters (e.g., SRMR, CFI, RMSEA, χ^2).

For this second-order analysis, the above-mentioned sample data of 544 student teachers (435 female; 108 male; 1 missing statement) from tertiary educational institutions was used again. (For more details concerning the sample see Reitinger, 2016, p. 49.)

The outcome stated below is based on Maximum Likelihood estimations. For all analyses, the software IBM AMOS was utilized.

Findings

The estimated model tested by Second-order CFA is pictured in Figure 1. The path diagram includes estimates of standardized regression weights and squared multiple correlations (R^2).

Table 4 comprises the unstandardized regression weights and shows significant effects of the central construct (*inle*) on all partial constructs (*exhy, auex, crdi, cotr*).

It has to be mentioned that the model described in Figure 1 and Table 4 is a corrected model with a manually determined value of one particular residual (r_2). The reason for this correction lies in the fact that the uncorrected calculated model lacks a thorough proper solution, as it shows one standardized regression weight and one squared multiple correlation (R^2) above 1 for the factor *auex*. According

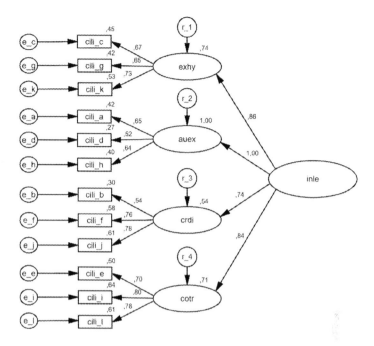

Figure 1. Second-order model of CILI derived from the theoretical approach TILA and tested by confirmatory factor analysis (CFA)

Table 4. Regression weights (unstandardized estimates) and factor loadings of the primary construct on the partial constructs (standardized estimates)

Path	Regr. weights (unstd.)	S.E.	C.R.	p	Loadings (std.)
exhy ← inle	1.000	–	–	–	.860
auex ← inle	1.190	.100	11.956	< .001	1.000
crdi ← inle	0.987	.088	11.195	< .001	.737
Cotr ← inle	1.085	.088	12.328	< .001	.840

to Chen, Bollen, Paxton, Curran, & Kirby (2001, p. 470) and Weber (2017, p. 132) such an outcome is invalid and indicates probable sample fluctuations, model misspecifications, underidentification (Byrne, 2010, p. 34), or the existence of outliers. As suggested by Chen et al. (2001, pp. 501–505), Weber (2017, pp. 132–133), and Newsom (2017), the problem can be compensated by an adaption of undue estimates of parameters, e.g., negative regression weights of residuals (negative error variances). If the corrected outcome converges, it can be assumed that the vagueness of the outcome is relatively small. Nevertheless, following the recommendations of statistics literature (e.g., Weber, 2017, p. 133) the entire result of a compensated analysis has to be treated with caution and, therefore, relativized.

As mentioned, Figure 1 and Table 4 depict the estimates of the corrected model (negative regression weight of residual r_2 set to zero). Regarding this outcome – basing on a compensated model – together with borderline parameters of model-fit like SRMR = .042 (threshold: < .050; Byrne, 2010, p. 77), CFI = .944 (threshold: > .950; Schreiber, Stage, King, Nora, & Barlow, 2006, p. 330), and RMSEA = .068 (threshold: < .070; Steiger, 2007), and a critical Chi-Square-Test (χ^2) for Goodness-of-Fit (χ^2 / df = 3.520; threshold: < 3; Weber, 2017, p. 131), the assumption of a statistically manifest Second-order factor (*inle*) concerning the four-dimensional CILI has to be treated with caution. The Target-coefficient *T* according to Marsh & Hovecar (1985), which is the ratio of the χ^2 of the First-order model to the χ^2 of the Second-order model, further underpins this conclusion with T = .842 (threshold: > .9; Spence, Barrett, & Turner, 2003, p. 615).

DISCUSSION AND FURTHER DIRECTIONS

The treatise at hand deals with the interrelationship of democratic education for responsibility and inquiry learning according to the Theory of Inquiry Learning Arrangements (TILA; Reitinger, 2013, pp. 186–189; Reitinger, Haberfellner, & Keplinger, 2016; cf. Patry, 2016). Following the considerations of several authors, including Dewey (1903, 1916, 1932/1985, 1933), an inherent affiliation between the constructs can be assumed.

Further, the chapter pursues the goal to pave the way for empirical investigations of the addressed interrelationship. To investigate the context an empirical inventory might be helpful. Within the chapter, such an inventory (Criteria of Inquiry Learning Inventory; CILI; Reitinger, 2016) is introduced and further tested. CILI measures the evolvement of inquiry learning within learning arrangements. It encompasses four inquiry-related criteria, (a) experience-based hypothesizing, (b) authentic exploration, (c) critical discourse, and (d) conclusion-based transfer. Within two independent studies (Reitinger, 2016), CILI has yet been tested according to Classical Test Theory (CTT; DeVellis, 2011), including the application of First-order Confirmatory Factor Analysis (First-order CFA), delivering good fit parameters for the presumed four-factor-model. Nevertheless, the statistical testing of the theoretically derivable second-order overall construct representing inquiry learning as a whole has not yet been performed and was, therefore, the attempt of the documented investigation at hand (see hypothesis [H]). Regarding the further up calculated fit parameters of the Second-order model, the following conclusion seems to be appropriate. Although the Second-order factor inquiry learning is theoretically reasonable, this central construct is statistically only limited verifiable. This means that H cannot be thoroughly confirmed. Overlooking the corrected improper solutions of the Second-order CFA (that relativize the investigation in a general manner), the outcome could also be an indicator for a heterogeneous nature of inquiry learning according to TILA and its four inquiry-related action domains (criteria) that is stronger than originally suggested (cf. Byrne, 2010, pp. 97–160). Hence, a summing-up of all CILI-items into one representative variable is not categorically wrong, but it should be taken with a grain of salt. In other words, I recommend an analysis of data, collected with CILI, differentiated according to the four partial-constructs.

Closing this treatise, I would like to return to the initial idea of my reflections concerning the interrelationship of democratic education and inquiry learning. In my estimation, an empirical investigation is worth being carried out regarding the hypothesis that endeavors of democratic education may concurrently support the evolvement of criteria of inquiry learning. Therefore, the introduced and advanced CILI could be applied. However, the chapter at hand may not clarify this supposition. However, it offers a standardized inventory to all interested scientists and may, therefore, help to motivate future research endeavors in that direction.

REFERENCES

Alt, D. (2012). Constructivist teaching methods. In D. Alt & R. Reingold (Eds.), *Changes in teacher's moral role: From passive observers to moral and democratic leaders* (pp. 121–131). Rotterdam, The Netherlands: Sense Publishers.

Alt, D., & Reingold, R. (2012). Current changes in teacher's role definition. In D. Alt & R. Reingold (Eds.), *Changes in teacher's moral role* (pp. 1–11). Rotterdam, The Netherlands: Sense Publishers.

Ansari, S. (2009). *Schule des Staunens: Lernen und Forschen mit Kindern* [School of amazement: Learning and exploring with children]. Heidelberg: Springer.

Aulls, M. W., & Shore, B. M. (2008). *Inquiry in education*. New York, NY: Routledge.

Benner, D. (2008). *Bildungstheorie und Bildungsforschung: Grundlagenreflexionen und Anwendungsfelder* [Theory of Bildung and educational research: Basic reflections and fields of application]. Paderborn: Schöningh.

Byrne, B. M. (2010). *Structural equation modeling with AMOS: Basic concepts, applications, and programming*. New York, NY: Routledge.

Campbell, D. T. (1988). Descriptive epistemology: Psychological, sociological, and evolutionary. In E. S. Overman (Ed.), *Methodology and epistemology for social science: Selected papers, Donald T. Campbell* (pp. 435–486). Chicago, IL: University of Chicago Press.

Chen, F. F., Bollen, K. A., Paxton, P., Curran, P. J., & Kirby, J. B. (2001). Improper solutions in structural equation models: Causes, consequences, and strategies. *Sociological Methods & Research, 29*(4), 468–508.

Chen, F. F., Sousa, H. K., & West, S. G. (2005). Testing measurement invariance of second-order factor models. *Structural Equation Modeling, 12*(3), 471–492.

DeVellis, R. F. (2011). *Scale development: Theory and applications*. Thousand Oaks, CA: Sage Publication.

Dewey, J. (1903). *Studies in logical theory*. Chicago, IL: University of Chicago Press.

Dewey, J. (1916). *Democracy and education*. New York, NY: Macmillan.

Dewey, J. (1932/1985). Ethics. In J. A. Boydston (Ed.), *John Dewey: The later works, 1925–1953* (Vol. 7). Carbondale, IL: Southern Illinois University Press.

Dewey, J. (1933). *How we think: A restatement of the relation of reflective thinking to the educative process*. Boston, MA: Heath & Co.

European Democratic Education Community. (2016). *EUDEC*. Retrieved from http://www.eudec.org

Garrison, J., Neubert, S., & Reich, K. (2016). *Democracy and education reconsidered: Dewey after one hundred years*. New York, NY: Routledge.

Gould, E. (2003). *The university in a corporate culture*. New Haven, CT: Yale University Press.
Gudjons, R., Teske, R., & Winkel, R. (1999). *Didaktische Theorien* [Theories of didactics]. Hamburg: Bermann und Helbig.
Hoy, W. K. (2001). The pupil control studies: A historical, theoretical, and empirical analysis. *Journal of Educational Administration, 39*, 424–444.
Knoester, M. (2012). *Democratic education in practice: Inside the mission hill school*. New York, NY: Teachers College Press.
Kohlberg, L., Wasserman, E., & Richardson, N. (1978). Die gerechte schul-kooperative [The just cooperation at school]. In G. Portele (Ed.), *Sozialisation und Moral: Neuere Ansätze zur moralischen Entwicklung und Erziehung* [Socialisation and morality: Contemporary approaches of moral development and education] (pp. 215–259). Weinheim: Beltz.
Lester, N. B., & Onore, C. S. (1990). *Learning change: One school district meets language across curriculum*. Portsmouth, NH: Boynton/Cook Publishers.
Littleton, K, Scanlon, E., & Sharples, M. (Eds.). (2012). *Orchestrating inquiry learning*. New York, NY: Routledge.
Marsh, H. W., & Hocevar, D. (1985). Application of confirmatory factor analysis to the study of self-concept: First- and higher-order factor models and their invariance across groups. *Psychological Bulletin, 97*, 562–582.
Newsom, J. (2017). *Improper solutions in SEM*. Retrieved from http://web.pdx.edu/~newsomj/semclass/
Oser, F., Dick, A., & Patry, J.-L. (1992). Responsibility, effectiveness, and the domains of educational research. In F. Oser, A. Dick, & J.-L. Patry (Eds.), *Effective and responsible teaching: The new synthesis* (pp. 3–13). San Francisco, CA: Jossey-Bass.
Patry, J.-L. (2013). Beyond multiple methods: Critical multiplism on all levels. *International Journal of Multiple Approaches, 7*(1), 50–65.
Patry, J.-L. (2014). Die Viabilität und der Viabilitäts-Check von Antworten [The viability and the viability-check of answers]. In C. Giordano & J.-L. Patry (Eds.), *Fragen! Antworten? Interdisziplinäre Perspektiven* [Questions! Answers? Interdisciplinary perspectives] (pp. 11–15). Wien: Lit.
Patry, J.-L. (2016). Inquiry learning arrangements from the perspective of critical multiplism and related concepts. In J. Reitinger, C. Haberfellner, E. Brewster, & M. Kramer (Eds.), *Theory of inquiry learning arrangements. research, reflection, and implementation* (pp. 171–186). Kassel: University Press.
Reitinger, J. (2013). *Forschendes Lernen: Theorie, Evaluation und Praxis in naturwissenschaftlichen Lernarrangements* [Inquiry learning: Theory, evaluation, and practice in science learning arrangements]. Immenhausen bei Kassel: Prolog.
Reitinger, J. (2014). Beyond reflection: Thinking outside the box of a necessary but not sufficient condition for successful education in a heterogeneous world. In D. Hollick, M. Neißl, M. Kramer, & J. Reitinger (Eds.), *Heterogenität in pädagogischen Handlungsfeldern: Perspektiven: Befunde: Konzeptionelle Ansätze* [Heterogeneity in educational fields of action: Perspectives: Findings: Conceptual approaches] (pp. 39–59). Kassel: University Press.
Reitinger, J. (2016). On the nature and empirical accessibility of inquiry learning: The Criteria of Inquiry Learning Inventory (CILI). In J. Reitinger, C. Haberfellner, E. Brewster, & M. Kramer (Eds.), *Theory of inquiry learning arrangements: Research, reflection, and implementation* (pp. 39–59). Kassel: University Press.
Reitinger, J., Haberfellner, C., & Keplinger, G. (2016). The Theory of Inquiry Learning Arrangements (TILA). In J. Reitinger, C. Haberfellner, E. Brewster, & M. Kramer (Eds.), *Theory of inquiry learning arrangements: Research, reflection, and implementation* (pp. 39–59). Kassel: University Press.
Ressissi, N. (2012). Social literacy curriculum: Education for significant democratic decision-making through integrative study of social problems. In D. Alt & R. Reingold (Eds.), *Changes in teacher's moral role: From passive observers to moral and democratic leaders* (pp. 73–80). Rotterdam, The Netherlands: Sense Publishers.
Roters, B., Schneider, R., Koch-Priewe, B., Thiele, J., & Wildt, J. (Eds.). (2009). *Forschendes Lernen im Lehramtsstudium: Hochschuldidaktik, Professionalisierung, Kompetenzentwicklung* [Inquiry learning in teacher education:Didactics, professionalization, development of competences]. Bad Heilbrunn: Klinkhardt.

Roth, K. (2007). Education for responsibility: Knowledge, ethics and deliberation. In K. Roth & I. Gur-Ze'ev (Eds.), *Education in the era of globalization* (pp. 105–121). Dordrecht: Springer.

Ryan, R. M., & Deci, E. L. (2004). An overview of self-determination theory: An organismic-dialectical Perspective. In E. L. Deci & R. M. Ryan (Eds.), *Handbook of self-determination research* (pp. 3–36). Rochester, NY: The University of Rochester Press.

Saether, J. (2012). Moral and democratic education in the context of science education. In D. Alt & R. Reingold (Eds.), *Changes in teacher's moral role: From passive observers to moral and democratic leaders* (pp. 181–200). Rotterdam, The Netherlands: Sense Publishers.

Schreiber, J. B., Stage, F. K., King, J., Nora, A., & Barlow, E. A. (2006). Reporting structural equation modeling and confirmatory factor analysis results. *The Journal of Educational Research, 6*, 323–337.

Spence, S. H., Barrett, P. M., & Turner, C. M. (2003). Psychometric properties of the Spence chrildren's anxiety scale with young adolescents. *Journal of Anxiety Disorders, 17*, 605–625.

Steiger, J. H. (2007). Understanding the limitations of global fit assessment in structural equation modeling. *Personality and Individual Differences, 42*(5), 893–898.

Töremen, F. (2011). The responsibility education of teacher candidates. *Educational Sciences: Theory & Practice, 11*(1), 273–277.

Waghid, Y. (2014). *Pedagogy out of bounds: Untamed variations of democratic education.* Rotterdam, The Netherlands: Sense Publishers.

Weber, C. (2017). *Elterliche Erziehung und externalisierende Verhaltensprobleme von Kindern* [Parental education and externalized behavioral problems of children]. Wiesbaden: Springer VS.

Weinberger, A., Patry, J.-L., & Weyringer, S. (2008). *Das Unterrichtsmodell VaKE (Values and Knowledge Education): Handbuch für Lehrerinnen und Lehrer* [The instructional model VaKE: Handbook for teachers]. Innsbruck: Studienverlag.

Johannes Reitinger
Private University College of Teacher Education of the Diocese of Linz, Austria
and
University of Kassel
Kassel, Germany

SARAH FORSTER-HEINZER

7. RESPONSIBILITY AS THE PRINCIPLE DENOMINATOR OF PEDAGOGICAL ETHOS

An Empirical Analysis of Pedagogical Responsibility from the Vocational Trainers' Perspective

INTRODUCTION

Nowadays it is broadly acknowledged that ethos is one important element of professionalism (e.g., Baumert & Kunter, 2006; Colby & Sullivan, 2008; Heikkerö, 2008; Tenorth, 2006). Within the context of education, Tenorth emphasized "[…] the question of how professionalism is established and how teaching becomes possible has to be addressed at two levels, which professionalism must join to unify: ethos and competence […]" (2006, p. 590; transl. author). A decisive criterion of professionalism – besides others – is often the specific responsibility professional members have to assume (Carr, 2010). As Oser, Dick, and Patry emphasized: "Responsibility is a 'control' that ensures that fairness, accountability, honesty, and care will be introduced into any decision-making process in a professional field" (1992, p. 12). Acting with professionalism, therefore, means to assume responsibility and entails making decisions. Professionalism is attributed to a person, but the content of professionalism (what it means to be and act professionally) needs to be defined by the profession's characteristics and its members (Forster-Heinzer, 2015). Without knowing the content of professionalism, no effective professional training program can be developed (Diehl, 2005). However, this is the very aim of every profession-related training institution. Therefore, to provide a basis for discussion about professionalism, professional ethics should explain the responsibility that professionals have towards their clients (Roth, 1995) but also towards the profession itself or the society as a whole (Colby & Sullivan, 2008). When delving into literature on professional ethos, it becomes obvious that researchers either focus on an individual subjective meaning or on a cultural objective meaning (for an overview see Forster-Heinzer, 2015, p. 13). On the objective level, the ethos of an institution or an occupation/profession is studied. The former finds its form of expression in an institution's overall guidelines, the latter in professional codes. Professional codes foster understanding of the profession by defining its underlying responsibilities, providing a monitory function at the same time. But, as Orlenius (2006) stressed, ethos is not a matter of law and jurisprudence but of personal responsibility and accountability. Moreover, in an earlier work, this chapter's author analyzed different ethos approaches such as understanding ethos as an attitude towards moral values (e.g., Brezinka, 1988; Latzko, 2012), an individual commitment to professional codes (e.g., Umstead et al., 2011; von Hentig, 2009), a virtue (e.g., Fenstermacher, 1992), or finding its highest expression in a discursive approach (e.g., Oser, 1998). Despite different theoretical perspectives, these ethos approaches agree upon the assumption that skills and knowledge are not enough to act professionally. And they consider ethos to be an important element of professionalism, that is closely linked to professional responsibility (Forster-Heinzer, 2015, p. 48). Therefore, ethos is understood as a person's active commitment to professional responsibility. Consequently, ethos is associated with the question of how individuals perceive their professional responsibility.

In this chapter, the focus lies on responsibility as the principle denominator of the professional ethos and is studied in the context of vocational company trainer's pedagogical responsibility. More precisely, this chapter questions the trainers' sense of pedagogical responsibility and how this sense is influenced by individual but also organizational characteristics. Thus, up to now, little research exists on the trainer's sense of pedagogical responsibility and its challenges. Besides skill training and providing knowledge, a trainer is held responsible for developing the trainee's professional identity, personal integrity, and critical self-reflection (Jalovaara, 2000). These social or societal expectations commit the trainer to ensure a comprehensive vocational education – one providing the trainee everything necessary to become a skilled and qualified specialist within a particular occupation. Therefore, trainers have to respond and give reasons to parents, occupational associations, and vocational departments when apprentices fail to pass their final practical exams or when they drop out of apprenticeship training early. However, being a vocational trainer and holding a pedagogical responsibility often consists merely of an additional function besides being the owner of the company, the factory manager, or the division manager. Consequently, the pedagogical responsibility is only one among others. Situations might occur in which differing responsibilities challenge each other. For instance, a trainer needs to decide whether to assign an apprentice to productive routine work (company's interest, financial responsibility) or to give him/her the best opportunity to foster professional skills (apprentice's best interest, educational responsibility). Since the pedagogical ethos is displayed in a trainer's commitment to the facets of pedagogical responsibility mentioned, one condition is the trainer's awareness of this responsibility. Without it, ethos is impossible.

PROFESSIONAL RESPONSIBILITY AS THE PRINCIPLE DENOMINATOR OF PEDAGOGICAL ETHOS

Archetypically, responsibility is given if one person is in charge of another or of an object. Within professional settings, these two forms of entrustment are often mixed (Hoff, 1995; Holderegger, 2006). Therefore, being responsible in a specific situation means having the power to decide and gives the person in charge control over the events (Hoff, 1995). The need to respond to one's actions and to the resulting consequences is required (Craig, 1998; Heid, 1997). Alternate possibilities, free will, accountability, and prospectivity are the most frequently discussed decisive criteria for responsibility (e.g., Auhagen, 1999; Becker & Charlotte, 2001; Roth, 1995). Consequently, a person is held responsible if there are alternatives of acting or behaving, if the person in charge needs to make a decision, for which he/she can be held accountable, and if this person is not forced into directing a decision. Thus, someone forced to do something would not be regarded as being held responsible for the action, because this person cannot be held liable under duress. Furthermore, a person should measure the consequences of the alternatives (ibid.). Linked to professional ethos, this signifies that one should to be aware of the scope of responsibility, to decide, to anticipate possible consequences, as well as to do so freely and in accord with the responsibility. Within the context of education, the construct of pedagogical responsibility is discussed as a social endeavor but also moral one. Due to the direct consequences on the development of entrusted individuals, professional responsibility is understood as having a moral character (e.g., Bergem, 1992; Damon, 1992, Reichenbach, 1994). The social dimension of responsibility constitutes the fact that holding someone responsible is linked to social expectations directly (Auhagen, 1999). Due to these characteristics of pedagogical responsibility, professional ethos becomes decisively important. But, as research shows, pedagogical responsibility is not only influenced by social and historical changes (which modify expectations held towards the person accountable) but also shaped by the situation and context. For instance, Diamond, Randolph, and Spillane (2004) found that, depending on the school district, teachers feel more or less committed to their responsibility. Youn (2016a) found a dependence of the teachers' responsibility sense from the level of their students' school readiness. But the author (Youn, 2016b) also emphasized the importance of a high sense of responsibility. Thus, she could trace a favorable learning growth trajectory of students taught by teachers with a high sense of responsibility compared to students taught by teachers of low responsibility sense. Furthermore, studies reported that societal expectations (Sherman, 2004), teaching role and experience (Stefanidis & Strogilos, 2015), as well as teaching emotions (Eren, 2014) alter or constrain the teachers' sense of responsibility. Since, as has been argued, ethos refers to the responsibility underlying any profession or occupation, it is important in any case to analyze these professional (or occupational) responsibilities first in order to define the ethos. But in order to foster the commitment to professional responsibility, one also needs to understand the perception of professional responsibility from the perspective of the person in charge as well as how the situation influences this perception. Therefore, the study's focus lies on the trainers' personal sense of pedagogical responsibility. In alignment with Youn (2016b, p. 578), this sense of responsibility is understood as the perceived willingness of trainers to hold themselves accountable for the learning and professional but also personal development of their apprentices.

METHODS AND DATA

Research Aims and Research Questions

The study's objective is to gain a deeper understanding of the vocational trainers' sense of pedagogical responsibility and how personal and company characteristics, as well as experiences, influence this sense. Due to little research in this area, the study has an explorative character. The specific research questions which led the instrument development, as well as the corresponding data analyses, are as follows:

1. Do company characteristics as well as personal characteristics influence the trainers' perception of responsibility?
2. Do the trainers' way of training involvement (whether they are concerned with administrative tasks and/or skill training) and differing training experiences predict the trainers' perception of responsibility?
3. Are there any occupation-specific differences with regard to the impacts mentioned above?

Research Design and Sample Characteristics

The study design was outlined as a mixed method approach consisting of two phases. In the first phase, a qualitative interview study was conducted (see below) and in the second phase a quantitative study. The latter consisted of an online survey with mainly closed questions. The questionnaire took about 30 minutes to complete. In-company vocational trainers in Switzerland were addressed with the questionnaire developed. Since little is known about the trainers' perspective on their responsibility and experiences with training, most of the scales have been newly developed. The trainer's survey was available in two versions: one for cook trainers, the other for automotive trainers. These two occupations were selected because they offer apprenticeship trainings that belong among the ten most often chosen. Both questionnaires were equal in their structure and format. However, due to occupation-specific characteristics, the content of the items was adapted to the respective training reality. In total, data from 222 automotive trainers as well as 348 cook trainers of 18 Swiss cantons is available.[1] It should be mentioned that the sample drawn does not correspond to a randomly selected sample. As Table 1 reveals, some socio-demographic trainers' characteristics and company characteristics have been collected. As becomes obvious, most trainers responding were male in both subsamples. Yet this proportion corresponds to reality. The averaged mean of both subsamples is about 44 years (with a slightly higher age range within the cook trainers' subsample). Interestingly, the subsamples do not differ in their averaged training experienced either (about 14 years). As the range of training experience shows, there are also trainers in the sample with less than a year of training experience.

Regarding the function of the trainers, it becomes obvious that most of the trainers surveyed have a manager function too. Only seldom are they exclusively

RESPONSIBILITY AS THE PRINCIPLE DENOMINATOR OF PEDAGOGICAL ETHOS

Table 1. Sample characteristics

	Automotive trainers	Cook trainers	Total sample
Total	222	348	570
Gender			
female	6 (2.7%)	48 (14%)	54 (9%)
male	213 (96%)	297 (85%)	510 (90%)
missing	3 (1.3%)	3 (1%)	6 (1%)
Age (years)	M = 44.23, SD = 10.38	M = 43.92, SD = 9.35	M = 44.04, SD = 9.7
Training experience (years)	M = 14.06, SD = 10.75	M = 13.96, SD = 9.31	M = 14.0, SD = 9.73
Function			
Owner of company	61 (27%)	64 (18%)	125 (22%)
Business manager	67 (30%)	55 (16%)	122 (21%)
Executive chief	59 (27%)	180 (52%)	239 (42%)
VET manager	14 (6%)	20 (6%)	34 (6%)
Productive employee	21 (10%)	29 (8%)	50 (9%)
Company Size			
micro (<10 employees)	103 (46%)	36 (10%)	139 (24%)
small (10–49 employees)	91 (41%)	142 (41%)	233 (41%)
medium (≥50 employees)	28 (13%)	170 (49%)	198 (35%)
# supervised apprentices	M = 3.18, SD = 3.25	M = 3.45, SD = 8.86	M = 3.34, SD = 7.2
# responsible vocational trainers within company	M = 3.02, SD = 2.12	M = 3.48, SD = 3.52	M = 3.3, SD = 3.06
% of total workload spent for VET	M = 17.11, SD = 15.71	M = 23.38, SD = 19.3	M = 21.12, SD = 18.3

responsible for vocational education and training (VET). It is also rare for them to be productive employees without any manager function. In the cook trainers' sample, 52% are executive chiefs. This corresponds to head chef with VET responsibility. In the automotive trainers' sample, most of the participating trainers work within a micro-sized (less than ten employees) or small-sized company (10–49 employees). The share of medium to big-sized companies was higher within the cook trainers' sample (13% vs. 49%). On average, the trainers questioned were responsible for three apprentices at the same time. But it should be noted that the range (from being in charge of one up to 145 apprentices) is huge. Somewhat disturbing is the fact that some trainers do not spend any of their employment time for the apprentices' vocational training, even though they are responsible for the in-company apprenticeship training. A closer look at the frequency distribution shows that only two trainers reported spending no working time in training apprentices (see Table 1). Nevertheless, 19% of the trainers questioned invested less than 10% of their employment on apprentice training.

Scales and Measures

In accord with the research interest, instruments were developed to measure trainers' perception of their training responsibility, the extent of their involvement in VET, as well as their experience regarding VET. In order to test the scales' dimensions, an Explorative Varimax Rotated Factor Analysis (EFA) was calculated as a first step, which revealed a factorial structure corresponding to the theoretical expectations. In a second step, the factorial structure obtained was confirmed by means of a latent modeled Confirmatory Factor Analysis (CFA). To evaluate the models' fit, the following fit indices were used (Hu & Bentler, 1999): the ratio between the chi-square (χ^2) and the degrees of freedom (*df*), the Comparative Fit Index (*CFI* >.95), the Root Mean Square Error of Approximation (*RMSEA* < .06), and the Standardized Root Mean Square Residuals (*SRMR* < .05). A robust Maximum Likelihood estimator (MLR) was used to calculate the model. The process of scale development will be described briefly for each scale separately. Table 2 depicts the scale characteristics, the reliability (*Cronbach's alpha*), as well as goodness of fit values.

Responsibility scale. Previous to the quantitative survey, an observation study was conducted within six companies combined with qualitative interviews (first phase of mixed method study). In addition, existing literature on trainers' responsibility was analyzed as were formal curriculum and other training related documents such as report forms. It was concluded that at least two dimensions of training responsibility could be found: (a) an understanding of responsibility focusing on apprenticeship training including the apprentices' professional development and (b) an understanding that broadens the responsibility perception considering the apprentices' personal development (see Forster-Heinzer, 2015, for more details). This second broader view on responsibility is illustrated by a trainer's statement collected within the interview study.

> [What belongs to a trainer's responsibility?] A lot! At first, meaningful leisure time. Young people are glued to the computer until 3 a.m., and you really can see it in the morning. They are totally exhausted and overtired (vocational trainer in the automotive trade).

In order to capture this two-dimensionality of responsibility, 15 items were developed. Table 2 summarizes the scales' characteristics. The two-dimensionality expected was confirmed by the EFA as well as the CFA. However, some items needed to be excluded due to low reliability. The factor *training responsibility* describes the first dimension of training responsibility with a focus on practical training but also covering professional development. The second-factor *broad responsibility* also considers the apprentices'

Table 2. Scale characteristics

	# items	Item example	Mean (SD)	Cronbach's Alpha	Goodness of Fit (CFA) c2(df)*p	CFI	RMSEA	SRMR
Responsibility[1]		*It belongs to a trainer's responsibility...*			73.766 (33)***	.956	.047	.044
Training responsibility	6	to impart to the apprentices all specific abilities (knowledge and skills) that are important for an automotive mechanic / cook.	5.43 (.50)	.79				
Broad responsibility	4	to support the apprentice in establishing meaningful leisure time activities.	3.99 (.92)	.67				
Training involvement[2]		*How often are you involved in the following training task?*			48.073 (18)***	.974	.054	.031
Administrative tasks	5	Selecting and choosing the apprentices (organizing taster courses, application procedure, signing the apprenticeship contract).	3.30 (.78)	.80				
Professional training	3	Controlling and providing feedback on the conducted tasks and apprentice's performance.	3.95 (.74)	.79				
Experiences[3]					40.706 (24)*	.977	.035	.034
Trainer's significance	3	As a vocational trainer, I have an important impact on the professional development of apprentices.	4.89 (.69)	.60				
Challenges	3	At times, I experience it as very difficult to bring together productivity demands and my educational responsibility.	2.88 (1.0)	.67				
Administrative overload	3	A vocational trainer needs to accomplish too much administrative work, which makes training suffer.	3.54 (1.2)	.72				

[1] Likert Scale with answer possibilities: (1) fully disagree up to (6) fully agree.
[2] Likert Scale with answer possibilities: (1) never (2) randomly (3) sometimes (4) often (5) very often.
[3] Likert Scale with answer possibilities: (1) does not apply up to (6) fully applies.
*** $p < .001$; ** $p < .01$; * $p < .05$

personal development as part of a trainer's responsibility. The Cronbach's *alpha* (.67) of the broad responsibility scale was considered acceptable but improvable. The goodness of fit obtained by the CFA reveals satisfactory values. However, one error correlation was allowed to improve the fit statistics. The latent measurement model showed a correlation between the two responsibility dimensions of .54; p < .001. The more the trainers agree on their training responsibility, the more they agree on their broad responsibility and vice versa.

Training involvement scale. One characteristic of in-company training is the diverse organization of actual training responsibility. In order to gain more information about the trainers' involvement within in-company training, items were developed based on findings extracted from earlier studies such as DBK (2005), Joho and Heinzer (2013) as well as Aff, Klusmeyer and Wittwer (2010). The calculated EFA distinguished between two factors, one concerning direct practical training and theoretical instruction (professional training), the other related to incoming administrative tasks. As depicted in Table 2, the Cronbach's alpha and the latent factorial measurement model's goodness of fit were satisfactory. One error correlation was allowed for. As the results of the latent measurement model revealed, the two dimensions extracted correlate with each other only slightly: 0.21; p < .001.

Trainer's experience scales. Trainers experience their VET responsibility and involvement differently (Forster-Heinzer, 2015; Joho & Heinzer, 2013). An instrument was developed to measure the trainers' experience regarding VET. An EFA showed a three-factorial structure. It was found that some feel more challenged by their training responsibility (scale: challenges); others experience the training-related administration as a burden (scale: administrative overload). But there are also differences in the trainer's significance attribution for the apprentice's development (scale: trainer's significance). Since each scale comprises only three items and due to an acceptable goodness of fit statistic the experience sub-scales were included in further calculations despite the improvable Cronbach's alpha (.60–.72).

Research Model and Hypotheses

A research model has been drawn in alignment with the aims and questions (see Figure 1). The model also shows the variables measured and included to test their influence on the trainers' responsibility perception.

As has been reported (literature review), it was found in earlier studies that the sense of responsibility is influenced by a professional's role, experience, emotions but also by external factors such as infrastructure and neighborhood. Up to now, research on vocational trainers' sense of responsibility is missing. The following hypotheses are to be tested in alignment with above discussed possible influences:

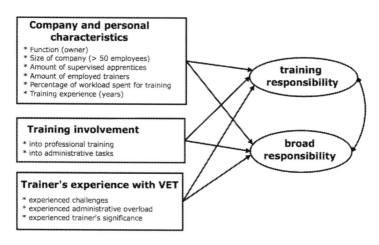

Figure 1. Research model

- Well educated apprentices are a seal of quality for companies. Therefore, an owner is expected to have a higher perception of one's training responsibility (*hypothesis H1*).
- Furthermore, it is assumed that the number of apprentices a trainer supervises, has a negative impact on the trainer's perception of broad responsibility. Conceivably with raising number of supervised apprentices the time resources for individual care decreases (*hypothesis H2*).
- Moreover, it is expected that being involved in practical skill training influences the perception of training responsibility positively. Thus, these vocational trainers have to respond, if the practical skills are not established at the end of apprenticeship (*hypothesis H3*).
- Due to organizational and occupational customs and traditions, differences were expected in the model of influences between the cook and the automotive trainers (*hypothesis H4*).

Data Analysis

In order to answer questions and test the hypotheses all data in the first step were included disregarding the occupation membership. Four different structural equation models (Byrne, 2012) were calculated after confirming the scales' reliability. The first model (see Table 3) included only company and personal characteristics, which all consisted of either binary or metric manifest items. The second model included only the two latent scales measuring trainers' involvement in practical skill training as well as involvement in training-related administrative duties. The third model concerned the three latent scales considering the trainers' experiences regarding VET, and the last model represented a combination of all influences tested in model

Table 3. Tested models with differing predictors of responsibility scales

Predictors	Model 1 Training responsibility	Model 1 Broad responsibility	Model 2 Training responsibility	Model 2 Broad responsibility	Model 3 Training responsibility	Model 3 Broad responsibility	Model 4 Training responsibility	Model 4 Broad responsibility
Owner	**.20*****	<.01; ns	—	—	—	—	**.19****	-.01; ns
Company > 50 employees	**.16****	-.01; ns	—	—	—	—	**.16****	-.02; ns
# Trainers	.01; ns	-.02; ns	—	—	—	—	-.02; ns	-.04; ns
# Apprentices	-.05; ns	.02; ns	—	—	—	—	-.06; ns	.04; ns
% of workload spent on training	**.23*****	**.10***	—	—	—	—	**.13***	-.03; ns
Training experience	**.23*****	.07; ns	—	—	—	—	**.21*****	.03; ns
Prof. training involvement	—	—	**.14***	**.19****	—	—	.06; ns	.093; ns
Administrative tasks involvement	—	—	**.27*****	**.19****	—	—	**.14***	.10, p = .06
Trainer's significance	—	—	—	—	**.43*****	**.48*****	**.36*****	**.43*****
Challenges	—	—	—	—	-.03; ns	-.12; ns	.05; ns	-.10; ns
Admin. overload	—	—	—	—	-.06; ns	-.06; ns	-.12; ns	-.07; ns
R^2	**.16**	**.02**	**.11**	**.09**	**.20**	**.26**	**.34**	**.29**
χ^2 (df)ᵖ	148.59 (81)**		246.974 (127)***		255.783 (141)***		733.619 (420)***	
CFI	.94		.95		.94		.92	
RMSEA	.038		.04		.04		.04	
SRMR	.036		.04		.05		.04	

Model 1 considers company and personal characteristics as predictors.
Model 2 considers the trainers' involvement as predictors.
Model 3 considers the trainers' VET experience as predictors only;
Model 4 represents a combination of all the predictors from model 1-3.
***$p < .001$; ** $p < .01$; * $p < .05$

1–3. In a follow-up step, a multi-group comparison was calculated (under constraints of partial scalar invariance[2]). First, all regression paths were freely estimated. But second, in a stepwise procedure, the regression paths were constrained to be equal between the two occupations. Testing determined if this assumption of equal influence on the dependent variables could be considered confirmed (see Table 4).

RESULTS AND DISCUSSION

Different Models of Influence on Responsibility Scale, n = 570

Table 3 summarizes results of the four structural equation models calculated with all data. If only company and personal characteristics are considered, the variance explained in the training responsibility construct is 16%, of the broad responsibility construct only 2%. As becomes obvious, the only predictor that has an actual relationship with the broad responsibility is the percentage of total workload a trainer spends on apprenticeship training. The amount of time a trainer spends on apprenticeship training seems to influence the perception of also being responsible for the apprentice's personal development in a small but positive way ($\beta = .10$; $p < .05$). Slightly stronger is this influence when focusing on training responsibility ($\beta = .23$; $p < .001$). Interestingly, this predictor is the only one that does not correlate with the other predictors of model 1. Equally high is the influence of training experience (years) on training responsibility. With regard to training responsibility, the two binary predictors were also significant. Vocational trainers who own the business at the same time tend to score slightly higher on training responsibility compared with non-owners. Furthermore, trainers working in a company with more than 50 employees also show higher scores on the training responsibility scale. Contrary to expectation, neither the number of supervised apprentices nor that of responsible trainers within a company had a significant effect on the perception of responsibility. These significant or non-significant paths remain almost the same when integrated into the whole model of influence. Only with regard to the percentage of workload spent on training does its influence decreases and even becomes non-significant with regard to the broad responsibility – at least when also including the trainers' involvement and VET experience as well. This outcome might be due to significant correlations with (a) involvement into administrative tasks ($r = .16$; $p < .01$), (b) involvement into training ($r = .34$; $p < .001$), or (c) the significance experienced ($r = .16$; $p < .01$). A similar result was found regarding trainers' involvement. When analyzed separately, both latent constructs regress positively on the responsibility scales. But only the path from administrative task's involvement on training responsibility remains significant in the comprehensive model. Trainers who are more involved in administrative tasks also seem to more inclined to consider comprehensive training among their responsibilities. The trainers' experienced significance for their apprentices and their education has the strongest influence on the responsibility scale. This influence also remains significant when including other

Table 4. Comparison of industry regarding model of influence (model 4)

Predictors	Automotive sample Training responsibility	Automotive sample Broad responsibility	Cook sample Training responsibility	Cook sample Broad responsibility	Constrained to be equal Training responsibility	Constrained to be equal Broad responsibility
Owner	.03; ns	-.01; ns	**.20***	.04; ns	.10; ns	-.04; ns
Company > 50 employees	.06; ns	-.06; ns	.02; ns	-.02; ns	-.02; ns	-.06; ns
# Trainers	**.18****	.08; ns	-.10; p = .06	-.08; ns	-.04; ns	-.03; ns
# Apprentices	-.08; ns	-.03; ns	-.05; ns	.10; ns	-.06; ns	.04; ns
% of workload spent on training	.06; ns	.04; ns	**.13***	-.08; ns	**.09* / .12***	-.04; ns
Training experience	**.15***	-.014; ns	**.26****	.04; ns	**.22****	.04; ns
Prof. training involvement	.05; ns	-.01;ns	.09; ns	**.22***	.02; ns	.06; ns
Administrative tasks involvement	.19; p = .06	.15; p = .07	.07; ns	.07; ns	**.11* / .15***	**.12***
Trainer's significance	**.39****	**.50****	**.31****	**.37****	**.32*** / .38****	**.43*** / .46****
Challenges	.19; ns	-.04; ns	.14; ns	-.06; ns	.12; ns	-.10; ns
Administrative overload	-.15; ns	-.17; ns	-.22; p = .06	-.03; ns	**-.18* / -.21***	-.08; ns
R^2	**.31**	**.36**	**.33**	**.28**	**.24 / .34**	**.26 / .31**
χ^2 (df)ᵖ	1289.224 (876)***				1313.326 (898)***	
AIC	56860.180				56839.621	
CFI	.90 (.896)				.90	
RMSEA	.04				.04	
SRMR	.05				.06	

*** $p < .001$; ** $p < .01$; * $p < .05$

variables. With regard to the explained variance, the third model explains the most when comparing model 1 to 3 (20% and 26%). While more variance in the training responsibility construct than in the broad responsibility construct was explained in model 1 and 2 it was the opposite in model 3. Unsurprisingly, the rate of explained variances in the comprehensive model 4 is the highest (34% and 29%).

Comparison of Industry Regarding the Comprehensive Model

As mentioned, in a follow-up step a multi-group comparison was tested regarding the comprehensive model (see Table 4). Some differences were found when allowing the regression paths to vary between the occupation groups. The respective predictors explained slightly more variance when regressing on the training responsibility construct within the sample of cook trainers (31% to 33%). But more variance was explained in the sample of automotive trainers (36% to 28%) when regressing on the broad responsibility construct. It was found, that the regressive path from the binary item '*owner*' or '*not-owner*' was only significant in the cook sample ($\beta = .20$; p < .05). Moreover, the percentage of total workload spent on training only showed a significant path in the cook sample ($\beta = .13$; p < .05). On the other hand, a significant influence from the number of responsible trainers on training responsibility ($\beta = .18$; p < .05) was found only within the automotive sample. It seems that trainers score higher on their perception of training responsibility when the automotive repair shop employs more responsible trainers. The experienced trainer's significance has a high positive impact ($\beta = .31-.50$; p < .001) in both samples for both dependent variables. With regard to the broad responsibility construct, an occupation-specific difference was found concerning the predictor of involvement in professional training. Higher involvement seems to be related to a higher perception of broad responsibility within the cook sample. In a stepwise procedure, the regressive paths between the two occupational groups were constrained to be equal. It was found that a model with all regressive paths constrained does not differ significantly in its fit from the unconstrained model ($\Delta\chi^2 = 24.10$; $\Delta df = 22$; ns). The results of the constrained model are displayed in Table 4. All unstandardized coefficients between the two occupation groups were equal. But due to non-constraints of error correlations and construct correlations the standardized *beta*-coefficients may vary slightly between the two subsamples despite the constraints. Some differences become obvious when comparing the combined model 4 (Table 3) with the multi-group constrained model (Table 4).

When taking the two different occupations into account, some paths on the training responsibility construct (from the binary variable of being the owner and of working in a company with at least 50 employees) are no longer significant. But the regressive path from the trainers' involvement in administrative tasks on the broad responsibility scale is significant under the control of the occupational groups. The high impact of the experienced trainers' significance on both dependent variables is unchanged. Surprisingly – when accounting for the group-specificity – is the fact that the perception of training responsibility is negatively regressed on the experienced administrative overload. One possible explanation is the fact that the multi-group comparison allowed for different correlations between predictors. A significant negative correlation was found within the cook sample between (a) the involvement in administrative tasks ($r = -.17$; $p < .05$) as well as (b) involvement in professional training ($r = -.24$; $p < .001$), and c) companies with at least 50 employees ($r = -.14$; $p < .05$) with the experienced administrative overload. But it was not found within the automotive sample. On the other hand, the number of responsible trainers correlated negatively with the experienced overload ($r = -.18$; $p < .05$) in the automotive sample, while this correlation was not significant in the cook sample.

CONCLUSIONS

Disregarding occupational membership, it was found – as expected – that company and personal characteristics, as well as the kind of VET involvement and trainer's VET experience, influence the perception of pedagogical responsibility. In alignment with hypothesis 1, owners scored slightly higher on the perception of training responsibility than non-owners did. Contrary to expectations (hypothesis 2), the number of supervised apprentices did not have an influence. Nor did training involvement (hypothesis 3). On the contrary, trainers more involved in administrative tasks scored higher on training responsibility. This might be due to the fact that trainers involved in administrative tasks must also fill in training forms confirming a comprehensive education. Even though they might be less responsible for the practical skill training, they have to respond concerning it. When respecting occupational membership, some differences regarding significant regression paths were found (hypothesis 4). However, these differences seem negligible, given the fact that the fit statistic does not decline significantly when constraining the regression paths to attain equality. But we have to keep in mind, that error correlations as well as correlations between the latent constructs were not constrained to be equal. Yet the most meaningful result was found with regard to the experienced trainer's significance for the apprentice's training success. A highly significant influence was found over all calculated models and for both responsibility constructs. A trainer seems more committed to pedagogical responsibility when he or she feels needed and believes that he or she has an impact and can make a difference. In a different research setting, Eren (2014) found that efficacy (understood as a sub-dimension of teaching optimism) positively influenced the sense of responsibility. These findings might indicate that the commitment to responsibility (and hence the pedagogical ethos too) is to some extent relational and fostered by societal but also individual recognition. This consideration is therefore not only interesting from an empirical but also theoretical point of view. It has been argued in the introduction that an important contribution to ethos is the sense of responsibility. Now it was found that this sense is to some extent influenced by situation and circumstances but also the trainers' experience of being significant for the apprentices' development. The character of this variable should be more profoundly discussed. Is it an attitude/ belief, influenced and shaped by knowledge or by relational experience? Therefore, the result regarding the experienced significance is also of practical value, not only for training institutions but for professional associations, company managers, and society in general. Training institutions should discuss a trainer's pedagogical responsibility but also their influence on the development of their apprentices. They should also know about some aspects of youth development and the importance of significant others for identity development. Training companies could reconsider their attitude or spirit of what apprenticeship training means. Thus, as has been argued, ethos is not only found on the individual but also institutional level, and interdependences are to expect. Professional association and society can contribute to the establishment of a trainer's ethos by acknowledging their doing and importance more explicitly. However, more research is needed not only to understand the trainers' sense of pedagogical responsibility but also their commitment to it, which is understood to constitute the professional ethos. The study presented was conducted in a very specific setting (Swiss VET) with a not-randomly drawn cross-sectional sample (cook and automotive trainers), and some scales need improvement. More research also with longitudinal design is needed to overcome this study's limitations.

NOTES

[1] This sample represents a subsection of the one described in Forster-Heinzer (2015). The study excluded all trainers who were responsible for interplant-courses but not directly involved in-company training. Furthermore, the company's human resources managers were also excluded due to differing technical education.

[2] Scalar invariance of the measurement model is considered an important condition for comparing the means of groups (Cheung & Rensvold, 2002). Therefore, the factor loadings as well as the intercepts were constrained to be equal between the two sub-samples. One intercept in each latent construct needed to be freely estimated. Yet these unconstrained intercepts are not considered to have an important influence on the measurement model (Byrne, 2012). Therefore, group-comparisons regarding the model of influence were calculated nonetheless.

REFERENCES

Aff, J., Klusmeyer, J., & Wittwer, W. (2010). Berufsausbildung in Schule und Betrieb. In R. Nickolaus, G. Pätzold, H. Reinisch, & T. Tramm (Eds.), *Handbuch Berufs- und Wirtschaftspädagogik* [Handbook of vocational and business education] (pp. 330–337). Bad Heilbrunn: Klinkhardt.

Auhagen, A. E. (1999). *Die Realität der Verantwortung* [The reality of responsibility]. Göttingen: Hogrefe.

Baumert, J., & Kunter, M. (2006). Stichwort: Professionelle Kompetenz von Lehrkräften [Keyword: Professional competence of teachers]. *Zeitschrift für Erziehungswissenschaften (ZfE), 4*, 469–520.

Becker, L. C., & Charlotte, B. B. (2001). Professional ethics. In L. C. Becker & B. B. Charlotte (Eds.), *Encyclopedia of ethics* (2nd ed., Vol. 3, pp. 1384–1386). New York, NY: Routledge.

Bergem, T. (1992). Teaching the art of living: Lessons learned from a study of teacher education. In F. Oser, A. Dick, & J.-L. Patry (Eds.), *Effective and responsible teaching: The new synthesis* (pp. 349–364). San Francisco, CA: Jossey-Bass.

Brezinka, W. (1988). Die Lehrer und ihre Berufsmoral [Teachers and their professional morality]. *Pädagogische Rundschau, 42,* 541–563.
Byrne, B. M. (2012). *Structural equation modeling with mplus: Basic concepts, applications and programming.* New York, NY: Routledge.
Carr, D. (2010). Personal and professional values in teaching. In T. Lovat, R. Toomey, & N. Clement (Eds.), *International research handbook on values education and student wellbeing* (pp. 63–74). New York, NY: Springer.
Cheung, G. W., & Rensvold, R. B. (2002). Evaluating goodness-of-fit indexes for testing measurement invariance. *Structural Equation Modeling, 9*(2), 233–255.
Colby, A., & Sullivan, W. M. (2008). Formation of professionalism and purpose: Perspectives from the preparation for the professions program. *University of St. Thomas Law Journal, 5*(2), 404–427.
Craig, E. (1998). Responsibility. In E. Craig (Ed.), *Routledge encyclopedia of philosophy* (Vol. 8, pp. 290–294). New York, NY: Roudledge.
Damon, W. (1992). Teaching as a moral craft and developmental expedition. In F. Oser, A. Dick, & J.-L. Patry (Eds.), *Effective and responsible teaching: The new synthesis* (pp. 139–153). San Francisco, CA: Jossey-Bass.
DBK. (2005). *Handbuch betriebliche Grundbildung* [Handbook vocational education]. Luzern: Deutschschweizerische Berufsbildungsämter-Konferenz.
Diamond, J. B., Randolph, A., & Spillane, J. P. (2004). Teachers' expectations and sense of responsibility for student learning: The importance of race, class, and organizational habitus. *Anthropology & Education Quarterly, 35*(1), 75–98.
Diehl, T. (2005). Pädagogische Professionalität: Möglichkeiten ihrer empirischen Erfassung. In A. Frey, R. Jäger, & U. Renold (Eds.), *Kompetenzdiagnostik: Theorien und Methoden zur Erfassung und Bewertung von beruflichen Kompetenzen* [Competence diagnostic: Theories and methods for assessment and evaluation of vocational competences] (pp. 116–135). Landau: Verlag Empirische Pädagogik.
Eren, A. (2014). Uncovering the links between prospective teachers' personal responsibility, academic optimism, hope, and emotions about teaching: A mediation analysis. *Social Psychology of Education, 17,* 73–104.
Fenstermacher, G. D. (1992). The concepts of method and manner in teaching. In F. Oser, A. Dick, & J.-L. Patry (Eds.), *Effective and responsible teaching: The new synthesis* (pp. 95–108). San Francisco, CA: Jossey-Bass.
Forster-Heinzer, S. (2015). *Against all odds: An empirical study about the situative pedagogical ethos of vocational trainers.* Rotterdam, The Netherlands: Sense Publishers.
Heid, H. (1997). Erziehung zur Verantwortungsbereitschaft: Ideologiekritische Analyse. In Comenius-Institut (Ed.), *Handbuch Religionsunterricht an berufsbildenden Schulen* [Handbook religious education in vocational schools] (pp. 81–85). Gütersloh: Deutscher Katechetenverein, Gütersloher Verlagshaus.
Heikkerö, T. (2008). How to address the volitional dimension of the engineer's social responsibility. *European Journal of Engineering Education, 33*(2), 161–168.
Hoff, E.-H. (1995). Berufliche Verantwortung. In E.-H. Hoff & L. Lappe (Eds.), *Verantwortung im Arbeitsleben* [Responsibility in vocations] (pp. 46–63). Heidelberg: Roland Asanger Verlag.
Holderegger, A. (2006). Verantwortung. In J.-P. Wils & C. Hübenthal (Eds.), *Lexikon der Ethik* [Encyclopedia of ethics] (pp. 394–403). Paderborn: Ferdinand Schöningh.
Hu, L., & Bentler, P. M. (1998). Fit indices in covariance structure modeling: Sensitivity to underparameterized model misspecification. *Psychological Methods, 3*(4), 424–453.
Jalovaara, A.-M. (2000). Berufliche Bildung in Finnland. In G. Bös & H. Ness (Eds.), *Ausbilder in Europa: Probleme und Perspektiven* [Vocational trainers in Europe: Problems and persepctives] (pp. 232–246). Bielefeld: W. Bertelsmann Verlag GmbH & Co.
Joho, C., & Heinzer, S. (2013). Eine facettenreiche Rolle: Zu den Aufgaben der betrieblichen Berufsbildenden. In F. Oser, T. Bauder, P. Salzmann, & S. Heinzer (Eds.), *Ohne Kompetenz keine Qualität: Entwickeln und Einschätzen von Kompetenzen bei Lehrpersonen und Berufsbildungsverantwortlichen* [No competence without quality: Developing and assessing competences of teachers and vocational trainers] (pp. 217–231). Bad Heilbrunn: Klinkhardt.

Latzko, B. (2012). Educating teachers' ethos. In D. Alt & R. Reingold (Eds.), *Changes in teachers' moral role* (pp. 201–210). Rotterdam, The Netherlands: Sense Publishers.
Orlenius, K. (2006, September). *Professional ethics and values education in school practice*. Paper presented at the EERA Conference, Geneva.
Oser, F. (1998). *Ethos – die Vermenschlichung des Erfolgs: Zur Psychologie der Berufsmoral von Lehrpersonen* [Ethos – the humanization of success: On the psychology of the professional morality of teachers]. Opladen: Leske + Budrich.
Oser, F., Dick, A., & Patry, J.-L. (1992). Responsibility, effectiveness, and the domains of educational research. In F. Oser, A. Dick, & J.-L. Patry (Eds.), *Effective and responsible teaching: The new synthesis* (pp. 3–13). San Francisco, CA: Jossey-Bass.
Reichenbach, R. (1994). *Moral, Diskurs und Einigung: Zur Bedeutung von Diskurs und Konsens für das Ethos des Lehrberufs* [Morality, discourse and agreement: About the importance of dicourse and consensus for the ethos of teachers]. Bern: Peter Lang.
Roth, J. K. (1995). Professional ethics. In J. K. Roth (Ed.), *International encyclopedia of ethics* (pp. 703–706). London: Fitzroy Dearborn Publishers.
Sherman, S. (2004). Responsiveness in teaching: Responsibility in its most particular sense. *The Education Forum, 68*, 115–124.
Stefanidis, A., & Strogilos, V. (2015). Union gives strength: Mainstream and special education teachers' responsibility in inclusive co-taught classrooms. *Educational Studies, 41*(4), 393–413.
Tenorth, H.-E. (2006). Professionalität im Lehrerberuf: Ratlosigkeit der Theorie, gelingende Praxis [Professionalism in the teaching occupation: Helplessness of the theory, success in practice]. *Zeitschrift für Erziehungswissenschaften (ZfE), 9*(4), 580–597.
Umpstead, R., Brady, K., Lugg, E., Klinker, J., & Thompson, D. (2011). *Educator ethics: A look at teacher professional responsibility through case law in four states*. Paper presented at the American Educational Research Association, New Orleans, LA.
Von Hentig, H. (2009). Das Ethos der Erziehung: Was ist in ihr elementar? [The pedagogical ethos. What is elementary?] *Zeitschrift für Pädagogik, 55*(4), 509–527.
Youn, M. (2016a). Inequality from the first day of school: The role of teachers' academic intensity and sense of responsibility in moderating the learning growth gap. *The Journal of Educational Research, 109*(1), 50–67.
Youn, M. (2016b). Learning more than expected: The influence of teachers' attitudes on children's learning outcomes. *Early Child Development and Care, 186*(4), 578–595.

Sarah Forster-Heinzer
Institute of Education
University of Zurich
Zurich, Switzerland

ALFRED WEINBERGER

8. EDUCATION FOR PROFESSIONAL ETHOS THROUGH V*A*KE (VALUES *AND* KNOWLEDGE EDUCATION) IN TEACHER EDUCATION

A Cognitive-Affective Process System Analysis of Pre-Service Teachers' Moral Judgments Concerning a Socio-Scientific Issue

INTRODUCTION

The moral dimension and the ethical nature of the teacher's professional responsibilities have been attracting increased attention in teacher education since the end of the last century (e.g., Goodlad, Soder, & Sirotnik, 1985; Oser, Dick, & Patry, 1992; Tom, 1984). The increased number of publications in the field points out to the view that teaching is considered inherently a moral endeavor (Maxwell & Schwimmer, 2016). In the context of this "ethics boom" (Glanzer & Ream, 2007), several approaches and strategies have been developed to foster the moral self. These approaches focus on the development of moral attitudes and capacities in pre-service teachers (e.g., Blumenfeld-Jones, Sennefield, & Crawford, 2013; Ehrich, Millwater, Kimber, & Cranston, 2011; Warnick & Silverman, 2011). Among these capacities, some authors deem moral judgment a cornerstone of high-quality teaching and professional dispositions (Chan, 1994; Johnson, 2008; Pritchard, 1999; Reiman & Johnson, 2003; Weinberger, 2014). Being able to make informed moral judgments is considered a core element of a teachers' professional ethos (Weinberger, 2016). It is the universities' moral responsibility to foster the ability to make informed moral judgments in prospective professionals (Sandalow, 1991).

However, the implementation of methods for fostering moral judgment into the crowded curriculum seems to be the most challenging task. The constructivist didactical approach V*a*KE (Values *and* Knowledge Education; Patry, Weinberger, Weyringer, & Nussbaumer, 2013) provides a possible solution to this problem since it combines moral education with knowledge acquisition and thus permits accounting for both simultaneously in the curriculum. Therefore, V*a*KE can be implemented in different content related courses aiming to facilitate moral judgment as well as in-depth knowledge.

In the present study, V*a*KE was used in a course for pre-service teachers addressing science contents. The application of V*a*KE in science education is particularly beneficial because of several reasons. First, scientific knowledge is never values-free (Kincaid, Dupre, & Wylie, 2007). Second, scientific literacy involves morality as its core element

(Kim & Roth, 2008) because responsible judgments concerning socio-scientific issues are always based on moral reasoning (Sadler & Zeidler, 2003). Socio-scientific issues refer to controversial social issues relating to science (e.g., reproductive cloning, animal testing, climate change), Third, teachers often rely on their subjective theories in scientific argumentation and do not include facts as support for their argument (Sampson & Blanchard, 2012). Finally, opportunities for students to participate in authentic scientific argumentation inside the classroom are rare because of the teachers' lack of knowledge regarding instructional practices (Simon, Erduran, & Osborne, 2006).

The applicability and effectivity of VaKE have already been shown in teacher education and in pre-service teacher courses on science (Keast & Marangio, 2015; Weinberger, 2014; Weinberger, Patry, & Weyringer, 2016); the present study adds new insights into how moral judgments are generated when learning with VaKE. The study aims to shed light on pre-service teachers' mental processes when making moral judgments concerning a socio-scientific issue to understand better how values and knowledge interact. For this, the cognitive-affective process system analysis is applied that allows to explore the individuals' networks of cognitions (e.g., values) and affects induced by situational features (e.g., knowledge) which underlie a moral decision.

THEORETICAL BACKGROUND

VaKE (Values and Knowledge Education)

VaKE is a didactical approach that combines moral education and knowledge acquisition based on social and cognitive constructivist principles of learning. Social constructivism posits that knowledge construction is the product of social interaction, interpretation, and understanding (Vygotsky, 1962). Cognitive constructivism posits that meaningful learning is initiated by a cognitive conflict that refers to a problem which is challenging for the learner (Piaget, 1975). Moral dilemmas are such problems: They trigger moral questions ("What should be done? And why should it be done?"). Moral dilemmas are particularly challenging because they provide at least two possible solutions and each solution violates an essential moral principle (Jonassen, 2000). The discussion of moral dilemmas (Blatt & Kohlberg, 1975; Lind, 2003) has been shown to be an effective method to foster moral judgment (Berkowitz & Bier, 2007; Schläfli, Rest, & Thoma, 1985). It can be used for moral education in different educational settings, including the education of professionals (Pritchard, 1999). According to Kohlberg (1984), an individual's moral judgment develops in six stages starting with an egoistic and self-referred view and going up, in the optimal case, to a principle oriented perspective that involves the needs of all involved persons.

VaKE draws on the dilemma discussion method but refines it by using content related moral dilemmas that trigger not only moral questions but also questions related to missing knowledge ("What do I need to know to come to a satisfying solution?"). To answer the moral questions through discussing the dilemma, the learners strive to answer the questions related to missing knowledge through inquiry learning. Inquiry learning, i.e., asking questions and trying to answer them through different means, is an essential constructivist learning strategy (Loyens & Rikers, 2010). Research in the context of teacher education indicates that inquiry learning fosters the acquisition of in-depth knowledge (Wagner, Stark, Daudbasic, Klein, Krause, & Herzmann, 2013), which is an essential goal in each education.

The basic framework for the learning process in V*a*KE consists in eleven steps emphasizing the crucial role of moral reasoning (see Figure 1); depending on the specific needs the structure can be adapted (e.g., Weyringer, 2008).

V*a*KE (Values *and* Knowledge Education)

(1) Introducing the dilemma: Which values are at stake?
(2) First decision: Who is in favor, who against?
(3) First arguments (dilemma discussion): Why are you in favor, why against? Do we agree with each other?
(4) Exchange experience and missing information: Exchange of arguments; what more do I need to know to be able to argue further?
(5) Looking for evidence: Get the information, using any source available!
(6) Exchange of information: Present the information! Is the information sufficient?
(7) Second arguments (dilemma discussion): Why are you in favor, why against?
(8) Synthesis of information: Present your conclusions!
(9) Repeat 4 through 8 if necessary
(10) General synthesis: Closing the sequence capitalizing on the whole process!
(11) Generalization: Discussion about other related topics

Figure 1. Prototypical steps in VaKE (adapted from Patry et al., 2013)

V*a*KE starts with the introduction of a content-related moral dilemma. The critical issues of the story and the competing moral values at stake are analyzed (step 1). Subsequently, the learners reflect on their decision, write down their argument, and announce their decision. They recognize the different justifications for a decision (step 2). In small groups, the learners discuss the dilemma. The discussion is guided by questions like (i) which consequences are likely to follow the protagonist's action?; (ii) would it be okay if every person solved the dilemma in this way?; (iii) how would you be treated as an affected person in such a situation?; (iv) what do you think the person feels and thinks in this particular situation?; (v) are any moral rules relevant?. These questions aim to stimulate moral reasoning (step 3). The group's experiences regarding the results of the discussion are exchanged although the dilemma discussion is usually not finished yet. More important at this stage of learning is that open questions regarding missing knowledge are collected (step 4). Then the learners organize themselves into groups which search for the missing knowledge using different sources of knowledge, while the teacher acts as a counselor and manager of the whole endeavor. The teacher may also provide necessary information upon request by taking the role of an expert (step 5). The learners exchange their acquired knowledge and discuss it so that all learners have the same level of knowledge (step 6). After that, the dilemma discussion in small groups is continued. The learners integrate the new knowledge into their moral arguments (step 7). In a general discussion, the groups present the results of the dilemma discussion (current state of negotiation), and all learners discuss their favored arguments (step 8). If there are still open questions, the steps 4 to 8 can be repeated once again (step 9). In the final synthesis, the learners present the solved problem or the current state of the solution of the whole group (step 10). Finally, in the generalization, the learners deal with similar issues to broaden the perspective (step 11).

The final moral judgment is based on repeated phases of individual and collective thoughtful moral reflection (see also Weyringer, 2008). The learners reflect on different moral values (step 1), different moral arguments (step 2, 3, 7, and 8), various moral principles (step 3 and 8), and relevant knowledge (step 5 and 6) aiming to come to the morally best solution.

Research on moral reasoning shows that moral judgments are caused not only by cognitions based on thoughtful reflection but also by affects based on intuitive processes (Green, Nystrom, Engell, Darley, & Cohen, 2004; Haidt, 2001). The present study aims to explore the cognitions and affects mediating individual moral judgments in a V*a*KE-unit. It is suggested that the cognitive-affective process system analysis is an appropriate method to shed light on the mental representations involved in making a moral judgment.

Cognitive-Affective Process System Analysis

The cognitive-affective process system analysis can best be elucidated by referring to the cognitive-affective process system (CAPS; Mischel & Shoda, 1995, 2008) which conceptualizes personality as a dynamic model. According to Mischel and Shoda (1995) CAPS is based on two fundamental propositions: The *first proposition* is that people differ in the chronic accessibility, that is, in the degree of readiness with which particular cognitive and affective mental representations or units (CAUs) become activated. The CAUs include all thoughts and feelings a particular person can potentially experience. These involve an individual's encodings, expectancies and beliefs, affects, goals and values, as well as competencies and self-regulatory plans (see Table 1 for descriptions of each).

CAUs become activated through specific situational features, such as external features or internal processes which are perceived by the subject who encounters a situation. A situation is defined according to Patry (this volume) as a set of elements of the environment which the protagonist can perceive and discriminate. Such a situation is, for example, a V*a*KE-dilemma, while the situational features refer for example to the different pieces of information which are provided by the V*a*KE-dilemma. An external feature can be input, for example, specific information included in a V*a*KE-dilemma. This can cause new thoughts and feelings to arise, while previously activated thoughts and feelings may fade. Internal processes, for example

Table 1. Cognitive-affective units (CAUs) (adapted from Mischel & Shoda, 1995)

CAU	
Encodings	Constructs which refer to how individuals perceive, comprehend, and interpret the world around them; constructs are categories for encoding the self, people, events, and situations; representations of the self and other people. These can be either external or internal. Examples: God guides my life. The new technique is dangerous.
Expectancies and beliefs	One's personal beliefs and expectations for the self and about the social world, about outcomes for behavior, and about one's self-efficacy. Examples: Reproductive cloning is wrong because it is unnatural. Genetic cloning is right because it can save lives.
Affects	An individual's feelings, emotions, and affective responses (including physiological reactions). Examples: Being or feeling angry, disappointed or frustrated.
Goals and values	An individual's goals, values and life projects; both, desirable outcomes and affective states, and aversive outcomes and affective states. Examples: Life must be preserved. Medical progress is crucial to me.
Competencies and self-regulatory plans	The potential behaviors and scripts that one can do and plans and strategies for organizing action and for affecting outcomes and one's behavior and internal states. Examples: I can argue convincingly by using evidence as backing for my argument. If I take a deep breath three times, I will calm down.

taking the perspective of a victim in a V*a*KE-dilemma, can result in the feeling of "being affected" which can diminish or replace the activation of indifference one may have been experiencing before.

The *second proposition* is that individuals differ in the distinctive organization of relationships among their CAUs which forms a unique associative network. This organization guides and constrains the activation of cognitions and affects that are available within the system, which in turn results in a particular reaction.

Based on their experiences, cultural background, and learning history, specific groups of individuals share cognitive-affective intra-individual dynamics. This assumption is based on the socio-cultural theory of Vygotsky (1987) which postulates that cognitive development is a process of co-construction characterized by the interrelatedness of cognitive and affective elements (p. 282). If features of a situation activate these shared networks, this group of individuals may generate similar reactions to that situation. It is proposed that V*a*KE-dilemmas referring to socio-scientific issues are some of such situations. CAPS is a super-ordinate theory (Patry, 2013) providing the possibility to generate locally optimized domain-specific theories. This study is a first attempt to build such a domain-specific theory about moral judgment in the context of a socio-scientific issue addressed in V*a*KE.

A cognitive-affective process system analysis tries to bring the network of CAUs in a particular situation to light. Thus, such an analysis can illuminate the network of cognitions and affects elicited by the specific information provided by a VaKE-dilemma and the discussions about it. This network is shared – with the reservation of different interpretations – by all group members. It underlies the moral judgments and can be visualized in the form of a domain map (see Figure 2).

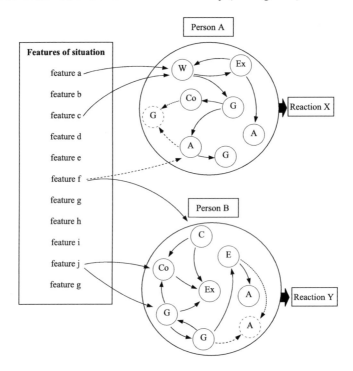

Figure 2. Schematic illustration of the cognitive-affective processing system (CAPS) for two hypothetical persons (i.e., Person A and Person B). Each person's mind is conceptualized by a stable network of interconnected cognitions and affects (E: Encodings; Ex: Expectancies and beliefs; A: Affects; G: Goals and values; Co: Competencies and self-regulatory plans) that mediates the effect of situational features on behavior. Solid lines within and outside of the network represent excitatory associations (e.g., activation of one situational feature or CAU automatically activates associated CAUs). Dashed lines within and outside of the network represent inhibitory associations (e.g., activation of one situational feature or CAU decreases the degree of readiness that the associated CAU becomes activated). In the above illustration, each person faces the same situation (e.g., a VaKE-dilemma) that consists of a common set of psychological features a through g (e.g., different information regarding the dilemma). Because not all features are meaningful for all people, Person A and Person B differ in the situational features which activate (or inhibit) certain CAUs within each person's network, which in turn leads to a particular reaction. (adapted from Shoda, Wilson, Whitsett, Lee-Dussud, & Zayas, 2015)

A domain map represents the cognitive-affective intra-individual dynamics of a particular group of persons who share many relevant experiences, the cultural background, and the learning history. In the present study, it is assumed that pre-service teachers from one Austrian teacher training institution will represent such a particular group. In contrast to the groups studied by Mendoza-Denton, Ayduk, Shoda, and Mischel (1997), where the groups were based only on ethnicity, in the present study, the participants share a collective experience, namely a VaKE procedure. The research question is how these situational features, cognitions and affects mediate pre-service teachers' moral judgments in a VaKE-unit.

METHOD

Participants and Context

81 pre-service teachers (four classes; 23 males) of a teacher education institution in Austria participated in this study. The mean age was 22.8 years (range: 19.2 to 45.5 years). All participants were undergraduate students and born in Austria. Three students had a migration background. The student population in this institution is regional with students coming from near High Schools. The study was embedded in the course "values education" (workload: 1 ECTS) which aims at (i) equipping pre-service teachers with different strategies for moral education, such as VaKE, and (ii) fostering their moral capacities, such as their moral judgment. Most of the pre-service teachers (85%) were preparing for teaching main disciplines (e.g., biology, geography, history, chemistry, physics, mathematics). The participants gave informed consent to take part in this study.

Procedure and Data Collection Method

Participants learned according to the VaKE-approach discussing a VaKE-dilemma about the socio-scientific issue reproductive cloning, which was as follows:

Future decision

We live in the year 2030. In a faraway country, there lives a 14-year-old boy. During a routine health examination, the school doctor finds an indication of a dangerous disease at this boy. The doctor makes the diagnosis leukemia. For medical treatment, the boy needs blood transfusions, bone marrow transplants, and tissue transplantations. Because there are no closely related compatible donors, the doctor explains to the parents that the only medically sensible alternative is the method of reproductive cloning. The cloned brother of the ill boy would be a genetical copy of their son and the ideal donor for him. The parents always wanted to have another child. They looked at each other. Their son's life is at stake. What should they do? Why?

The data collection method was an essay after having finished VaKE. The pre-service teachers were assigned to write a dialogue between a proponent and an opponent of reproductive cloning. They were also asked to write down their position regarding reproductive cloning. No time limit or limited word count was given for writing the dialogue. They accomplished this assignment as homework. Permission was obtained from each student to use the data. They were assured that the data would be treated confidentially.

Data Analysis

To identify the features of the situation (i.e., information regarding the dilemma), the participants considered essential, and the CAUs that participants generated, their essays were subject to a qualitative content analysis. The categories were generated inductively according to Mayring (2014). The content analysis consisted of two steps. In the first step the situational features, i.e., particular information regarding the dilemma which activated specific CAUs, were analyzed. Unit of analysis were words and phrases referring to the categories. Each text unit which referred to specific information regarding the dilemma was coded as a situational feature. In the second step, the CAUs were analyzed. The data did not allow to distinguish between the different types of cognition (i.e., encodings, expectancies and beliefs, goals and values, and competencies and self-regulatory plans). Therefore, each text unit that referred to a type of cognition or affect was coded as CAU. The author of this chapter coded all text material according to the following rules, which was similar to the one used by Mendoza-Denton et al. (1997): If a category was not represented in a dialogue, that category was coded 0. If it was mentioned only once, it was coded 1. If it was mentioned more than once within the same dialogue, it was coded 2. Each dialogue was also coded for agreement or disagreement with reproductive cloning.

To estimate intercoder reliability, a second coder, who was a trained research assistant, coded 50% of all dialogues according to the rules mentioned above. Intercoder reliabilities as indexed by Krippendorf's alpha were acceptable for situational features (.63 < KALPHA < .72) and satisfactory for CAUs (.69 < KALPHA < .78). Conflicting codings were discussed between the two coders after the calculation of the reliability index and resolved through consensus about the proper coding. This final coding was used in all subsequent analysis.

Construction of Domain Maps: Operationalization of Situational Features, Accessibility and Activation Pathways

The construction of the domain maps was done following the procedure described by Mendoza-Denton et al. (1997). Situational features and accessibility of CAUs were conceptualized as the frequency with which each information regarding the V*a*KE-dilemma or CAU was mentioned among those who agreed with reproductive cloning ($N = 21$) and those who disagreed ($N = 60$). Only those CAUs that were differentially accessible to one group over the other, i.e., mentioned more often (based on a chi-square analysis applying a Bonferroni-corrected significance level), were thought of as belonging to that group. The activation pathways between a) the situational features and the accessible CAUs, and b) among the accessible CAUs were identified by way of correlation (Spearman's Rho) computed among all the situational features, and CAUs coded for, respectively. CAPS is based on the assumption that individual differences exist in the accessibility of CAUs, as well as in the networks of activation. This study concentrates on testing the first of these assumptions while holding the second assumption constant. It is assumed that relevant pathways are societally shared given the similar educational and social background of the participants. Thus, correlations including all situational features and CAUs were computed using all participants (c.f. Mendoza-Denton et al., 1997). A positive correlation was interpreted as an excitatory link, meaning that the activation of one situational feature or CAU will likely lead to the activation of an associated CAU. A negative correlation was interpreted as an inhibitory link, meaning that the activation of one situational feature or CAU will likely lead to the inhibition of an associated CAU.

The domain maps were generated considering the following rules: (1) If a CAU was significantly more accessible to one group than another, it was grounds for including it into the former's domain map. (2) The darkness of the CAU node depicts the strength of accessibility (i.e., frequency) of each CAU. The darker the node, the more often this CAU was mentioned by the participants. (3) A dashed node, in contrast, represents an inhibited CAU. (4) In representing the activation pathway between the situational features and the CAUs and between the CAUs, only those links significantly below $p < .001$ in the correlational analyses were included in the domain map. This adjusted confidence interval resulted from the Bonferroni-correction which was applied in response to the problems caused by multiple comparisons (Dunn, 1961). (5) Solid arrows represent positive correlations (activating links) between a situational feature and a CAU or between CAUs. (6) Dashed arrows represent negative correlations (inhibitory links) between a situational feature and a CAU or between CAUs. Although inhibited CAUs had activation links to other CAUs, they were not included in the domain map since it is assumed that a deactivated CAU cannot influence another CAU.

RESULTS

Situational Features

Table 2 shows the percentage of participants for whom each situational feature (i.e., information concerning the VaKE-dilemma) played an essential role in activating specific CAUs. The participants mentioned 24 different situational features. Among those, nine features refer to information included in the VaKE-dilemma, while 15 features (italics in Table 2) refer to new information participants acquired during their information search in VaKE-step 7.

The results indicate that each group perceived or reported different information concerning the VaKE-dilemma as significant. If the learners perceive the information "Terminally ill (suffering)", "Organ transplantation", "Desire to have children",

Table 2. *Situational features (information concerning the VaKE-dilemma; italics: information acquired in VaKE-step 7)*

Situational feature (if ...)	Agree with cloning (%) N = 21	Disagree with cloning (%) N = 60
1. Terminally ill (suffering)	47.6	11.7
2. Organ transplantation	38.3	0
3. Desire to have children	28.6	0
4. *Medical achievement*	*23.8*	*6.7*
5. No organ donor	23.8	0
6. *Clone shaped by environment*	*23.8*	*0*
7. Clone is own child	14.3	0
8. *Cloning of food*	*9.6*	*0*
9. Cloning is legal	9.6	0
10. *Predetermined purpose*	*4.8*	*0*
11. Clone is organ donor	0	53.3
12. *Health hazard*	*0*	*38.3*
13. *Genetic defects*	*0*	*31.6*
14. *Clone is other-directed*	*0*	*28.3*
15. Genetical copy	0	26.7
16. *Embryos killed*	*0*	*26.7*
17. Medical treatment	9.5	24.4
18. *Sheep Dolly*	*9.5*	*23.3*
19. *Faster aging*	*4.8*	*23.3*
20. *Organ trade*	*9.5*	*20.0*
21. Designer babies	0	18.4
22. *Cloning is expensive*	*0*	*11.7*
23. *Danger for mother*	*0*	*10.0*
24. *Rejection reactions*	*0*	*3.3*

"Medical achievement", "No organ donor", "Clone shaped by environment", "Clone is own child", "Cloning of food", "Cloning is legal" and "Predetermined purpose", they rather tend to agree with genetic cloning.

In contrast, if they perceive information of the dilemma such as "Clone is organ donor", "Health hazards", "Genetic defects", "Clone is other-directed", "Genetical copy", "Embryos killed", "Medical treatment", "Sheep Dolly", "Faster aging", "Organ trade", "Designer babies", "Cloning is expensive", "Danger for mother",

Table 3. Accessibility of CAUs

Cognitive-Affective Unit (CAU)	Agree with cloning (%) N = 21	Disagree with cloning (%) N = 60
COGNITIONS		
1. Life has to be preserved	76	0**
2. Suffering should be reduced	19	0**
3. I do not want to feel guilty	5	5
4. Every child has right to be loved	0	12
5. Medical progress is important to me	71	2**
6. All options should be exploited	28	0**
7. Improvement of quality of life is important	28	3
8. New life should be created	43	2**
9. We are all human beings	24	4
10. Everyone has a purpose	14	0
11. Diseases should be cured	71	0**
12. Do not spend too much money on useless things	9	15
13. Parents always love their child	24	2
14. Absolute truth does not exist	14	0
15. Interventions into nature are common	39	0**
16. Humans should not be used as a means to an end	0	76**
17. We have no right to act like god	0	50**
18. Human beings should not be copied	0	65**
19. Do not take too much risk	0	76**
20. Parents should love their child	0	12
21. Human dignity shall be inviolable	0	70**
22. Stress should be avoided	0	30
23. Do not interfere with nature	5	68**
24. Negative consequences to society should be avoided	0	47**
25. I am against experiments with human beings	0	47**
26. It is not worth the expenses	9	15
27. Cloning leaves too many open questions	0	23
28. We are responsible for our actions	0	20
29. Problems can be solved differently	5	25

(Continued)

Table 3. (Continued)

Cognitive-Affective Unit (CAU)	Agree with cloning (%) N = 21	Disagree with cloning (%) N = 60
COGNITIONS		
30. Misuse is always a potential risk	0	32
31. Everyone should have the right to decide autonomously	0	37
32. Negative feelings should be avoided	24	55
AFFECTS		
1. Empathic concern	9	2
2. Fear	0	15
3. Indignation	0	7
4. Delight	0	2
5. Anger	0	7
6. Sadness	0	3

Note: Percentages with ** differ significantly at p < .001 by the chi-square significant difference test; chi-square comparisons of cells with small N may be unreliable.

and "Rejection reactions", they rather tend to disagree with genetic cloning. It is important to note, that the dilemma was for all participants the same but for each participant different information regarding the dilemma was important. Both groups perceive some information as important (e.g., "Terminally ill (suffering)", "Medical achievement", and "Medical treatment") indicating that this information can activate CAUs from those who agreed as well as from those who disagreed.

Accessibility (Frequency) of CAUs

Table 3 shows the percentage of participants who addressed the different CAUs, i.e., these were accessible, as a function of their opinion about the solution to the VaKE-dilemma. Participants mentioned 32 cognitions and six affects in their dialogues.

The results of the chi-square analysis show that the cognitions "Life has to be preserved", "Suffering should be reduced", "Medical progress is important to me", "All options should be exploited", "New Life should be created", "Diseases should be cured", and "Interventions into nature are common" are significantly more accessible to those who agreed. In contrast, for those who disagreed the cognitions "Humans should not be used as a means to an end", "We have no right to act like god", "Human beings should not be copied", "Do not take too much risk", "Human

EDUCATION FOR PROFESSIONAL ETHOS THROUGH VAKE

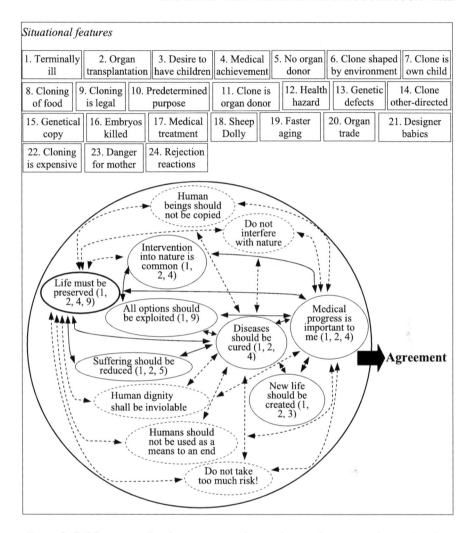

Figure 3. CAPS associated with agreement with reproductive cloning. Numbers in brackets indicate the situational features (i.e., information regarding the VaKE-dilemma) that activated the relevant CAU. Sold lines indicate positive (activating) links. Dashed lines indicate negative (inhibitory) links. Solid nodes indicate activated CAUs. Dashed nodes indicate inhibited CAUs

dignity shall be inviolable", "Do not interfere with nature", "Negative consequences to society should be avoided", and "I am against experiments with human beings" are significantly more accessible. There was no significant difference found concerning the frequencies of the affects.

119

A. WEINBERGER

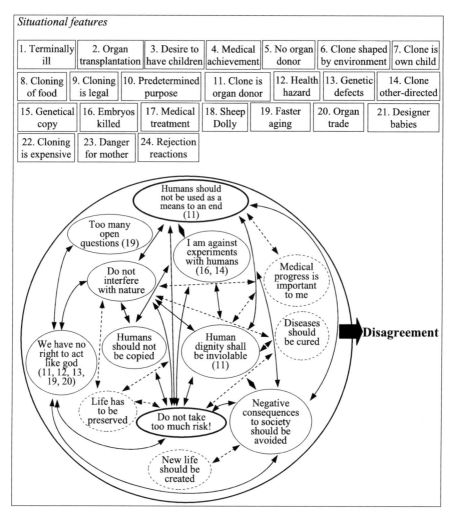

Figure 4. CAPS associated with disagreement with reproductive cloning. Numbers in brackets indicate the situational features (i.e., information regarding the VaKE-dilemma) that activated the relevant CAU. Sold lines indicate positive (activating) links. Dashed lines indicate negative (inhibitory) links. Solid nodes indicate activated CAUs. Dashed nodes indicate inhibited CAUs

Domain Maps

The results of the content analysis show that the participants' moral judgment is based on different types of cognitions and affects that were activated in relation to specific knowledge they perceived as important. The CAPS model allows taking a more differentiated look at the generation of moral judgments than just describing simple reactions to a VaKE-dilemma. It prompts us to "look inside the heads" of individuals and to consider their thought patterns and emotions and the situational features when describing their reactions. In what follows, the thought patterns for those who agreed and those who disagreed are traced using cognitive-affective domain maps (Mendoza-Denton et al., 1997; Miller, Shoda, & Hurley, 1997). The domain maps are drawn based on the analyses of the situational features and the accessible CAUs. The resulting networks of CAUs do not allow to conceptualize the chronology of their activation. Thus, different activation pathways are possible. One possible pathway is described. Note that the domain maps represent how one thought activates or inhibits another one. Since the correlational analysis does not allow to determine the directionality of activation, these inferences are based on the author's common sense (nurtured by the texts) and may be considered as arbitrary.

Figure 3 illustrates the CAPS for the group agreeing with reproductive cloning. A possible activation pathway is as follows: The information contained in the dilemma that the boy is terminally ill (1) and that organs need to be replaced to save his life (2) activated the thought "Life must be preserved". This thought is strengthened by the information that cloning is a pioneering medical achievement (4) and that it is legal (9). It activated, on the one hand, the thoughts that "Suffering should be reduced", "Diseases should be cured", and "Medical progress is important to me", while on the other hand, it inhibited the thoughts "Human beings should not be copied", "Do not interfere with nature", "Human dignity shall be inviolable", "Humans should not be used as a means to an end", and "Do not take too much risk".

The activated thought that "Diseases should be cured", which was strengthened by the information that the boy is terminally ill (1), organs need to be replaced (2), and cloning is a pioneering medical achievement (4) – the same information used for "Life must be preserved" –, activated in turn the thoughts "New life should be created" and "All options should be exploited". The latter in turn activated the thought "Intervention into nature is common". As a result of this network, the person agrees with reproductive cloning.

Figure 4 illustrates the CAPS which generated disagreement with reproductive cloning. A possible activation pathway is as follows: The information that the clone is an organ donor (11) and that reproductive cloning can cause genetic defects (12) activated the cognition that "We have no right to act like god". With this activated thought, the information that cloning can cause health hazards (12), faster aging (19), and organ trade (20) became important and the cognitions "Do not interfere with nature", "Too many open questions", "Do not take too much risk", and "Negative consequences to society should be avoided" became activated. The activated cognitions "Do not interfere with nature" and "Do not take too much risk" inhibited the thought "Life has to be preserved". The activated thought "Negative consequences to society should be avoided" inhibited the thought "New life should be created". With these activated thoughts the information that the clone is other-directed and embryos are killed activated the thoughts "I am against experiments with humans" which in turn activated the thoughts "Human dignity shall be inviolable". This network results in disagreement with reproductive cloning.

CONCLUSION AND IMPLICATIONS

This study took place in the context of fostering professional ethos which is considered in this chapter as the ability to make informed judgments in morally relevant situations. It tried to bring the cognitions and affects to light which are being activated when pre-service teachers make moral judgments in a V*a*KE-dilemma discussion. Based on the results of the cognitive-affective process system analysis the following conclusions and implications can be drawn:

CAPS has proven to be an appropriate model to generate a domain-specific theory of moral judgment in the context of a V*a*KE-dilemma discussion using the example of a socio-scientific issue. It could be shown that moral judgments are based on a complex network of cognitions and affects elicited by different situational features.

The construction of domain maps can visually illustrate what is going on "in the heads" of a person when facing a morally relevant decision situation. It is assumed that when learners are provided with the opportunity to draw their domain maps in V*a*KE, they can become aware of their cognitions and affects and the importance of particular factual knowledge. Drawing their domain maps about socio-scientific issues could support pre-service teachers to avoid relying on their subjective theories in scientific argumentation and to include facts to support their argument. Further, it could foster the awareness that scientific knowledge is not values-free. These propositions need to be examined in future studies.

Although affects are included in moral judgments, they are not mentioned as often as cognitions. This finding can be explained by the hypothetical content of the V*a*KE-dilemma in this study. In personal dilemmas, which are dilemmas persons encounter in their life, affects play a more critical role than in hypothetical dilemmas (Green et al., 2004; Weinberger, 2016).

V*a*KE has shown to be an appropriate method for discussing a socio-scientific issue. The learners can elaborate their scientific arguments through repeated phases of individual and collective thoughtful moral reflection and by considering relevant knowledge. The complex networks visualized in the domain maps show that the final scientific arguments include moral principles and facts which are related to each other. By this, it is assumed that V*a*KE can foster scientific literacy which has to be examined in future studies. Future studies addressing the formation of professionals' ethos through V*a*KE should also aim to investigate the cognitions and affects of teachers in the context of authentic decision situations.

The results of this study are in line with findings of similar studies in teacher education exploring the potential impact of V*a*KE on making responsible judgments (e.g., Weinberger, 2016). They are also in line with similar studies in the context of learning in schools exploring the argument-chains of pupils in a V*a*KE learning process (e.g., Nussbaumer, 2007; Patry, Weyringer, & Weinberger, 2010). However, by exploring the individuals' mental representations using CAPS, this study goes a step further showing how V*a*KE contributes to integrating knowledge and values effectively.

REFERENCES

Berkowitz, M. W., & Bier, M. C. (2007). What works in character education. *Journal of Research in Character Education, 5*, 29–48.
Blatt, M. M., & Kohlberg, L. (1975). The effects of classroom moral discussion upon children's level of moral judgment. *Journal of Moral Education, 4*(2), 129–161. Retrieved from https://doi.org/10.1080/0305724750040207
Blumenfeld, D., Senneville, D., & Crawford, M. (2013). Building an ethical self: Awareness of many modes of ethical thinking and acting. In M. N. Sanger & R. D. Osguthorpe (Eds.), *The moral work of teaching and teacher education* (pp. 60–75). New York, NY: Teachers College Press.
Chan, F.-Y. (1994). School teachers' moral reasoning. In J. R. Rest & D. Narváez (Eds.), *Moral development in the professions: Psychology and applied ethics* (pp. 71–84). Hillsdale, NJ: Lawrence Erlbaum.
Dunn, O. J. (1961). Multiple comparisons among means. *Journal of the American Statistical Association, 56*(293), 52–64.
Ehrich, L. C., Kimber, M., Millwater, J., & Cranston, N. (2011). Ethical dilemmas: A model to understand teacher practice. *Teachers and Teaching, 17*(2), 173–185.
Glanzer, P. L., & Ream, T. C. (2007). Has teacher education missed out on the "ethics boom"? A comparative study of ethics requirements and courses in professional majors of christian colleges and universities. *Christian Higher Education, 6*(4), 271–288.
Goodlad, J. I., Soder, R., & Sirotnik, K. A. (1990). *The moral dimensions of teaching*. San Francisco, CA: Jossey-Bass.
Greene, J. D., Nystrom, L. E., Engell, A. D., Darley, J. M., & Cohen, J. D. (2004). The neural bases of cognitive conflict and control in moral judgment. *Neuron, 44*(2), 389–400.
Haidt, J. (2001). The emotional dog and its rational tail: A social intuitionist approach to moral judgment. *Psychological Review, 108*(4), 814–834.
Johnson, L. E. (2008). Teacher candidate disposition: Moral judgement or regurgitation? *Journal of Moral Education, 37*(4), 429–444.
Jonassen, D. H. (2000). Toward a design theory of problem solving. *Educational Technology Research and Development, 48*(4), 63–85.
Keast, S., & Marangio, K. (2015). Values and Knowledge Education (V*a*KE) in teacher education: Benefits for science pre-service teachers when using dilemma stories. *Procedia: Social and Behavioral Sciences, 167*, 198–203.
Kim, M., & Roth, W.-M. (2008). Rethinking the ethics of scientific knowledge: A case study of teaching the environment in science classrooms. *Asia Pacific Education Review, 9*(4), 516–528.
Kincaid, H., Dupré, J., & Wylie, A. (Eds.). (2007). *Value-free science?: Ideals and illusions*. Oxford: Oxford University Press.
Kohlberg, L. (1984). *The psychology of moral development: The nature and validity of moral stages*. San Francisco, CA: Harper & Row.
Lind, G. (2003). *Moral ist lehrbar: Handbuch zur Theorie und Praxis moralischer und demokratischer Bildung*. München: Oldenbourg.
Loyens, S. M. M., & Rikers, R. M. J. P. (2011). Instruction based on inquiry. In R. E. Mayer & P. A. Alexander (Eds.), *Handbook of research on learning and instruction* (pp. 361–380). New York, NY: Routledge.
Maxwell, B., & Schwimmer, M. (2016). Professional ethics education for future teachers: A narrative review of the scholarly writings. *Journal of Moral Education, 45*(3), 354–371.

Mendoza-Denton, R., Ayduk, O. N., Shoda, Y., & Mischel, W. (1997). Cognitive-affective processing system analysis of reactions to the O. J. Simpson criminal trial verdict. *Journal of Social Issues, 53*(3), 563–581.

Miller, S. M., Shoda, Y., & Hurley, K. (1996). Applying cognitive-social theory to health-protective behavior: Breast self-examination in cancer screening. *Psychological Bulletin, 119*(1), 70–94.

Mischel, W., & Shoda, Y. (1995). A cognitive-affective system theory of personality: Reconceptualizing situations, dispositions, dynamics, and invariance in personality structure. *Psychological Review, 102*(2), 246–268.

Mischel, W., & Shoda, Y. (2008). Toward a unified theory of personality: Integrating dispositions and processing dynamics within the cognitive-affective processing system. In O. John, R. W. Robins, & L. A. Pervin (Eds.), *Handbook of personality: Theory and research* (3rd ed., pp. 208–241). New York, NY: Guilford Press.

Nussbaumer, M. (2007). *Das Unterrichtskonzept VaKE in Verbindung mit der Argumentationsstruktur von Max Miller* [VaKE in relation to the argumentation structure of Max Miller] (Unpublished Bachelor-thesis). University of Salzburg, Salzburg.

Oser, F., Dick, A., & Patry, J.-L. (Eds.). (1992). *Effective and responsible teaching: The new synthesis* (1st ed.). San Francisco, CA: Jossey-Bass.

Patry, J.-L. (2013). Beyond multiple methods: Critical multiplism on all levels. *International Journal of Multiple Research Approaches, 7*(1), 50–65.

Patry, J.-L., Weinberger, A., Weyringer, S., & Nussbaumer, M. (2013). Combining Values and Knowledge Education (VaKE). In B. Irby, G. Brown, R. Lara-Alecio, & S. Jackson (Eds.), *The handbook of educational theories* (pp. 561–580). Charlotte, NC: Information Age Publishing.

Patry, J.-L., Weyringer, S., & Weinberger, A. (2010). Kombination von Moral- und Werterziehung und Wissenserwerb mit VaKE: Wie argumentieren die Schülerinnen und Schüler? [Combination of values education and knowledge acquisition with VaKE: How do students argue?]. In B. Latzko & T. Malti (Eds.), *Moralische Entwicklung und Erziehung in Kindheit und Adoleszenz* [Moral development and education in childhood and adolscence] (pp. 241–260). Göttingen: Hogrefe.

Piaget, J. (1975). *L'équilibration des structures cognitives: Problème central du développment* [The development of thought: Equilibration of cognitive structures]. Paris: PUF.

Pritchard, M. S. (1999). Kohlbergian contributions to educational programs for the moral development of professionals. *Educational Psychology Review, 11*(4), 395–409.

Pritchard, M. S. (2006). *Professional integrity: Thinking ethically.* Lawrence, KS: University Press of Kansas.

Reiman, A. J., & Johnson, L. E. (2003). Promoting teacher professional judgment. *Journal of Research in Education, 13*(1), 4–14.

Sadler, T. D., & Zeidler, D. L. (2004). The morality of socioscientific issues: Construal and resolution of genetic engineering dilemmas. *Science Education, 88*(1), 4–27.

Sampson, V., & Blanchard, M. R. (2012). Science teachers and scientific argumentation: Trends in views and practice. *Journal of Research in Science Teaching, 49*(9), 1122–1148.

Sandalow, T. (1991). The moral responsibilities of universities. In D. L. Thompson (Eds.), *Moral values and higher education: A notion at risk* (pp. 149–171). New York, NY: Brigham Young University.

Schlaefli, A., Rest, J. R., & Thoma, S. J. (1985). Does moral education improve moral judgment? A meta-analysis of intervention studies using the defining issues test. *Review of Educational Research, 55*(3), 319–352.

Shoda, Y., Wilson, N. L., Whitsett, D. D., Lee-Dussud, J., & Zayas, V. (2015). The person as a cognitive-affective processing system: Quantitative ideography as an integral component of cumulative science. In M. Mikulincer, P. Shaver, M. L. Cooper, & R. J. Larsen (Eds.), *APA handbook of personality and social psychology, Volume 4: Personality processes and individual differences* (pp. 491–513). Washington, DC: American Psychological Association.

Simon, S., Erduran, S., & Osborne, J. (2006). Learning to teach argumentation: Research and development in the science classroom. *International Journal of Science Education, 28*(2–3), 235–260.

Tom, A. R. (1984). *Teaching as a moral craft.* New York, NY: Longman.

Vygotsky, L. S. (1962). *Thought and language.* Cambridge, MA: MIT Press.

Vygotsky, L. S. (1987). 'Thinking and speech' (N. Minick, Trans.). In R. W. Rieber & A. S. Carton (Eds.), *The collected works of L. S. Vygotsky, Vol. 1: Problems of general psychology* (pp. 39–285). New York, NY: Plenum. (Original work published 1934)

Wagner, K., Stark, R., Daudbasic, J., Klein, M., Krause, U.-M., & Herzmann, P. (2013). Effektivität integrierter Lernumgebungen in der universitären Lehrerbildung: eine quasiexperimentelle Feldstudie [Effectivity of integrated learning settings in university-based teacher education: A quasi-experiment]. *Journal for Educational Research Online, 5*(1), 115–140.

Warnick, B. R., & Silverman, S. K. (2011). A framework for professional ethics courses in teacher education. *Journal of Teacher Education, 62*(3), 273–285.

Weinberger, A. (2014). Diskussion moralischer Fallgeschichten zur Verbindung moralischer und epistemischer Ziele [Promoting moral and epistemic goals through discussion of moral cases]. *Beiträge zur Lehrerinnen- und Lehrerbildung, 32*(1), 60–72.

Weinberger, A. (2016). Konstruktivistisches Lernen in der Lehrerinnenbildung: Die Förderung des Professionsethos mit dem Unterrichtskonzept VaKE [Constructivist learning in teacher education: Fostering professional ethos through the didactical approach VaKE]. *Journal für LehrerInnenbildung, 2*, 28–39.

Weinberger, A. (2016, July). *The Cognitive Affective Processing System (CAPS) model: How do pre-service teachers act in different ethically challenging situations during their practicum.* Paper presented at the EARLI SIG 13-conference "Teachers' Ethos and Education for Responsibility," Salzburg, Austria.

Weyringer, S. (2008). *VaKE (Values and Knowledge Education) in einem internationalen Sommercampus für (hochbegabte) Jugendliche* [VaKE in an international summercamp for high-ability students] (Uupublished Dissertation doctoral thesis). Universität Salzburg, Salzburg.

Alfred Weinberger
Department of Research and Innovation
Private University of Education of the Diocese of Linz
Linz, Austria

YARIV ITZKOVICH AND DORIT ALT

9. THE DARK SIDE OF TEACHERS' BEHAVIOR AND ITS IMPACT ON STUDENTS' REACTIONS

A Comprehensive Framework to Assess College Students' Reactions to Faculty Incivility

INTRODUCTION

The pedagogical assignment of educators' concerns, among other aims, the general personality development of students, their socio-emotional development, and their moral development (Klaassen, 2008). These aims form an integral part of the professional profile of teachers. In this respect, the ethics of teachers in schools is considered an important prerequisite for accomplishing these pedagogical tasks and has triggered an extensive research (Alt & Reingold, 2012) however, thus far, there appears to be a paucity of literature which extensively conceptualizes or details its practical applications (Alt, 2014; Alt & Itzkovich, 2015b).

Ethics in higher education, in the context of faculty-student communication, has been recently linked to tremendous changes in educational pedagogies, characterized by an increased demand for adapted teaching strategies that focuses attention on student's needs and wellbeing (Itzkovich & Alt, 2015a). Those changes impose growing challenges for educators and academic institutions alike. As teachers are the very center of pedagogical effort, their professional ethos should support the evolving pedagogical arena. To a great extent, characteristics of teachers' ethos, which in turn can support these tendencies, are centered on two complementary domains: the moral domain of teaching and the instructional domain, both can be adapted either positively to support the aforementioned changes (Van Veen et al., 2003) or negatively as in the case of faculty incivility (FI, Itzkovich & Alt, 2015b).

Broadly defined, incivility is a disrespectful deviant organizational behavior (Andersson & Pearson, 1999). As a low-intensity deviant behavior, incivility is manifested through a range of inappropriate social interactions (Andersson & Pearson, 1999; Pearson & Porath, 2005) which might be active in nature when someone is making demeaning remarks, for example, or passive when an employee is ignored (Schilpzand et al., 2015). A wider viewpoint of incivility enabled studying this phenomenon in academia while focusing on uncivil interactions between faculty members (i.e. lecturers) and students as well as between faculty members (Caza & Cortina, 2007; Clark, 2008a, 2008b; Clark & Springer, 2007; Lasiter, Marchiondo, & Marchiondo, 2012; Marchiondo, Marchiondo, & Lasiter, 2010).

Despite increased interest in incivility and specifically FI (Clark et al., 2012a; Del Prato, 2013; Johnson-Bailey, 2015), it is noteworthy that very little is empirically known about the relationships between this phenomenon and its antecedents or outcomes (Schilpzand, De Pater, & Erez, 2016). Additionally, previous work has presented a quantitative model for measuring contemporary reactions of students to FI (Itzkovich & Alt, 2015). However, the qualitative data gathered to conceptualize this model were not introduced thus far. Therefore, the purpose of the current chapter is to describe the qualitatively assessed consequences of the dark side of teachers' behavior in academia, namely FI, as expressed by students.

LITERATURE REVIEW

Defining Academic Incivility

Incivility is defined as a low-intensity deviant behavior which violates workplace norms for mutual respect (Andersson & Pearson, 1999). As such, incivility is displayed through a wide range of inappropriate behaviors (Porath & Pearson, 2013), some can be categorized as active, for example, when someone is making demeaning remarks, and others as passive for example, when an employee is ignored (Paulin & Griffin, 2016). Although initially attributed to deviant organizational behaviors, incivility was also utilized to uncivil attitudes and behaviors in academia (Alt & Itzkovich, 2015b; Clark & Farnsworth, 2009; Clark et al., 2012).

For example, a recent study (Alt & Itzkovich, 2015b) was aimed at mapping features of FI as perceived by students. This study presented a new scale for measuring those features which represents adverse attitudes of faculty. Klaassen (2010) argues that by displaying a particular attitude, a teacher can fulfill a certain exemplary function that students can follow. This role model function forms an essential element in the ethos procedure which can stimulate the moral and social development of students and colleagues. Thus, FI may impair teachers' professional ethos and their role as educators. In turn, such behavior may have several implications for the institution atmosphere or culture as well as for the social and moral development of students. This issue is of prime importance, as students are affected by the culture patterns in the institution. Creating a positive atmosphere can lead students toward a self-respect and responsible behavior. In contrast, a negative atmosphere, created by FI encounters, may elicit student responses with special characteristics in the academic context, as discussed in this study.

Implications of Incivility

Incivility does not come without a price tag. The financial cost of being subjected to workplace incivility is assessed as a yearly cost of US$14,000 per employee, who might react emotionally and behaviorally in manners that distract him/her from work (Schilpzand et al., 2016). Some of these responses can be categorized as retaliation responses (Itzkovich, 2016), while others can be considered as withdrawal behaviors (Porath & Pearson, 2013).

Despite the profound inventory of reactions to workplace incivility, only recently a comprehensive theoretical framework to capture implications of incivility was introduced (Itzkovich, 2015). This conceptualization was not focused only on behavioral responses of targets of incivility but also on perceptual outcomes, such as withdrawal intentions, job insecurity perceptions, retaliation reactions toward the organization, and protest measures which were integrated by the conceptualization of the EVLN model (as described below), utilized to assess reactions to stressful situations (Hagedoorn, Yperen, Vliert, & Buunk, 1999; Liljegren, Nordlund, & Ekberg, 2008; Naus, van Iterson, & Roe, 2007). This suggested theoretical framework was recently assessed quantitatively (Itzkovich & Alt, 2015), and to some extent qualitatively (Clark, 2008a).

Academic incivility is as costly as its counterpart in workplaces (i.e., workplace incivility): it interferes with learning and safe clinical performance in nursing education; it decreases program satisfaction and retention (Lasiter et al., 2012), and impacts adjustment to college (Alt & Itzkovich, 2015a). Additionally, students who were exposed to uncivil behaviors of lecturers, have experienced stress, felt disrespected, unprotected and helpless, used to avoid interactions with the perpetrator, reduced their help-seeking behaviors and, in general, disconnected themselves from the learning process (Altmiller, 2012).

Responses to Stressful Situations: Model Development

Several theoretical models which mapped optional reactions to stressful situations such as incivility were presented thus far. Hirschman (1970) presented a conceptualization of employees', customers' and/or citizens' responses driven by a decline in firms and other social systems. In his model, Hirschman presented three optional responses: *exit*, a reaction which describes departure from the organization/state or its services; *voice*, which represents protest engagements aimed to amend the unfavorable situation; and *loyalty* which conveys the need to choose a temporary response before choosing between *exit* and *voice* (Farrell, 1983), or express devotion (Si & Li, 2012).

Hirschman's model was later utilized to explain reactions of employees' dissatisfaction (Farrell, 1983). This conceptualization shifted the focus of the model from the macro level to the micro level. In addition, for the first time, the '*neglect*' response was addressed and integrated into the model (Rusbult, Farrell, Rogers, & Mainous, 1988). The *neglect* response represents a wide variety of behaviors, such as lateness, absenteeism, and increased error rates (Farrell, 1983). Altogether, the extended model consists of four categories stretched upon two dimensions of destructiveness and constructiveness. While *exit* and *neglect* pertain to the destructive end, *voice* and *loyalty* pertain to the constructive end. Additionally, while *exit* and *voice* are viewed as active responses, *loyalty* and *neglect* are considered passive (Hagedoorn et al., 1999; Si & Li, 2012). The *exit, voice, loyalty* and *neglect* model

(EVLN) in its extended outlook, was primarily focused on reactions to employee's dissatisfaction (Farrell, 1983). Yet, several studies have also utilized the model to address responses to problematic events in general (Hagedoorn et al., 1999) and specifically to stressful situations such as job insecurity (Berntson, Naswall, & Sverke, 2010; Sverke & Hellgren, 2001), and psychological contract violation (Rousseau, 1995).

Rousseau (1995) presented a different interpretation to the models' categories that warrants mentioning. The main addition of Rousseau is expressed through her aptitude to present a wider variety of destructive reactions, some of them were considered by others as constructive (Itzkovich, 2015). Specifically, a wider, destructive in part, interpretation has been given to *loyalty*, referred to as *silence*. In her view *silence* refers to inaction due to pessimism. In addition, she suggested addressing the *neglect* reaction as a more active reaction, such as vandalism and theft, defined as destructive reactions. Lastly, she maintained that *voice* can be threatening at times.

It should be noted that Rousseau (1995) was not the only one to stress that *loyalty* can be driven out of weakness. Hirschman (1970) also indicated that *loyalty* can be driven out of low potential to *exit* or raise *voice* (Itzkovich, 2015). In a similar vein, Hagedoorn et al. (1999) noted that *voice* reactions should be divided into two forms: *considerate voice* and *aggressive voice* – which is characterized by a lack of consideration and aspirations to win the situation rather than to fix it. Indeed, Rousseau's (1995) model is more inclined toward destructive reactions and, therefore, seems as a useful perspective for framing an empirically based understanding of responses to incivility. Yet, to date, although the EVLN model in its extended outlook was assessed qualitatively, only the original assembly (i.e., Hirschman, 1970) was measured by a qualitative research array as a framework for understanding reactions to FI (Clark, 2008b).

In summary, Clark (2008b) was the first to suggest the EVLN theoretical structure while assessing reactions to FI. Still, her insightful conceptualization was limited to three possible reactions to FI in accordance with the three categories of responses initially presented by Hirschman (1970). Therefore, the model suggested by Clark could not capture a wider scope of contemporary responses to FI, presented through the comprehensive and more recent developments of the model.

Based on the literature presented above, the aims of this study were to map features of responses to FI (as perceived by students) and validate the EVLN structure by analyzing qualitative data.

METHOD

Sample and Procedure

The study was conducted in a peripheral college in Israel. The college consists of about 3,000 students from two large schools: Social Sciences and Humanities and

Engineering. Semi-structured interviews with 12 undergraduate third-year social-science students were conducted during one semester (seven females and five males). The students have volunteered to participate in the study and were assured that no specific identifying information about them would be processed.

The students were asked to describe an incivility incident in which a faculty member acted as a perpetrator of an uncivil behavior. They were asked to focus their descriptions on incidents in which they were involved or incidents they witnessed in college. They were also asked to describe their reactions toward it. The interviews were held in the colleges, in a separate room which allowed privacy and intimacy. The length of each interview was 20–30 minutes.

Research Tools and Data Analysis

Semi-structured interviews allow gathering rich and varied data. This technique enabled capturing the depth and many layers of the incivility experience and recognizing individual emotions, appraisals, and intentions to react which cannot be revealed by other measures. While the same guideline was used with all interviewees, the time allotted for each question, the detailed follow-up questions and the order of some of the questions differed across interviews and were modified according to the interviewees' responses. This flexibility allows for a free-form interaction and ensures that the interviewees do not only elaborate on topics that they find most compelling but may also raise new issues which were not referred to in the initial list of questions. Furthermore, by allowing researchers to clarify, probe, and understand meanings, such interviews promote a broad and deep understanding of the topics under discussion. Data were recorded and transcribed by research assistants.

A thematic analysis, a "method for analysing and reporting patterns (themes) in the data" (Braun & Clarke, 2006, p. 79), was employed. Each of the researchers created a thematic analysis of the data performed on all interviews. The themes and codes were then presented to the other researcher and were examined in order to get an agreement among the different codes and data. Inter-rater Cohen's Kappa (k) reliability, which is commonly assessed in psychological research, was used. The raters (the two researchers, which are experts in the field of incivility and moral education) were asked to rate the data. The k values were interpreted as follows, $k < 0.20$ poor agreement; $0.21 < k < 0.40$ fair agreement; $0.41 < k < 0.60$ moderate agreement; $0.61 < k < 0.80$ good agreement; $0.81 < k < 1.00$ very good agreement. Results of $0.61 < k < 1$ were considered acceptable for the purposes of the current study.

FINDINGS

General Incivility Descriptions

In general, the interviews demonstrated that FI exists and it is manifested through a wide array of behaviors, some are active as one student described:

> In the last day of the course, the lecturer gave us some example questions. I asked for an additional explanation when I failed to understand the question, right after the lecturer explained the issue twice. When I raised my hand, the lecturer told me that nothing is wrong with the question and that it is most likely that I have difficulty *understanding* it. He also said that he doesn't have any intention to explain it again.

Other manifestations of incivility were more passive as another student described: "One of our lecturers used his cell phone during class time" or, "we have a lecturer that arrives 25 minutes after class starts and he lets us go 20 minutes before class ends. In between, he only reads off his presentations. It is obvious that he was not into teaching".

Category of Responses

Students reacted differently to these FI behaviors. In their stories, we identified four categories of reactions which collapsed into the EVLN theoretical model. The first notable reaction observed was *Exit* which is a voluntary termination of the affiliation/relationships with the lecture/college. Yet, our results showed that the termination of relationship is limited to class attendance. Students did not report leaving college or course as sometimes it is an obligatory course with no alternative, and leaving college is costly, for example,

> When one of the students asked for an explanation, the lecturer shut her up saying that she disturbs her. When the student asked again, the lecturer threatened her saying that if she will disturb once again she will send her to the discipline committee. The student stepped out of class and never came back. She only attended the final exam.

The second category of reactions was *Voice*. Voice is defined as any action which is intended to remedy the situation. Indeed, students in the Israeli higher education system feel comfortable to approach their lecturers as described by one of the students:

> In one of the classes the lecturer was belittling me as a response to my misunderstanding ... after class I tried to talk to the lecturer. I explained him my discontent with his behavior during class, and he understood and agreed that he should have said things differently.

Our third observed reaction was *Loyalty*, defined as a non-response, represented mostly by the willingness to endure unfavorable conditions mostly due to lack of alternatives, in line with Rousseau's (1995) interpretation. In the students' words:

> As a freshman, I attended an *introduction to statistics* course. I asked the lecturer a simple question, but instead of explaining the issue, he shouted "what is not clear? How can't you understand the obvious?" I was in a complete shock and continued sitting there with no ability and intention to respond.

I asked the professor a question regarding the learning material. The professor ridiculed me in front of the class. I felt very unpleasant. I was asking a simple question, and instead of answering me he mocked me in front of the entire class. Instead of explaining the material pleasantly he made a joke at my expense. I sat quietly until the end of the lesson.

The last category of responses was *Neglect* which is a passive negligence or active destruction which can be manifested in destructive interpersonal relations. The most destructive response we identified was 'complaining'. This reaction defers from voicing as the purpose is to hurt the offender, for example,

One of our lecturers was impatient toward students, aggressive and very irritated when students did not understand the material. She even, at times, left class in the middle of the lesson to use her mobile phone. She also told us more than once that she gets paid and it does not really matter if we complained or not. I filed a complaint against her, but nothing happened.

DISCUSSION

The primary goal of this study was to map responses to FI which demonstrates the implications of the dark side of teachers' behavior. A qualitative method approach was applied in this research. The results foregrounded four categories: (1) *exit* (2) *voice* (3) *loyalty* and (4) *neglect*, which together assembled the EVLN theoretical model (Farrell, 1983). Classifying potential responses to incivility was merely introduced by Clark (2008a) who suggested the outdated three-dimensional model of Hirschman (1970) as a framework of mapping responses to FI. The present study elaborates on previous work by corroborating the EVLN four-dimensional model, which allows delving deeper into the dark side of teachers' behavior and its implications for students. While school teachers' ethos is commonly addressed in research, this study illustrates its relevance to higher education. These findings may suggest that while promoting positive values is of importance and widely investigated, recognizing and detaining negative behaviors should not be overlooked.

This study enhances the understanding of FI implications for colleges and could promote a proactive policy of zero tolerance for FI. In this respect, colleges should establish *'voice'* mechanisms to enable targets of FI to speak up. By doing so, students might refrain from *exit* and would prefer *voice* channels as well as *loyalty* based on attachment, and not as a silent reaction based on weakness and absence of opportunities.

Klaassen (2010) suggests several tools that can serve to initiate the teachers' sensitivity for a concrete behavior that meets ethical standards of their profession namely teachers' ethos. These may also be useful for faculty. First is helping teachers to implement reflection on and dialogue about ethical questions, known as the 'ethos procedure'. Faculty can, and should, create a package of activities that they can work through and apply to their own experiences. Such tools can stimulate teachers in academia to think about the ethical aspects of their profession. The instrument might fit in with experiences of the teachers and the value dependent character of the professional decisions with which they must make every day. The second tool is helping faculty to formulate their own personal ethical codes. Developing a professional code by the teachers may help them to justify their own experiences and expectations with relation to their profession. Third, the teachers' own code should be confronted with the official formal professional code. In the context of FI, such codes are scarce. Alt and Itzkovich (2015a) maintain that in these codes, incivility toward others should be considered as a direct violation of academic ethics, and the faculty moral responsibility to deter such unethical behaviors should be recognized. These initiatives should also be accompanied by activities aimed at nurturing common moral values. In this process, teachers should discuss with their students which moral values are important and how moral norms could be collectively constructed. Teachers should negotiate the meaning of civil codes in the context of collaborative environments. Although rarely takes place in academic settings, Alt and Itzkovich argue that open discourses on expected academic behavior should be seen as important socialization tools aimed at confronting unethical behaviors. Such discussions should involve faculty and students in order to shape a mutual code of ethics and code of conduct. In keeping with the code of ethics, faculty should condemn any behavior that demonstrates bias against or disrespect for any individual. The mutual acknowledgment in these codes of ethics is considered vital to creating a positive learning environment that will allow students to admit mistakes without fear of being humiliated.

Nevertheless, this study was conducted in a single country and was limited to one regional college; therefore, the results cannot necessarily be generalized to students of other regions or countries. A cross-cultural validation of the results is needed to substantiate these findings. While the only association between incivility and the EVLN model was either theoretical (Itzkovich, 2015) quantitative (Itzkovich & Alt, 2015) or partial (Clark, 2008a) so far, despite its limitations, the present study introduced an additional validation to a general model of responses (EVLN) to FI and showed that this behaviour might elicit all four responses indicated in theory.

REFERENCES

Alt, D. (2014). Assessing the connection between students' justice experience and attitudes toward academic cheating in higher education new learning environments. *Journal of Academic Ethics, 12,* 113–127.

Alt, D., & Itzkovich, Y. (2015a). Adjustment to college and perceptions of faculty incivility. *Current Psychology, 35*(4), 657–666. Retrieved from http://doi.org/10.1007/s12144-015-9334-x

Alt, D., & Itzkovich, Y. (2015b). Assessing the connection between students' justice experience and perceptions of faculty incivility in higher education. *Journal of Academic Ethics, 13*(2), 121–134. Retrieved from http://doi.org/10.1007/s10805-015-9232-8

Alt, D., & Reingold, R. (Eds.). (2012). *Changes in teachers' moral role: From passive observers to moral and democratic leaders.* Rotterdam, The Netherlands: Sense Publishers.

Altmiller, G. (2012). Student perceptions of incivility in nursing education: Implications for educators. *Nursing Education Perspectives, 33*(1), 15–20.

Andersson, L. M., & Pearson, C. M. (1999). Tit for tat? The spiraling effect of incivility in the workplace. *Academy of Management Review, 24*(3), 452–471. Retrieved from http://doi.org/10.2307/259136

Berntson, E., Naswall, K., & Sverke, M. (2010). The moderating role of employability in the association between job insecurity and exit, voice, loyalty and neglect. *Economic and Industrial Democracy, 31*(2), 215–230. Retrieved from http://doi.org/10.1177/0143831X09358374

Braun, V., & Clarke, V. (2006). Using thematic analysis in psychology. *Qualitative Research in Psychology, 3*(2), 77–101. Retrieved from http://doi.org/10.1191/1478088706qp063oa

Caza, B. B., & Cortina, L. M. (2007). From insult to injury: Explaining the impact of incivility. *Basic and Applied Social Psychology, 29*(4), 335–350. Retrieved from http://doi.org/10.1080/01973530701665108

Clark, C. M. (2008a). On faculty incivility in nursing education: A conceptual model. *Nursing Education Perspectives, 29*(5), 284–289.

Clark, C. M., & Farnsworth, J. (2009). Development and description of the Incivility in Nursing Education (INE) survey. *The Journal of Theory Construction & Tes, 13*(1), 54–62. Retrieved from http://web.a.ebscohost.com.georgefox.idm.oclc.org/ehost/pdfviewer/pdfviewer?vid=15&sid=1ed74a49-e89a-4e30-8fd8-5614c31428fd@sessionmgr4002&hid=4212

Clark, C., Juan, C., Allerton, B., Otterness, N., Ya, J. W., & Wei, F. (2012a). Faculty and student perceptions of academic incivility in the people' republic of China. *Journal of Cultural Diversity, 19*(3), 85–93. Retrieved from http://content.ebscohost.com/ContentServer.asp?T=P&P=AN&K=2011680779&S=R&D=c8h&EbscoContent=dGJyMNXb4kSeprM4yOvsOLCmr0uep7FSsK64S7KWxWXS&ContentCustomer=dGJyMOGssUq0p7FQuePfgeyx43zx\n
http://ezproxy.sunderland.ac.uk/login?url= http://search.ebscohost.com/lo

Clark, C. M., & Springer, P. J. (2007). Thoughts on incivility: Student and faculty perceptions of uncivil behavior in nursing education. *Nursing Education Perspective, 28*(2), 93–98.

Del Prato, D. (2013). Students' voices: The lived experience of faculty incivility as a barrier to professional formation in associate degree nursing education. *Nurse Education Today, 33*(3), 286–290. Retrieved from http://doi.org/10.1016/j.nedt.2012.05.030

Farrell, D. (1983). Exit, voice, loyalty, and neglect as responses to job dissatisfaction: A multidimensional scaling study. *Academy of Management Journal, 26*(4), 596–607. Retrieved from http://doi.org/10.2307/255909

Hagedoorn, M., Yperen, N. W., Van Vliert, E., & Buunk, B. P. (1999). Employees' reactions to problematic events: A circumplex structure of five categories of responses, and the role of job satisfaction. *Journal of Organizational Behavior, 20*(3), 309–321. Retrieved from http://doi.org/10.1002/(SICI)1099-1379(199905)20:3<309::AID-JOB895>3.0.CO;2-P

Hirschman, A. O. (1970). *Exit, voice, and loyalty: Responses to decline in firms, organizations, and states*. Cambridge, MA: Harvard University Press.

Itzkovich, Y. (2015). *Uneconomic relationships: The dark side of interpersonal interactions in organizations*. Tel-Aviv: Resling.

Itzkovich, Y. (2016). The impact of employees' status on incivility, deviant behaviour and job insecurity. *EuroMed Journal of Business, 11*(2), 304–318. Retrieved from http://doi.org/doi:10.1108/EMJB-09-2015-0045

Itzkovich, Y., & Alt, D. (2015). Development and validation of a measurement to assess college students' reactions to faculty incivility. *Ethics & Behavior, 26*(8), 621–637. Retrieved from http://doi.org/10.1080/10508422.2015.1108196

Johnson-Bailey, J. (2015). Academic incivility and bullying as a gendered and racialized phenomena: Roadrunner Search discovery service. *Adult Learning, 26*(1), 42–47. Retrieved from http://doi.org/10.1177/1045159514558414

Klaassen, C. (2008, August). *The professional ethos of teachers*. Paper presented at the meeting of Moral and Democratic Education, Florina, Greece.

Klaassen, C. (2010). The professional ethos of teachers. In C. Klaassen & N. Maslovaty (Eds.), *Moral courage and the normative professionalism of teachers* (pp. 225–243). Rotterdam, The Netherlands: Sense Publishers.

Lasiter, S., Marchiondo, L., & Marchiondo, K. (2012). Student narratives of faculty incivility. *Nursing Outlook, 60*(3), 121–126. Retrieved from http://doi.org/10.1016/j.outlook.2011.06.001

Liljegren, M., Nordlund, A., & Ekberg, K. (2008). Psychometric evaluation and further validation of the Hagedoorn et al. modified EVLN measure: Personality and social sciences. *Scandinavian Journal of Psychology, 49*(2), 169–177. Retrieved from http://doi.org/10.1111/j.1467-9450.2007.00620.x

Marchiondo, K., Marchiondo, L. A., & Lasiter, S. (2010). Faculty incivility: Effects on program satisfaction of BSN students. *The Journal of Nursing Education, 49*(11), 608–614. Retrieved from http://doi.org/10.3928/01484834-20100524-05

Naus, F., van Iterson, A., & Roe, R. (2007). Organizational cynicism: Extending the exit, voice, loyalty, and neglect model of employees' responses to adverse conditions in the workplace. *Human Relations, 60*(5), 683–718. Retrieved from http://doi.org/10.1177/0018726707079198

Paulin, D., & Griffin, B. (2016). The relationships between incivility, team climate for incivility and job-related employee well-being: A multilevel analysis. *Work & Stress, 8373*, 1–20. Retrieved from http://doi.org/10.1080/02678373.2016.1173124

Porath, C., & Pearson, C. (2013). The price of incivility. *Harvard Business Review, 91*(1–2), 115–121. Retrieved from http://doi.org/10.1080/14616696.2013.767923

Rousseau, D. M. (1995). *Psychological contracts in organizations: Understanding written and unwritten agreements*. Thousand Oaks, CA: Sage Publications.

Rusbult, C. E., Farrell, D., Rogers, G., & Mainous, A. G. (1988). Impact of exchange variables on exit, voice, loyalty, and neglect: An integrative model of responses to declining job status satisfaction. *Academy of Management Journal, 31*(3), 599–627. Retrieved from http://doi.org/10.2307/256461

Schilpzand, P., De Pater, I. E., & Erez, A. (2016). Workplace incivility: A review of the literature and agenda for future research. *Journal of Organizational Behavior, 37*, S57–S88. Retrieved from http://doi.org/10.1002/job.1976

Si, S., & Li, Y. (2012). Human resource management practices on exit, voice, loyalty, and neglect: Organizational commitment as a mediator. *The International Journal of Human Resource Management, 23*(8), 1705–1716. Retrieved from http://doi.org/10.1080/09585192.2011.580099

Sverke, M., & Hellgren, J. (2001). Exit, voice and loyalty reactions to job insecurity in Sweden: Do unionized and non-unionized employees differ? *British Journal of Industrial Relations, 39*(2), 167–182. Retrieved from http://doi.org/10.1111/1467-8543.00195

Van Veen, K., Theunissen, M., Sleegers, P., Bergen, T., Klaassen, C., & Hermans, C. (2003). Relations between teachers' professional and religious orientations and their behavior during morally critical incidents. *Educational Research and Evaluation, 9*(1), 51–74. Retrieved from http://doi.org/10.1076/edre.9.1.51.13551

Yariv Itzkovich
Kinneret College on the Sea of Galilee
Israel

Dorit Alt
Kinneret College on the Sea of Galilee
Israel

KARIN HEINRICHS AND SIMONE ZIEGLER

10. COMMITMENT TO DEVELOP APPRECIATIVE RELATIONSHIPS IN SCHOOL

Nonviolent Communication as an Approach to Specify a Facet of Teacher Ethos

APPRECIATIVE RELATIONSHIPS IN SCHOOL – RELEVANCE FOR AN APPROACH TO TEACHER ETHOS?

A teacher noticed that one student has been changing his behavior in school for some time in a conspicuous way. He/She is now very inattentive, and in group work, he/she stands out through apathy. The teacher does not want to neglect this irritative development in the student's behavior. He decides to talk to the student after the lesson. To get insights why the student shows this changed behavior the teacher asks for reasons and intends to find an appropriate solution. So, he asks how the student could be supported in school. Although the student does not express any reason for his/her behavior, he/she starts to participate in lessons again. After some time, the student tells the teacher that his/her behavior has been linked to his parents' divorce. (Adaptive scenario according to Oser, 1998)

This situation demonstrates one option how teachers could act in such a case of irritative student's behavior. The teacher apparently felt committed to scrutinize the students' change in negative behavior and to support him/her to solve underlying problems. The teacher took responsibility. He tried to get in contact with the student and wanted to understand his/her situation and needs.

The teachers' willingness to assume responsibility for students' well-being and learning as well as to award students' (self-)responsibility can be considered as core elements of teachers' daily work. Therefore, the role of teachers as professionals should not be reduced to "knowledge mediators," and the requirements of professional and effective teaching in the sense of teaching should not be reduced to strictly targeting at good learning outcomes. Instead, responsible teaching should aim to shape individuals' potentials for achieving the intended knowledge and skills in a particular domain or subject as well as for being prepared to lifelong learning, to participate and to get integrated into society. It is well known that students differ in perceiving and exploiting offered learning opportunities. So, teachers should take into account individuals' opportunities and preconditions for learning while preparing their lessons. During the last decades, the discussion about teachers' professional (moral) responsibility was hardly mentioned in the debate on competences. However, Baumert and Kunter (2006) describe in their framework model of teacher competency that not only teachers' professional content knowledge, pedagogical content knowledge, or pedagogical knowledge, but also motivation, metacognition, self-regulation, attitudes as well as beliefs and values are important for teaching and students' learning. Values, such as care, justice, and truthfulness unite to general (moral) principles and ideals, which teachers feel committed. Moreover, these values are regarded as core elements of professional ethos, in particular of teacher ethos (see, e.g., Bauer, 2007; Forster-Heinzer, 2015; Harder, 2014; Noddings, 1992; Ofenbach, 2006; Orth & Fritz, 2013; Oser, 1998). Teacher ethos represents a point of reference for the concrete and value-oriented behavior (Konrad, 1986). In some discussions, Oser and co-authors (1992) have already offered ideas how teachers could implement these values, how to deal with value conflicts and, furthermore, how even to foster students' (moral) competences. Teacher ethos in that sense goes beyond the critical dimension of the commitment, which focuses on supporting students in gaining knowledge and developing domain-specific competencies (Harder, 2014); moreover, teacher ethos has a moral core. Furthermore, the already mentioned values may be fruitful for teachers to deal with individual differences in the classroom as well as to offer sophisticated learning environments (Becker & Lauterback, 2010; Latzko, 2012). Teachers who were asked about their professional values pointed out another vital facet of teacher ethos that focuses on forming trustful relationships between teachers and students as well as among students (Harder, 2014). However, forming appreciative relationships additionally plays an essential role in teaching and for the individual learning process (Bauer, 2007; Furrer & Skinner, 2003; Harder, 2014; Hattie, 2012; Martin & Dowson, 2009). Appreciative relationships are considered as appropriate preconditions for establishing fairness, caring and truthfulness in the classroom, for dealing with diversity or conflicts as well as for fostering effective learning.

The approach of nonviolent communication (NVC) according to Rosenberg (2005) offers underlying assumptions as well as practical implications of how to get into appreciative relationships. Thus, NVC provides fruitful ideas how to improve communication, social climate and, finally, responsible teaching as well as learning. NVC offers a framework and methods for considering individual differences in experiences or values, for creating a social atmosphere and allows dealing with conflicts, caring for one's self as well as others' needs (Rosenberg, 2005). Therefore, this chapter suggests NVC as a concept to specify a facet of teacher ethos that focuses on how to develop appreciative relationships, particularly teacher-student relationships. Teacher ethos in this sense considers taking care and feeling responsible for students as a standard, which professional teachers individually feel committed to (Beck, 1997). Additionally, NVC might support balancing students' as well as the teachers' needs.

This chapter will try to answer the question, what is the potential of the NVC as a facet of teacher ethos to create positive relations between teachers and students?

The next section explains a preconception of teacher ethos focusing on forming appreciative relationships. Teacher ethos is considered as an identity intention influencing teachers' self-commitment and professional actions (Beijaard et al., 2000). Additionally, in the following section, it will be explained in which situations teacher ethos is assumed to become visible in many situations in everyday working life, not only in odd situations or moral dilemmas. Further, it will be described a facet of teacher ethos focusing on building appreciative relationships that can be theoretically specified referring to the concept of NVC developed by Rosenberg. Then, some likely effects on teaching environments will be derived which are based on that kind of teacher ethos. Finally, the future perspectives and implications for research will be discussed.

TEACHER ETHOS – A PEDAGOGICAL VERSION OF PROFESSIONAL VALUES, COMMITMENT, AND BEHAVIOR

Professional Ethos and Teacher Ethos – Based on Values and Focus on Creating Effective Student Learning Development

Ofenbach (2006) shows that many different concepts of ethos coexist. In general, professional ethos integrates general principles and ideals of a profession that affect professionals' performance. Because most comprehensions remain on a very abstract level (Forster-Heinzer, 2015), professional ethos is linked to a kind of idealistic understanding of the profession and illustrates how a professional should act (Terhart, 1987). To approach this abstractness, Harder (2014) and Lewin (1951) remarked that (teacher) ethos does not only depend on professional, but also on individual moral values. In this regard, teacher ethos is considered as a compression of job-specific values (Konrad, 1986) and as a personal factor, subjective theory, individual awareness, and attitude. Furthermore, it involves the professional self as well as habitualized self-control (Ofenbach, 2006), and determines teachers' actions in everyday working life (Oser, 2004).[1]

In Oser's (1998) concept, teacher ethos is claimed mainly to become visible in odd situations. Within these odd situations, teachers violate a fundamental moral value such as justice or caring to create a different essential value like truthfulness. For example, the teacher would like to take care of an individual student, but at the same time, he or she knows that the justice in the classroom cannot be realized. To find a solution in such an odd situation different (moral) values have to be balanced. To reach such a balanced status the agent probably uses one out of five types of (realized ways of) decision-making (Oser et al., 1998). (1) Avoidance: The protagonist refuses his or her competences which means that he or she decides not to take over responsibility even though he or she realizes that he or she would be responsible. (2) Delegation: He or she accepts the responsibility, but at the first opportunity he or she hands it over to another person. (3) Single decision: The teacher decides alone and intuitively what to do in the present odd situation, but he or she does not give reasons for it. (4) Incomplete discourse: The protagonist discusses with the concerned persons about the odd situation, but he or she finally decides alone. (5) Complete discourse: The teacher assumes that all concerned persons could balance between contradictory values and want to accept responsibility. All involved persons equally participate when searching for solutions. Given these underlying assumptions, Schönknecht (2005) defined teacher ethos as, in the best case, an attitude characterized by responsibility and commitment. Forster-Heinzer (2015, p. 10) agrees and describes pedagogical ethos "[…] as a commitment to pedagogical responsibility and the effort to create a learning environment conducive to positive development of the person in the trainer's care".

Thus, pedagogical ethos is based on an attitude that includes social and individual components (Schwer et al., 2014). In this sense, the pedagogical ethos is accompanied by a commitment that is linked to professional responsibility and morality (Forster-Heinzer, 2015). Teachers feel obliged to perform regarding profession-related and individual, ethical norms (Zutavern, 2001). Furthermore, teacher ethos integrates the commitment to the engagement to take care of, be responsible for as well as support the development of each learner. Thus, teacher ethos in the presented understanding involves the willingness to prepare good learning conditions. This learning condition notably includes the willingness to become aware of the students' and teachers' needs, to balance the students' and the teacher's well-being, to form proper teacher-student relationships and a supportive climate in the whole class (Hattie, 2012). Hence, teacher ethos has a principal function and determines professional conduct (Feather, 1990; Oser, 1998, 2004; Schwer et al., 2014).

The Influence of Teacher Ethos on Teachers' Behavior and Relationships in School

In that sense, professional and in particular teacher ethos stresses that pedagogical actions cannot be successful without combining effectiveness as well as responsibility, moral aspects, and values (Ofenbach, 2006). So, teacher ethos includes, among others, a moral core and determines professional actions. However, approaches to teacher ethos differ greatly regarding the visibility of ethos. In Oser's (1998) discourse model teacher ethos is assumed to be apparent in odd situations. When teachers have to balance conflicting values, such as truthfulness, care or justice to decide and act ethically, teacher ethos is in line with procedures of moral decision-making. This process of decision-making is based on risk assessments and connected to the associated assumption about the efficacy of the decision. Teacher's patterns of acting vary in quality of the reactions to moral conflicts as already described in Oser's model (complete or incomplete discourse, "lonely decider", delegating or avoiding actions). This model includes that individual decisions and actions differ concerning situational conditions and values. Thus, some challenges, like odd situations in everyday working life, might call for a reflective mode of decision-making; others might indicate reactions developed in an intuitive or habitual mode of data processing (Heinrichs, 2005).

Forster-Heinzer's approach (2015) to pedagogical ethos focused on vocational trainers and also considers ethos to be visible in morally relevant, odd situations. Teacher ethos is seen as a pedagogically professional attitude. Such an ethical, attentive, pedagogical attitude could also be evident in the teacher's effort to support and balance individuals' needs as well as in the willingness to take responsibility for the learning outcomes (Hattie, 2012). In this sense, ethos has a greater efficacy and becomes visible in many areas of work (Forster-Heinzer, 2015; Schönknecht, 2005). So, different types of behavior could indicate teacher ethos, such as teachers' actions to establish a caring environment that supports a students' successful development, teachers' focus on social or political issues which are important for students, or teachers' beliefs that guide relationships with students (Hansen, 2001). Thus, it could be expected that teacher ethos contributes to forming trustful and respectful social relationships in school. Both a trustful relationship between students and teachers as well as trustful relationships among students are fruitful to establish coherence with one another. This coherence of care and respectful cooperation is one necessary requirement to build up a fruitful learning or working environment (Noddings, 1992).

ONE FACET OF TEACHER ETHOS – NONVIOLENT COMMUNICATION AS AN APPROACH TO DEVELOP APPRECIATIVE RELATIONSHIPS IN SCHOOLS

To identify teacher beliefs and values which are relevant for forming appreciating relationships regarding honest, open and empathic connections between teachers and students, in this chapter, we suggest an approach to teacher ethos specified by referring to NVC according to Rosenberg. The fundamental aim of NVC is to get in contact with each other. Thus, teacher ethos in this sense focuses on how to form appreciative and supporting relationships in school and a fruitful class climate (Orth & Fritz, 2013).

Attitudes as open-mindedness towards everyone's needs, the awareness of one's own and the foreign autonomy as well as the concession to take responsibility for the own feelings are of great importance within the concept of NVC. Empathy is considered as an essential ability that enables and allows implementing appreciation. Applying empathy to oneself or others helps to communicate and solve conflict situations. The awareness of others', but also one's own needs is the basis of appreciative relationships as well as open and unprejudiced recognition of all members of a community (Rosenberg, 2015; Ziemen, 2013). In addition to other factors, the appreciative attitude towards fellow human beings seems to be a key factor for successful interaction at school and in learning processes. Rosenberg denotes such an appreciative learning environment as the requirement of "life-enhancing education". Although the NVC aims to fulfill the needs of all interactors, usually it is not possible to realize all the needs completely (Bitschnau, 2008). Thus, it is important that at least the needs of each person are adequately perceived. It is necessary for the NVC to balance different components, such as those described within the ethos model of Oser (1998). To get an overview of how to balance different components regarding NVC Rosenberg suggests the following four steps. These four steps help one to learn and to apply the NVC as well as to gain a deeper understanding of the basic appreciative attitude:

1. *Observation* regards the recognition of what happened in a situation. This first step recommends describing simply what could be perceived via senses and what could be "observed" without interpreting, judging or evaluating.
2. The next step is to be aware of and to manifest the *feelings* arising from the situation. It is relevant to understand that emotions are not the effect of the behavior of others but a result of (un-)satisfied needs of one's self.
3. In every situation, the emerging feelings provide information about which *needs* are relevant. In particular, negative feelings point to unfulfilled needs. So, it is comprehensible that needs are unavoidably linked with feelings.
4. The fourth step is the *request*. The request refers to what we need within the experienced situation (from the interaction partners) so that all involved parties contribute to the improvement of the situation (Rosenberg, 2015).

Based on the assumption that every human being could experience similar kinds of feelings and needs, these four steps are claimed to be helpful to understand and communicate one's own and others' feelings and needs. So, the method of the NVC does not just integrate the observation, feelings, needs, and requests of one's self. The four steps could also be useful to perceive and understand the counterpart. Thereby, the four steps promote identifying four essential types of information of the interaction partners, which are essential to transfer appreciation in daily communication as well as to act empathically in unusual, odd situations (Orth & Fritz, 2013).

In cases of classroom disruptions, it may help to apply these four steps to draw the attention of the students to the observed situation and to sensitize them to others' and maybe also to draw the teacher's attention to his or her actual emotional background and needs. Also, teachers can be sensitized to the students' actual background and needs. Thus, NVC allows both, the students and the teacher, to be involved in the process of dealing with conflicts and to reach a shared solution based on the current needs. Hence, NVC offers the potential that students feel respected and taken seriously. Such an atmosphere is essential to convey care and trust, which promote lively interpersonal contacts and dedicated learning (Hart & Kindle Hodson, 2006).

However, an unreflected use of the NVC also involves risks. If the NVC is applied as a method just to receive one's benefit, it can also be deliberately abused and used to establish violent structures (Bitschnau, 2008). This happens, for example, if a teacher already has pre-defined expectations regarding students in terms that he blames the students for his or her own emotions. If he or she wants to realize only his or her own needs and feelings by using the NVC and ignores the students' emotional states, it is near to manipulation or negative influence by teachers towards their students. That is exactly not the aim of the four steps of the NVC. Rather, the adequate use of the NVC should make accessible and convey an appreciative attitude which supports the creation of trustful bonds between people by consideration of the needs of all people involved in a specific situation (Larsson & Hoffmann, 2013). Although Rosenberg calls the NVC a language, the basis is not the words but rather the underlying attitude, which goes beyond the use of the four steps (Rosenberg, 2005). This kind of professional attitude refers to the basic personal attitude towards oneself as well as towards fellow human beings, towards the surrounding environments and the conditions for acting in a concrete situation (Nentwig-Gesemann et al., 2011). In this sense, the appreciative attitude includes a professional understanding of one's role in society and (professional) self-concept which is also essential regarding teacher ethos (Schwer et al., 2014). Additionally, the NVC emphasizes in line with different concepts of teacher ethos the balancing of different needs respectively different values. Therefore, the four steps of the NVC provide criteria that might help to find indicators of how to grasp teacher ethos in teacher-student interactions or teacher-student relationships. Accordingly, in this chapter, NVC is considered an appropriate fundamental concept for approaching teacher ethos that focuses on the development of appreciative relationships and supportive social class climate.

THESES ON THE EFFECTS OF TEACHER ETHOS WITH A FOCUS ON APPRECIATIVE RELATIONSHIPS

The attitude of open-mindedness explained above, and the commitment towards fulfilling one's own and others' needs are claimed as main facets of teacher ethos in this chapter. Among other facets of teacher ethos,[2] these main facets also affect the action of teachers in a variety of interaction situations (Forster-Heinzer, 2015; Hansen, 2001; Oser, 1998; Schönknecht, 2005). They have an important role in terms of supporting a trustful learning environment and a fruitful learning atmosphere (Davis, 2003; Mainhard, 2009; Patrick et al., 2003). One opportunity to create such positive climate and continuative appreciative relationships in classrooms is that teachers consider students' feelings and needs regarding the NVC. This might promote the feeling of autonomy of students. An effect of this feeling of autonomy could be that learning goals are perceived as students' own goals. Therefore, this participation of students in lessons could result in better learning and becoming more involved as well as gaining better learning success. In this case students experience their abilities and skills during the lessons. According to the assumption of Heid (1991) persons only can take responsibility if they are enabled to influence the situation. The experienced autonomy of students could also promote responsible action (Baumgartner et al., 2000; Ryan & Deci, 2000). Furthermore, the perceived autonomy in classrooms can positively influence the (intrinsic) motivation of students in terms of establishing positive students' attitudes towards school and teaching as well as developing students' interests

(Maulana, 2012; Niemiec & Ryan, 2009; Tsai et al., 2008). This motivation due to appreciative relationships could lead to another possible effect: adequate social behavior of students (Crosnoe et al., 2004; Fend, 1998). Watzlawick et al. (2000) pointed out that divergent perceptions or even ideas could lead to disturbances. The latter are often linked to learning blockades, stagnation in learning processes and prevention of efficient work (Wehner, 2012). To avoid these non-efficient processes, it is necessary to minimalize interruptions and to promote a similar understanding and assessment of situations by students and teachers (Weaver & Shannon, 1949). Applying NVC could support clear and dialogical communication within classes. The four steps of NVC enable describing situations in a differentiated and concise manner without moral evaluations or criticism (Rosenberg, 2015). Nevertheless, it is possible to reveal important information in terms of feelings and needs, which can lead to deeper understanding among all participants (Orth & Fritz, 2013). The NVC could improve communication and contact between students and teachers at "eye level" without neglecting their roles and somehow asymmetric structured relationship. So, the NVC could be a possibility for reducing teaching interruptions and classroom conflicts and could provide an important basis to educate with and for diversity and to unfold students' individual potentials. In this way, students may feel respected and cared about by the teacher which foster their willingness to deal with the prevalent values in the classroom (Ryan & Deci, 2000). Thus, the students' moral sensitivity, understood as their ability to judge and argue morally which is viewed as a key of successful social life, can be promoted (Dann et al., 2000). Furthermore, the development of moral judgments and understanding is often associated with moral emotions which for example enable to understand the emotions of victims and victimizers (Arsenio & Kramer, 1992). Referring to the NVC, there are first findings which demonstrate that the perception of feelings and needs is improved through a NVC training (Bitschnau, 2008). According to these findings, the potential of the NVC could be that trained teachers' ethical behaviors in terms of emotion- and need-orientation have an exemplary function. If students permanently experience positive emotions caused by teachers' just behavior, there is potential that students act in a similar ethical way. This could support the moral development of the students and strengthen the morality in the class community (Klaassen, 2012; Patrick et al., 2007).

According to the first situation at the beginning of this chapter, the coherence of care, appreciative and responsible attitude of teachers and their potential effect on students can be illustrated. On the one hand, the teacher's attitude becomes visible in an ordinary situation by perceiving the responsibility for and approaching the students actively. The teacher offers help to the student, signals that the student's current behavior is irritating and gives the student self-responsibility by asking for a shared solution. On the other hand, the student experiences autonomy through the demand of self-responsibility and is motivated by the teacher's care. Positive experiences of school and learning are increased. The social behavior of the student changed again, and it can be interpreted that he or she perceived truthfulness as a moral value.

In summary, the facet of teacher ethos based on Rosenberg's NVC which this chapter presented points to the possibility and importance of establishing trustful relationships. Within this trustful relationship, teachers take care of and are responsible for the development of each learner. It initiates mutual appreciation and leads to a favorable learning atmosphere (Orth & Fritz, 2013) if the teacher manages to balance also his or her own needs.

PERSPECTIVES AND IMPLICATIONS

The focus of this chapter was to explain a particular facet and concept of teacher ethos based on NVC. Rosenberg's approach was selected because it offers methods and underlying assumptions of how to develop productive and appreciative relationships (Rosenberg, 2015). So, the facet of teacher ethos specified here is not only visible in conflict situations but also through a caring environment that supports successful learning. It is assumed that, via integrating the opposite and one's feelings and needs in communication, dialogical and symmetrical communication will develop. This kind of communication and the values mediated thereby enable considering interactions differentially and develop a good and appreciative relationship within the class (Lind, 2000) which is a valuable opportunity to support successful teaching-learning processes (Ryan & Deci, 2000). The previous theoretical explanations about how this kind of teacher ethos can be used are the first step in approaching this particular facet of teacher ethos. A further step could be to analyze the literature intensively regarding some similar theoretical constructs, like teacher attitudes, teacher beliefs as well as skills to separate the different constructs quite accurately and to assess their respective influence on creating appreciative relationships. Furthermore, the development of measures to grasp teacher ethos in the sense of the NVC attitude is necessary. Therefore, research in emotional psychology offers a great potential. Here, some measurements, such as the Mayer-Salovey-Caruso Test (MSCEIT) (Jauk et al., 2016; Steinmeyr et al., 2011) or vignettes as a stimulus (Schnurr, 2003) could be used to train and evaluate some emotional abilities (Röhr-Sendlmeier & Schmitz, 2010). Moreover, research on teacher ethos has already been planned or even started. So, the laddering technique (Botschen et al., 1999) has been applied to receive the first findings regarding the content of the "NVC attitude" and intending to identify in which situations or through which behaviors the NVC attitude becomes visible. Another important goal is to study the NVC attitude empirically within the school context. It is interesting to examine if students could perceive and verbalize differences between teachers regarding their ability to create appreciative relationships. Moreover, it is interesting to ask teachers if applying NVC enables them to get in contact with their students in a more differentiated way. So, all in all, the presented concept focuses on the role of relationships in schools that was almost a neglected issue during the wave of research on competences. The proposed approach to teacher ethos will have to be further developed to get theoretically precise. It also needs to be related to different approaches and findings of other disciplines, such as the humanistic or emotion psychology, identity development or on professional competence of teachers. This chapter provides a theoretical idea as a starting point for theory progress and empirical studies in the future on this facet of teacher ethos.

NOTES

[1] This assumption is closely linked to Beck's (1997) perspective on modern professionalism in the context of vocational education. His concept of modern professionalism integrates a kind of metacognition, which allows individuals to justify their work in terms of a socially extended value through reflecting working conditions and recognizing the social and environmental consequences of their own work (ibid).
[2] Bauer (2007) splits teachers' ethos into the four dimensions (1) teacher-personality, (2) teacher-student-relationship, (3) interpretation of the profession, and (4) philosophy of life.

REFERENCES

Arsenio, W., & Kramer, R. (1992). Victimizers and their victims: Children's conceptions of the mixed emotional consequences of moral transgressions. *Child Development, 63*, 915–927.
Bauer, M. (2007). *Zum Berufsethos von Hauptschullehrer/innen und dessen Zusammenhang mit dem Kollegium* [The professional ethos of primary school teachers and its connection with the college]. Hamburg: Dr. Kovač.
Baumert, J., & Kunter, M. (2006). Stichwort: Professionelle Kompetenz von Lehrkräften [Keyword: Professional competence of teachers]. *Zeitschrift für Erziehungswissenschaft, 9*(4), 469–520.
Baumgartner, P., Laske, S., & Welte, H. (2000). Handlungsstrategien von LehrerInnen: ein heuristisches Modell. In C. Metzger, H. Seitz, & F. Eberle (Eds.), *Impulse für die Wirtschaftspädagogik* [Impulses for business education]. St. Gallen: Verlag des schweizerischen kaufmännischen Verbandes (SKV).
Beck, K. (1997). Die Zukunft der Beruflichkeit: Systematische und pragmatische Aspekte zur Gegenwartsdiskussion um die prospektiven Voraussetzungen der Berufsbildung. In M. Liedtke (Eds.), *Berufliche Bildung: Geschichte, Gegenwart, Zukunft* [Vocational education. History, present, future]. Bad Heilbrunn: Klinkhardt.
Becker, R., & Lauterbach, W. (2010). Bildung als Privileg: Ursachen, Mechanismen, Prozesse und Wirkungen dauerhafter Bildungsungleichheiten. In R. Becker & W. Lauterbach (Eds.), *Bildung als Privileg: Erklärungen und Befunde zu den Ursachen der Bildungsungleichheit* [Education as a privilege: Explanations and findings on the causes of educational inequality]. Wiesbaden: VS-Verlag für Sozialwissenschaft.
Beijaard, D., Verloop, N., & Vermunt, J. D. (2000). Teachers' perceptions of professional identity: An exploratory study from a personal knowledge perspective. *Teaching and Teacher Education, 16*, 749–764.
Bitschnau, K. (2008). *Die Sprache der Giraffen* [The language of giraffes]. Paderborn: Junfermann.
Botschen, G., Thelen, E., & Pieters, R. (1999). Using means-end structures for benefit segmentation. *European Journal of Marketing, 33*(1–2), 38–58.
Crosnoe, R., Johnson Kirkpatrick, M., & Elder, G. H. (2004). Intergenerational bonding in school: The behavioral and contextual correlates of student-teacher relationships. *Sociology of Education, 77*(1), 60–81.
Davis, H. A. (2003). Conceptualizing the role and influence of student-teacher relationships on children's social and cognitive development. *Educational Psychologist, 38*(4), 207–234.
Dunn, J., Cutting, A. L., & Demetriou, H. (2000). Moral sensibility, understanding others, and children's friendship interactions in the preschool period. *British Journal of Developmental Psychology, 18*, 159–177.

Feather, N. T. (1990). Bridging the gap between values and actions: Recent applications of the expectancy-value model. In E. T. Higgins & R. M. Sorrentino (Eds.), *Handbook of motivation and cognition: Foundations of social behavior* (pp. 151–192). New York, NY: Guilford Press.

Fend, H. (1998). *Qualität im Bildungswesen: Schulforschung zu Systembedingungen, Schulprofilen und Lehrerleistung* [Quality in education: School research on system requirements, school profiles and teacher performance]. Weinheim: Juventa.

Forster-Heinzer, S. (2015). *Against all odds: An empirical study about the situative pedagogical ethos of vocational trainers*. Rotterdam, The Netherlands: Sense Publishers.

Furrer, C., & Skinner, E. (2003). Sense of relatedness as a factor in children's academic engagement and performance. *Journal of Educational Psychology, 95*(1), 148–162.

Hansen, D. T. (2001). *Exploring the moral heart of teaching: Toward a teacher's creed*. New York, NY: Teachers College Press.

Harder, P. (2014). *Wertehaltungen und Ethos von Lehrern: Empirische Studie zu Annahmen über den guten Lehrer* [Values and ethos of teachers: Empirical study on assumptions about the good teacher]. Bamberg: University of Bamberg Press Bamberg.

Hart, S., & Kindle Hodson, V. (2006). *Empathie im Klassenzimmer: Gewaltfreie Kommunikation im Unterricht: Ein Lehren und Lernen, das zwischenmenschliche Beziehungen in den Mittelpunkt stellt* [Empathy in the classroom. Nonviolent communication in the classroom. A teaching and learning that focuses on interpersonal relationships]. Paderborn: Junfermann Verlag.

Hattie, J. (2012). *Visible learning for teachers: Maximizing impact on learning*. London: Routledge.

Heid, H. (1991). Problematik einer Erziehung zur Verantwortungsbereitschaft [Problems in the education to the readiness to take on responsibility]. *Neue Sammlung, 31*, 459–481.

Heinrichs, K. (2005). *Urteilen und Handeln: Ein Prozessmodell und seine moralpsychologische Spezifizierung Reihe: Konzepte des Lehrens und Lernens* [Judgments and actions: A process model and its moral psychological specification]. Frankfurt am Main: Peter-Lang-Verlag.

Jauk, E., Freudenthaler, H. H., & Neubauer, A. C. (2016). The dark triad and trait versus ability emotional intelligence: Emotional darkness differs between women and men. *Journal of Individual Differences, 37*(2), 112–118.

Klaassen, C. (2012). Just a teacher or also a moral example? In D. Alt & R. Reingold (Eds.), *Changes in teachers' moral role from passive observers to moral and democratic leaders*. Rotterdam, The Netherlands: Sense Publishers.

Konrad, H. (1986). Gedanken zur Frage nach einem pädagogischen Ethos [Thoughts on the question of an educational ethos]. *Vierteljahrsschrift für die Wissenschaftliche Pädagogik, 62*(1), 547–558.

Larsson, L., & Hoffmann, K. (2013). *42 Schlüsselunterscheidungen in der GFK: Für ein tieferes Verständnis der gewaltfreien Kommunikation* [42 main differences in the NVC: For a deeper understanding of nonviolent communication]. Paderborn: Jungfermann.

Latzko, B. (2012). Educating teachers'ethos. In D. Alt & R. Reingold (Eds.), *Changes in teachers' moral role from passive observers to moral and democratic leaders*. Rotterdam, The Netherlands: Sense Publishers.

Lewin, K. (1951). *Field theory in social science: Selected theoretical papers*. New York, NY: Harper & Row.

Lind, G. (2000). Ansätze und Ergebnisse der "Just-Community"-Schule [Approaches and results of the "just-community"-school]. *Zeitschrift für Erziehungswissenschaft und Gestaltung der Schulwirklichkeit*. Retrieved from https://www.uni-konstanz.de/ag-moral/pdf/Lind-1987_Just-Community-Schule.pdf

Mainhard, M. T. (2009). *Time consistency in teacher-class relationships* (Unpublished doctoral dissertation). University of Utrecht, Utrecht. Retrieved from https://www.researchgate.net/publication/27717883_Time_Consistency_In_Teacher-Class_Relationships

Martin, A. J., & Dowson, M. (2009). Interpersonal relationship, motivation, engagement, and achievement: Yield for theory, current issues, and practice. *Review of Educational Research, 79*, 327–365.

Maulana, R. (2012). *Teacher-student relationships during the first year of secondary education* (Unpublished doctoral dissertation). University of Groningen, Groningen.

Nentwig-Gesemann, I., Fröhlich-Gildhoff, K., Harms, H., & Richter, S. (2011). *Professionelle Haltung: Identität der Fachkraft für die Arbeit mit Kindern in den ersten drei Lebensjahren* [Professional attitude – the identity of the specialist for working with children in the first three years of life]. Retrieved from http://www.weiterbildungsinitiative.de/uploads/media/WiFF_Expertise_Nentwig-Gesemann.pdf

Niemiec, C. P., & Ryan, R. M. (2009). Autonomy, competence, and relatedness in the classroom: Applying self-determination theory to educational practice. *Theory and Research in Education, 7*(2), 133–144.

Noddings, N. (1992). *The challenge to care in school: An alternative approach to education.* New York, NY: Teachers College Press.

Ofenbach, B. (2006). *Geschichte des pädagogischen Berufsethos: Realbedingungen für Lehrerhandeln von der Antike bis zum 21 Jahrhundert* [History of the pedagogical profession-ethos. Real requirements for teacher actions from the antiquity to the 21st century]. Würzburg: Königshausen & Neumann.

Orth, G., & Fritz, H. (2013). *Gewaltfreie Kommunikation in der Schule* [Nonviolent communication in school]. Paderborn: Junfermann.

Oser, F. (1998). *Ethos: Die Vermenschlichung des Erfolgs: Psychologie der Berufsmoral von Lehrpersonen* [Ethos: The humanization of success: Psychology of the professional morality of teachers]. Opladen: Leske + Budrich.

Oser, F. (2004). Standardbasierte Evaluation der Lehrerbildung [Standard-based evaluation of teacher education]. In S. Blömeke, P. Reinhold, G. Tulodziecki, & J. Wildt (Eds.), *Handbuch Lehrerbildung* [Handbook teacher education] (pp. 184–206). Bad Heilbrunn: Klinkhardt.

Oser, F., Dick, A. & Patry, J.-L. (1992). *Effective and responsible teaching: The new synthesis.* San Francisco, CA: Jossey Bass.

Patrick, H., Ryan, A. M., & Kaplan, A. (2007). Early adolescents' perceptions of the classroom social environment, motivational beliefs, and engagement. *Journal of Educational Psychology, 99*, 83–98.

Patrick, H., Turner, J. C., Meyer, D. K., & Midgley, C. (2003). How teachers establish psychological environments during the first days of school: Associations with avoidance in mathematics. *Teachers College Record, 105*(8), 1521–1558.

Röhr-Sendlemeier, U. M., & Schmitz, M. (2010). Sozial-Emotionale Kompetenz: Längsschnittstudie zu Effekten einer kurzzeitigen Förderung für Grundschulkinder [Social-emotional competence: Longitudinal study on the effects of short-term support for primary school children]. *Bildung und Erziehung, 63*(3), 347–369.

Rosenberg, M. B. (2005). *Speak peace in a world of conflict: What you say next will change your world.* San Francisco, CA: PuddleDancer Press.

Rosenberg, M. B. (2015). *Nonviolent communication: A language of life.* Encinitas: PuddleDancer Press.

Ryan, R. M., & Deci, E. L. (2000). Intrinsic and extrinsic motivations: Classic definitions and new direction. *Educational Psychology, 25*, 54–67.

Schnurr, S. (2003). Vignetten in quantitativen und qualitativen Forschungsdesigns. In H. U. Otto, G. Oelerich, & H.-G. Micheel (Eds.), *Empirische Forschung und Soziale Arbeit: Ein Lehr- und Arbeitsbuch* (pp. 393–400). München: Luchterhand.

Schönknecht, G. (2005). Die Entwicklung der Innovationskompetenz von Lehrerinnen aus (berufs) biographischer Perspektive [The development of the innovation competence of teachers from (occupational) biographical perspective]. *Berufs- und Wirtschaftspädagogik.* Retrieved from http://www.bwpat.de/spezial2/schoenknecht_spezial2-bwpat.pdf

Schwer, C., Solzbacher, C., & Behrensen, B. (2014). Annäherung an das Konzept „Professionelle pädagogische Haltung" [Approaching the concept of "professional pedagogic attitude"]. In C. Schwer & C. Solzbacher (Eds.), *Professionelle pädagogische Haltung* [Professional pedagogical attitude]. Bad Heilbrunn: Klinkhardt.

Steinmeyr, R., Schütz, A., Hertel, J., & Schröder-Abé, M. (2011). *MSCEIT: Mayer-Salovey-Caruso test zur Emotionalen Intelligenz (Mayer, Salovey, and Caruso emotional intelligence test)* [MSCEIT: Mayer-Salovey-Caruso test for emotional intelligence]. Bern: Huber.

Terhart, E. (1987). Vermutungen über das Lehrerethos [Assumptions about the teacher ethos]. *Zeitschrift für Pädagogik, 33*(6), 787–804.

Tsai, Y., Kunter, M., Lüdtke, O., Trautwein, U., & Ryan, R. M. (2008). What makes lessons interesting? The role of situational and individual factors in three school subjects'. *Journal of Educational Psychology, 100*, 460–72.

Watzlawick, P., Bavelas, J. B., & Jackson, D. (2000). *Menschliche Kommunikation: Formen, Störungen, Paradoxien* [Human communication: Forms, disturbances, paradoxes]. Bern: Huber.

Weaver, W., & Shannon, C. E. (1949). *Mathematical theory of communication.* Illinois, IL: University of Illinois.

Wehner, L. (2012). *Dicke Luft: Konfliktmanagement in Gesundheitsberufen* [Thick air: Conflict management in health care professions]. Berlin: Springer-Verlag.

Ziemen, K. (2013). *Kompetenz für Inklusion: Inklusive Ansätze in der Praxis umsetzen* [Competence for inclusion: Implementation of inclusive approaches in practice]. Göttingen: Vandenhoeck & Ruprecht.

Zutavern, M. (2001). *Professionelles Ethos von Lehrerinnen und Lehrern: Berufsmoralisches Denken, Wissen und Handeln zum Schutz und Förderung von Schülerinnen und Schülern* [Professional ethos of teachers. Professional meditative thinking, knowledge and action to protect and promote students]. St. Gallen: Universität Freiburg CH.

Karin Heinrichs
Business Education, Department of Social Sciences and Economics
Otto-Friedrich-University Bamberg
Bamberg, Germany

Simone Ziegler
Business Education, Department of Social Sciences and Economics
Otto-Friedrich-University Bamberg
Bamberg, Germany

BRIGITTE LATZKO AND ANNE-CATHRIN PAESZLER

11. PROFESSIONALS' ETHOS AND EDUCATION FOR RESPONSIBILITY

Teachers' Ethos as an Example of Professionals' Ethos

INTRODUCTION

Demands for Teachers' Ethos in Today's Society

Our contemporary educational system is confronted with huge challenges caused by flows of refugees. Diversity among students' values, for instance, gets a new qualitative dimension; teachers' own values might be questioned by foreign cultures, and even those teachers who are convinced that subject related matters have priority in class will be affected by the outcomes of this development. Against this background the demand of most school curricula (e.g., Australian Institute for Teaching and School Leadership, 2011; Kultusministerkonferenz [KMK], 2014) for imparting knowledge *and* educating students never before was as salient as today. However, how can we raise awareness among in-service teachers and future teachers for their twofold task, particularly for the educational duties in their work as a teacher? Moreover, what is even more important, how can we raise awareness among teacher educators towards teacher education itself to be seen as a promising way meeting the challenges outlined above?

Besides, there are numerous tasks which need to be fulfilled within the daily business of the teaching profession which are not associated with education explicitly. To name a few, teachers prepare and teach lessons, make copies, attend conferences, talk to students, parents, colleagues, and headmasters, clean blackboards, develop, correct, and grade papers, fill in school reports, pick up paper from the ground, organize and lead parent-teachers' conferences, and organize field or class trips. Even though these daily hustles are, at a first glance, not related to education they are at a second. Referring to the educational theory and *Didaktik* by Klafki (1991) which claims that transmitting knowledge is always tied to educating students morally, it is obvious that education in general and moral education, in particular, are inherent parts of teachers' daily work in classrooms. In this sense teaching itself, in its nature, is a moral endeavor (e.g., Buzzelli & Johnston, 2001; Sanger, 2007; Sherman, 2006; Tirri, 2003).

It seems reasonable that educational scientists call for "professional ethos" as a "tool" allowing teachers to fulfill all tasks named above thoroughly, mainly their educational duties, and to educate their pupils accordingly (Brezinka, 2016). This demand appears ordinary, as it seems relatively easy to determine the ethos of other professions. One example is the *Hippocratic oath* of physicians which binds the professional group of doctors to save and recover lives and furthermore binds them to foster the wellbeing of humans with their professional actions. Another example would be the ethos of the legal profession which broadly speaking is beaconed by a people's respective law and seeks to bring peace and justice to their living as a community (Böckenförde, 2010).

So far, only von Hentig (1993) strived to formulate essential obligations titled *Sokratischer Eid (Socratic oath)* which could be considered the teachers' ethos. The same aims at teachers' obligation and provision to protect every child's unique personality as well as every child's rights and rules of living. He furthermore argues that those values, protecting and ensuring the teachers' care for the students entrusted to him or her, are a stronghold against any political despotism, general regulations or what could be considered a relentless demand of transmitting knowledge. Von Hentig emphasizes that the practice of the values named above can only be assured by a teacher's self-commitment provoked by reflection. Although von Hentig's ideas on the *Sokratischer Eid* seem appealing when searching a precise definition of the meaning of teachers' ethos the former fall short when it comes to determine precise educational goals as guidelines for teachers which they could possibly commit themselves to such as being a role model, teaching students always to be orderly or promoting a respectful working atmosphere within class. As a consequence, educational goals for teachers with regards to their ethos can only be derived vaguely. These considerations concerning the ethos of different professional groups entail teachers' ethos to be a comparatively vague concept.

Against this background, it is not surprising that university curricula of teacher education fall short of taking a stance of how to teach professional ethos. Nevertheless, looking at the requirements of the Kultusministerkonferenz [KMK], a German political institution, we wish to implement teacher ethos into the German curricula of teacher education. However, to be able to do so concerning the academic character of teacher education it is urgently needed to take a step backward trying to find out what teacher ethos is on a theoretical level. Only by doing so, it will be possible to detect what needs to be part of teacher education. Moreover, wishing to foster the development of teacher ethos within teacher education a clear-cut concept is needed to specify the developmental goal. Admittedly, "providing education is a highly normative activity" as Klaassen and Maslovaty (2010, p. 1) already emphasized. This implies the demand for a normative educational goal to promote teachers' professionalism systematically in accordance with a normative curricular standard.

Therefore, in a first step, this chapter aims at clarifying on a conceptual level what teacher ethos is and whether there is a clear-cut core of the same that is shared by most concepts on teachers' ethos. First, prominent theoretical concepts on teacher ethos will be taken into consideration. By doing so, we wish to find overlapping features shared by all concepts of teacher ethos sketched out below. Proceeding like this will allow to draw conclusions with regards to the questions of (a) *which elements – what* – should be implemented into teacher education to educate a teacher's ethos and (b) *how* it shall be done.

TEACHERS' ETHOS – A CONCEPTUAL ANALYSIS

Even though many in-service-teachers are fascinated by the topic of teachers' ethos, their questions remain: What are researchers talking about when speaking about ethos? Is it about the teacher him- or herself, about teachers' personality, or about a teacher's charisma when talking about teachers' ethos?

Taking a closer look at the literature on teacher's ethos we become aware of the fact that current research on and relevant concepts of teachers' ethos embrace the same differently. Moreover, many researchers are engaged in investigating professionals' ethos – more or less explicitly. Oser (1998) and Forster-Heinzer (2015), for example, conceptualize teacher ethos as a process model put into practice in various situations. Patry (1991) and Weinberger (2016) speak of teacher ethos referring to constructive didactics and by doing so, defining teachers' ethos as a didactical decision making on how to conduct lessons. Furthermore, ethos is spoken of in the realms of professional identity and sensitivity (Tirri, 1999), focusing on moral identity sensu Blasi (1984). Noddings (1992), Veugelers (2011) and Abs (2016) choose yet another approach by emphasizing professional care and responsibility when speaking and conceptualizing teacher ethos. Bauer and Prenzel (2016) and Biedermann (2016) speak of teacher ethos about teachers' judgment, closely linked to the ideas of Oser (1998) and Forster-Heinzer (2015). Forster-Heinzer, for example, defines teacher ethos as a commitment to pedagogical responsibility and the effort to create learning environments conducive to a positive development of the students/children (2015, p. 66). Finally, Sayers (2010), Berliner (1992) and Heid (2006, 2016) understand teachers' ethos from a systemic point of view. Taken together, concepts on teachers' ethos address professional identity, professional procedural morality, professional responsibility and care, moral judgment as well as moral attitudes.

Hence, the literature on ethos reveals that morality, ethics, and responsibility seem to be related concepts to the concept of teacher ethos (e.g., Alt & Reingold, 2012; Klaassen, 2010; Latzko, 2012). We are lead to this assumption as the concepts named above many times were used either synonymously or closely linked to the concept of ethos. This, however, leads to confusion on a conceptual level and at the same time, frames a task we all need to face from now on. It is our task to make clear cuts between concepts on ethos, concepts on morality, and concepts on ethics. The confusion between the concepts arises from the shift between the theoretical considerations and operationalization which could be referred to as the gap between the theoretical background and the methodological approach. To exemplify this statement, we wish to give an example referring to a master thesis in research on educational goals done by Paeszler (2008). The results of her study were

153

presented at the EARLI conference in Amsterdam in 2009. However, they were not only presented in terms of educational goals, but rather they were also presented drawing conclusions on teachers' professional ethos. Now, several years later, we choose to question such a procedure as it is an example of inappropriate theoretical reduction and, with regards to methodological possibilities, scientifically narrow-minded work. Hence, today we call such a way of researching teachers' ethos a "single-item-approach". By giving this example, we wish to point towards other approaches exploring teachers' ethos in various domains, such as educational goals rather than understanding teachers' ethos in line with concepts that name the same as a component of teachers' professionalism.

First outcome: The concepts in sum seem to be a cluster of concepts understanding teachers' ethos in various ways – as for example the cluster of teachers' ability for moral judgments, teachers' moral decision making or teachers' responsibility. Furthermore, different concepts suggest different methodological approaches of how teachers' ethos can be fostered (see Selmo, 2017; Weinberger, 2016). Taken together, it seems to be an impossible task to point out what the concepts named above have in common. Which deliberately reveals the finding that even though the idea to analyze different concepts on teachers' ethos in order to find overlapping features shared with regards to its theoretical as well as methodological understanding was very promising, one needs to consider *Ethos* from a linguistic point of view as the discipline of linguistics is concerned about the morphological composition and semantic meaning of lexemes as well as utterances. Being well aware of the fact that concepts on teachers' ethos are embedded in the discipline of education the idea behind this "trip to a neighboring discipline" is to grasp the core of a phenomenon by visiting the roots of a term labeling the same.

TEACHERS' ETHOS: A LINGUISTIC ANALYSIS

To be able to do so, the science of linguistics dictates several steps. At first, etymological considerations shall be outlined, followed by an exposition of the theory of feature semantics. Finally, Rosch's (1978) prototype theory will be laid out as a promising way of finding the core of teachers' ethos.

The Greek Word Ethos

The word *ethos*,[1] in Greek, spelled out εθοσ translates into *habit, custom,* and *manner* and often occurs with the word ποιειν. This conjunction indicated in the dictionary can best be translated into *to get used to sth.* Moreover, as the former is often used in its perfect stem, it is suggested to translate the same into *to be used to sth.* Furthermore, Menge and Güthling (1913) highlight the phrase εν εθει εστι τινι which uses the noun ethos in its Dative form and is best described by *it is customary for sb. to do sth.* Looking at the verb εθω which belongs to the noun εθοσ one recognizes that the latter is often used in its participle form and therefore is best translated into *in accordance with one owns habit, custom,* and *manner.* Finally, within the ordinary changing process of language one cannot help but realizing its impact on the word εθοσ as well. Within this particular instance, one needs to refer to the vowel shift that has occurred commonly known in natural languages, such as the English or German language. This process of change applies to the Greek language as well. So besides finding εθοσ we also found ηθοσ which can be translated into the German language in different ways, always depending on the context it is used. Possible translations will be listed below:

1. *at the customary place, ordinary place of dwelling, flat, (geographical) position, home.* ηθοσ used with regards to animals, the word can also mean *pasture ground.* Also, ηθοσ can be used with regards to heavenly bodies and then can mean *the ordinary place of rising*
2. *habit, practice, tradition and custom*
   However, yet another possibility to translate ηθοσ into the German language needs to be recognized. When referring to the domain of morality, the following translations are possible:
3. *an inner moral nature of things, character, attitude, disposition, mindset, mode of thinking*

Second outcome: Now, taking a step back and trying to summarize these linguistic findings, specific nouns, such as *habit, custom, practice, attitude* and *character* stand out. However, from a linguistic point of view, one needs to point out that neither words, i.e., linguistic signs, are to be taken as the referent, which is the actual object human utterances may refer to in any situation. Nor does etymological research give any information about the intensional meaning of words, since language itself is subject to change through natural processes as well as a society's, i.e., humans', use and application of language (von Pohlenz, 2000). In short, the linguistic approach towards *Ethos* has not revealed its intensional or extensional meaning so far.

However, one cannot approach a lexeme searching for its meaning without looking at Saussure's dyadic model of language's symbolic character or Ogden's and Richards' (1923) understanding of the meaning of meaning expressed in the semiotic triangle. These models share the understanding that what is essential to grasp the meaning of any lexeme are the thoughts behind the use of the same. This means the relation between the linguistic sign and the object is artificial and is caused by a person's use and application of the former.

By this understanding of von Pohlenz (2000), Ogden and Richards (1923) as well as Saussure (1967) it is possible to draw conclusions regarding the elements which are part of the definition of teachers' ethos. Moreover, this research suggests of implementing the same into teacher education.

Nevertheless, and taking into account that this research, too, stresses the importance to normatively define teachers' ethos so conclusions can be drawn with regards to teacher education, we firstly wish to set that teachers' ethos, too, ought to be understood as an action that is habitual. Thereby teachers' ethos is to be regarded as a feature of a person's action recurring in various situations. Plainly spoken, one aspect of the definition of teachers' ethos is an action that can be found over and over again in teachers' behavior. However, its content is still unknown. Secondly, we come to the conclusion that, as the common conjunction of εθοσ ποιειν (= *to be used to sth.*, Menge & Güthling, 1913) as well as the phrase often used εν εθει εστι τινι (= *sth. is customary for somebody*, Menge & Güthling, 1913) suggest, εθοσ can be understood within the realms of reflection.

Drawing from these findings, we conclude that teachers' ethos can be educated by instructed, guided and supervised reflection of future teachers. In the light of previous considerations concerning von Hentig's *Socratic oath*, it seems to be reasonable that teaching experiences of student teachers within their educational training at university should be subject to their reflection (see also Weinberger, 2016).

This twofold outcome, finally, reminds of an old debate within the psychology of moral development which is the debate between "content" and "structure" and which will be elaborated on later in the text.

Feature Semantics

However, asking for the meaning of a lexeme within the field of linguistic research, one cannot help but taking a closer look at semantics. The latter focusses on finding the meaning of lexemes in various ways. One prominent way to determine meaning is captured within the traditional approach of feature linguistics, referring back to Aristoteles' way of categorizing. By proposing necessary and sufficient features, linguists strive to compose the meaning of words and/or categories. Hence, an entity belongs to a category and thereby has a certain meaning if, and only if, all the features named above are represented. Concerning ethos, this entails that ethos is a category composed of necessary and sufficient features. This entails that borders of categories are clear-cut and that all members have the same status within the category in question.

However, critics of this way of categorizing voice claim that by proceeding like described above, the meaning of words is constituted minimalistically, saying that the meaning of a word, i.e., a category, is only captured by a sufficient number of necessary features. Secondly, is has been criticized that all members of a category hold the same status within its borders. Proceeding like this leads to a problem which Bärenfänger (2002) in line with Wiegand and Wolski (1980, p. 209) refers to as "*Kontinuumsproblem*" and makes it difficult, even impossible to differentiate abstract terms such as *respect/awe or love*. Thirdly, meanings of words are, in accordance with the understanding of feature semantics, discrete categories showing clear-cut borders mentioned before. However, well-established terms and therefore concepts, such as *dawn*, clearly opposes this guiding principle. Finally, by comprehending necessary and sufficient features to determine the meaning of words, and thus, the meaning of categories, feature semantics neglect natural polysemy of words.

Third outcome: Again, this approach does not allow to clarify the core of teachers' ethos comprehensively. When applying the approach of feature semantics to the question of the core of teachers' ethos one cannot ignore the fact that the approach of feature semantics rests on necessary and sufficient features. Following this understanding of categorization implies that only concepts on teachers' ethos that do comprise certain features of teachers' ethos, such as morality, responsibility, care or judgment can qualify as a scientific concept on teachers' ethos. This finding clearly opposes the deliberations on teachers' ethos named and explained in the previous chapter.

Prototype Theory

It was in the late 70ies and the early 80ies within the *kognitive Wende* when this understanding of categorizing explained above was questioned. At first, it was questioned by research at the break of the 1970ies done by the anthropologists and experimental psychologists Berlin and Kay (1969) and Rosch (1973) on words of focal colors as well as Labov (1973) who investigated the cognitive representation of the concept of *cup*. The results of their research suggested that certain members of a category are privileged whereas others are marginal members, thus, marginal representatives of a category. These findings suggested the notion of *prototypes* as a *cognitive reference point* of a category (Rosch, 1973). Naturally, the findings and theoretical considerations and conclusions made by Berlin and Kay, Rosch and Labov initiated extensive research on the meaning of words. Moreover, with that, research on and considerations relating to the principle(s) of cognitive categorizing by the human mind expanded as well. Although the understanding of the term of *prototype* has been revised many times and hence reveals many facets of the scientific approach of cognitive psychology as well as cognitive linguistic, in the following we choose to focus on Rosch's statements on principles of categorization in 1978 as well as the conclusions she draws from them with reference to the term *prototype*. Finally, Rosch's new understanding on categorization leads to the emergence of the *prototype theory* which was adapted as *prototype semantics* and thus links cognitive psychology and cognitive linguistics.

However, with regard to the concept(s) of teacher ethos being established in the field of pedagogical psychology from now on, we will refer to *prototype theory* rather than *prototype semantics*. The former shall be introduced in the following. Prototype theory follows two essential principles of categorizing introduced by Rosch in 1978. The first principle addresses the function of a category system and embraces the idea "[...] that the task of category systems is to provide maximum information with the least cognitive effort" (Rosch, 1978, p. 28). The second principle, presupposing the first just mentioned, states that the principle of categorization "[...] has to do with the structure of information so provided and asserts that the perceived world comes as structured information rather than arbitrary or unpredictable attributes" (Rosch, 1978, p. 28). Drawing from these principles, Rosch defines the prototype of a category as a "convenient grammatical fiction" which refers to "judgements of degree of prototypicality" (1978, pp. 40–41) by the respective subject group in question. Furthermore, she points out that prototypes neither constitute any particular model for categories nor a theory of representation of categories. Equally important, she stresses, that although prototypes must be learned, they do not constitute any particular theory of category learning. In short, to speak of a prototype now points towards the salience and the cue validity of a member of a category.

With the help of the observations made, let us point towards further basic understandings of prototype theory which seem of great importance regarding our investigations concerning teachers' ethos:

1. Instead of describing members of a particular category by sufficient and necessary features (see *Feature Semantics*), typical features are used for describing categories of meaning.
2. Instead of deciding upon an entity belonging to a category by necessary and sufficient features, the decision is made on the basis of features shared by the members.
3. This leads to fuzzy borders of a category.
4. Finally, within *prototype theory*, one recognizes the concept of *family resemblance* introduced by Wittgenstein's finding on the category of *Spiel* in 1953. Hence, entities are to be realized within the same category in virtue of their sharing of features.

Fourth outcome: Drawing from this analysis on *prototype theory* it becomes clear that teachers' ethos needs to be understood as holistic concept embracing various approaches differently. When linking this finding with the aim of this chapter to answer the question what professional teachers' ethos means, several conclusions are suggested:

1. Teachers' ethos can be understood as a family. However, teachers' ethos on a theoretical level can only be understood this way because of the contribution of every single family member, i.e., every single concept on teachers' ethos. This means each theoretical concept on teachers' ethos contributes to teachers' ethos as an entity. By grasping the different concepts on teachers' ethos accordingly, the latter can be understood as a holistic concept (see Figure 1). We are in great favor of this idea, as approaching teachers' ethos like this allows to include all the existing concepts and pays reference to the theoretical background(s) and argumentation of the concepts in question.
2. Teachers' ethos in its full sense remains a secret as teachers' ethos as a holistic concept could be understood to be more than the sum of its constituents. This understanding would urge us to discard the idea that there is one concept on teachers' ethos that embraces all its dimensions (see Figure 1). This entails the impossibility to operationalize teachers' ethos with the help of only one method. Moreover, this observation results in the necessity to acknowledge that there is no core of teachers' ethos on a theoretical level. Rather, this idea proposes that each concept is needed to reveal teachers' ethos as a whole. Most important, we are left

unknowing how much of teachers' ethos theoretical considerations and empirical research actually gathers.

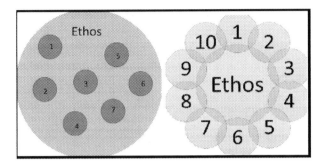

Figure 1. Ethos as a family versus ethos as a holistic concept (each number represents a single concept of teacher ethos)

OVERALL CONSIDERATIONS AND FURTHER DIRECTIONS

The remarks on the outcomes on different theoretical approaches towards teachers' ethos imply that the question of which elements teachers' ethos contains, i.e., how teachers' ethos can be grasped on a conceptual level and how the elements in its theoretical frame of a concept should be implemented into teachers' education demand empirical research. This research, however, needs to be aware of the fact that it can only provide answers to the teachers' ethos of the 21st century as its content strongly depends on the *Zeitgeist*, as argued before. As a result, the content of teachers' ethos is subject to change. Thus, studies on teachers' ethos content need be performed continuously to ensure teachers' education which cultivates teachers' ethos reflecting and acting upon societies' current demands. Concerning teachers' education, this research must be guided by the theoretical concepts of teachers' ethos. Thus, only by studying the concepts of teachers' ethos in depth, it will be possible to detect und derive further defining elements of teachers' ethos. Rosch's understanding of categorization in combination with the methodological approaches used by her has brought forth great examples of how this could be done in forthcoming research. Thereby, the considerations concerning *prototype theory* lead to new ways of investigating teachers' ethos.

Also, the analyses above remind of an old debate within the psychology of moral development which is the debate between "content" and "structure". In line with the claim of Bergem (2003, 2012) we cannot hide behind structure anymore. Teachers' ethos on a conceptual level needs to be filled with content which does not act exclusively. Morality, authority, and responsibility, for example, could all feed into teachers' ethos equally as several concepts named above suggest. We too, wish to consider this an outcome which shall guide future theoretical considerations and empirical research on teachers' ethos. This means the work concerning teachers' ethos combines both – a top down and bottom up process.

Finally, we, as a scientific community, need to do research on the content in which the defining elements of teachers' ethos can be found in. By doing so, we are convinced that the structural element derived theoretically can be filled with content successfully. Speaking in linguistic terms, we, as a scientific community, need to do theoretically guided research on the thoughts behind the use and application of the lexeme *ethos*.

NOTE

[1] The findings we wish to present in the following are concerned with the translations of the word ethos/ εθοσ and/or ηθοσ from the Greek into the German language.

REFERENCES

Abs, H.-J. (2016, January). *Aspects of general and domain specific teacher ethos*. Beitrag auf dem Symposium "Ethos von Lehrpersonen: eine Kernkompetenz professionell handelnder Lehrpersonen?" [Paper presented at the Symposium "Teachers' ethos: A core competence of professional teachers?"]. Otto-Friedrich-University Bamberg, Germany.

Alt, D., & Reingold, R. (Eds.). (2012). *Changes in teachers' moral role: From passive observers to moral and democratic leaders*. Rotterdam, The Netherlands: Sense Publishers.

Australian Institute for Teaching and School Leadership. (2011). *Australian professional standards for teachers*. Melbourne: Education Services Australia.

Bärenfänger, O. (2002). Merkmals- und Prototypensemantik: Einige grundsätzliche Überlegungen. *Linguistic Online, 12*, 3–17. Retrieved from https://bop.unibe.ch/linguistik-online/article/view/890/1550

Bauer, J., & Prenzel, M. (2016, January). *Approaches to investigate teachers' ethos in large scale studies: Exemplary findings on teachers' educational values*. Beitrag auf dem Symposium "Ethos von Lehrpersonen: eine Kernkompetenz professionell handelnder Lehrpersonen?" [Paper presented at the Symposium "Teachers' ethos: A core competence of professional teachers?"]. Otto-Friedrich-University Bamberg, Germany.

Bergem, T. (2003). The quest for teacher professionalism: The importance of commitment. In W. Veugelers & F. K. Oser (Eds.), *Teaching in moral and democratic education* (pp. 85–105). Bern: Peter Lang.

Bergem, T. (2012, June). *How to build ethical schools?* Key note address at the EARLI SIG 13 conference in Bergen, Norway.

Berlin, B., & Kay, P. (1969). *Basic color terms: Their universality and evolution*. Berkeley, CA: Berkeley University Press.

Berliner, D. C. (1992). The nature of expertise in teaching. In F. K. Oser, A. Dick & J.-L. Patry (Eds.), *Effective and responsible teaching: The new synthesis* (pp. 227–248). San Francisco, CA: Jossey-Bass.

Biedermann, H. (2016, January). *Sie wissen nicht was sie tun*. Beitrag auf dem Symposium "Ethos von Lehrpersonen: eine Kernkompetenz professionell handelnder Lehrpersonen?" [Paper presented at the Symposium "Teachers' ethos: A core competence of professional teachers?"]. Otto-Friedrich-University Bamberg, Germany.

Blank, A. (2001). *Einführung in die lexikalische Semantik für Romanisten* [Introduction to the lexical semantic for Romanists]. Tübingen: Max Niemeyer Verlag.

Blasi, A. (1984). Moral identity: Its role in moral functioning. In W. Kurtines & J. Gewirtz (Eds.), *Morality, moral behavior and moral development* (pp. 128–139). New York, NY: Wiley.

Böckenförde, E.-W. (2011). *Vom Ethos der Juristen* (2. Aufl.) [The ethos of lawyers]. Berlin: Duncker & Humblot.
Brezinka, W. (2016). *Education in a society uncertain of its values: Contributions to practical pedagogy* (J. S. Brice, Trans.). Newcastle: Cambridge Scholars Publishing. (Original work published in 1993)
Buzelli, C., & Johnston, B. (2001). Authority, power, and morality in classroom discourse. *Teaching and Teacher Education, 17*, 8, 873–884.
Forster-Heinzer, S. (2015). *Against all odds: An empirical study about the situative pedagogical ethos of vocational trainers*. Rotterdam, The Netherlands: Sense Publishers.
Heid, H. (2006). Werte und Normen in der Berufsbildung. In R. Arnold & A. Lipsmeier (Eds.), *Handbuch Berufsbildung* [Handbook on occupational education] (pp. 33–43). Wiesbaden: VS Verlag.
Heid, H. (2016, January). *Die Übertragung von Verantwortung*. Beitrag auf dem Symposium "Ethos von Lehrpersonen: eine Kernkompetenz professionell handelnder Lehrpersonen?" [Paper presented at the Symposium "Teachers' ethos: A core competence of professional teachers?"]. Otto-Friedrich-University Bamberg, Germany.
Hentig, H. von (1992). Der Sokratische Eid [The Socratic oath]. *Friedrich Jahresheft, X*, 114–115.
Klaassen, C. (2010). The professional ethos of teachers. In C. Klaassen & N. Maslovaty (Eds.), *Moral courage and the normative professionalism of teachers* (pp. 225–243). Rotterdam, The Netherlands: Sense Publishers.
Klaassen, C., & Maslovaty, N. (2010). Teachers and normative perspectives in education. In C. Klaassen & N. Maslovaty (Eds.), *Moral courage and the normative professionalism of teachers* (pp. 1–12). Rotterdam, The Netherlands: Sense Publishers.
Klafki, W. (1991). *Neue Studien zur Bildungstheorie und Didaktik: Zeitgemäße Allgemeinbildung und kritisch-konstruktive Didaktik* [New studies on educational theory and didactics: General education and critical-constructive didadctics]. Weinheim & Basel: Beltz.
Kultusministerkonferenz [KMK]. (2014). *Standards für die Lehrerbildung: Bildungswissenschaften* [Standards for teacher education: Educational sciences]. Berlin: Sekretariat der Kultusministerkonferenz.
Labov, W. (1973). The boundaries of words and their meanings. In C.-J. N. Bailey & R. W. Shuy (Eds.), *New ways of analyzing variation in English* (pp. 340–373). Washington, DC: Georgetown Universitypress.
Lakoff, G. (1990). *Women, fire and other dangerous things: What categories reveal about the mind*. Chicago, IL: The University of Chicago Press.
Latzko, B. (2012). Educating teachers' ethos. In D. Alt & R. Reingold (Eds.), *Changes in teachers' moral role* (pp. 201–210). Rotterdam, The Netherlands: Sense Publishers.
Menge-Güthling, H. (1913). *Griechisch-deutsches und deutsch-griechisches Schulwörterbuch, Teil 1: Griechisch-deutsch*. Berlin: Langenscheidt.
Noddings, N. (1992). *The challenge to care in schools: An alternative approach to education*. New York, NY: Teachers College Press.
Ogden, C. K., & Richards, I. A. (1923). *The meaning of meaning*. London: Routledge & Kegan Paul.
Oser, F. (1998). *Ethos: die Vermenschlichung des Erfolgs: Zur Psychologie der Berufsmoral von Lehrpersonen* [Ethos: The humanization of success: Psychology of teachers' ethos]. Opladen: Springer.
Paeszler, A.-C. (2008). *Die Schule braucht Schülerinnen, doch es kommen Kinder: Eine theoretische und empirische Auseinandersetzung mit Bildungskonzepten von Lehrerinnen* [The school needs students but it has to deal with children: A theoretical and empirical examination of teacher's concepts of Bildung] (Unpublished Masterthesis). University Leipzig, Germany.
Patry, J.-L. (1991). Normative Vorstellungen von Lehrerinnen und Lehrern: Konfrontation, Koexistenz oder Komplementarität im Lehrerethos. In F. M. Schmölz & P. Weingartner (Eds.), *Werte in den Wissenschaften* [Values in science] (pp. 119–139). Innsbruck: Tyrolia.
Polhenz, P. (2000). *Deutsche Sprachgeschichte vom Spätmittelalter bis zur Gegenwart* [German language history from mediaevel times present]. Berlin: Walter de Gruyter.
Rosch, E. (1973). Natural categories. *Cognitive Psychology, 3*, 328–350.
Rosch, E. (1978). Principles of categorization. In E. Rosch & B. B. Lloyd (Eds.), *Cognition and categorization* (pp. 27–48). Hillsdale, NY: Erlbaum.

Sanger, M. (2007). What we need to prepare teachers for the moral nature of their work. *Journal of Curriculum Studies, 40*(2), 169–185.
Saussure, F. (1967). *Grundfragen der allgemeinen Sprachwissenschaft* [Course in general linguistics] (2. Auflage). Berlin: de Gruyter.
Sayers, A. (2010). Class and morality. In S. Hitlin & S. Vaisey (Eds.), *Handbook of the sociology of morality: Handbook of sociology and social research* (pp. 163–178). New York, NY: Springer.
Selmo, L. (2017, July). *Improving the professional ethos in teaching through reflective practice and narration*. Paper presented at the 5th EARLI SIG 13 Conference "Professionals' Ethos and Education for Responsibility", University of Salzburg, Austria.
Sherman, S. (2006). Moral dispositions in teacher education: Making them matter. *Teacher Education Quarterly, 4*, 41–57.
Tirri, K. (1999, August). *In search of moral sensitivity in teaching and learning*. Paper presented at the European Conference for Research on Learning and Instruction (EARLI), Gothenburg.
Tirri, K. (2003). The teacher's integrity. In F. K. Oser & W. Veugelers (Eds.), *Teaching in moral and democratic education* (pp. 173–191). Bern: Peter Lang.
Veugelers, W. (2011). The moral and the political in global citizenship: Appreciating differences in education. *Globalisation, Societies and Education, 9*(3–4), 473–485.
Weinberger, A. (2016). Konstruktivistisches Lernen in der Lehrerinnenbildung: Die Förderung des Professionsethos mit dem Unterrichtskonzept VaKE [Constructivistic learning in teacher education: Fostering professional ethos through VaKE]. *Journal für LehrerInnenbildung, 2*, 28–39.
Wiegand, H., & Wolski, W. (1980). Lexikalische Semantik. In H. P. Althaus, H. Henne, & H. Wiegand (Eds.), *Lexikon der Germanistischen Linguistik* [Lexikon of the German linguistics] (pp. 155–180). Tübingen: Max Niemeyer Verlag.
Wittgenstein, L. (1953). *Philosophical investigations*. Oxford: Blackwell.
Wittgenstein, L. (2003). *Philosophische Untersuchungen: Auf der Grundlage der kritisch-genetischen Edition* [Philosophical investigation based on critical-genetic edition]. Frankfurt am Main: Suhrkamp Verlag.

Brigitte Latzko
Faculty of Education
University of Leipzig
Leipzig, Germany

Anne-Cathrin Paeszler
Faculty of Education
University of Leipzig
Leipzig, Germany

INDEX

A
Appreciative relationship, 8, 137–146
Aristoteles, 32, 156

C
CAPS, 5, 6, 48, 49, 51, 57, 58, 110–112, 115, 119–123
Cognitive conflict, 108
Conceptual change, 63–72

D
Decision-making, 4, 6, 7, 27, 29, 50–53, 75–77, 89, 139–141, 153, 154
Democracy, 6, 7, 75–85
Dependency, 5, 23, 24, 46, 91
Descriptive language, 12, 13, 15
Dilemma discussion, 7, 68, 108–110, 122
Discourse model of ethos, 5, 30–32, 140

E
Ethical behaviour, 144

I
Incivility, 7, 127–134
Inquiry learning, 6, 7, 75–82, 84, 85, 109

K
Kohlberg, L., 34, 49, 50, 77, 108

L
Linguistic analysis, 8, 11, 154–159

M
Metaethics, 5, 11–20

Moral dilemma, 6, 19, 65, 68, 108, 109, 139
Moral education, vii, 5, 6, 11–20, 107, 108, 113, 131, 151
Moral judgment, 4, 7, 33, 36n2, 107–123, 144, 153, 154
Moral reflection, 110, 122

N
Nonviolent communication, 8, 137–146

P
Pedagogical ethos, 89–103, 140, 141
Prescriptive language, 12, 14, 15, 17, 20n2
Professional code, 7, 89, 90, 134
Professional morality, 5, 25, 33

S
Situation-specificity of human actions, 5, 7, 41–58
Socio-scientific education, 6, 65, 107–123

T
Teacher education, 5, 23, 30, 78, 107–123, 151–153
Teacher ethos, 5–7, 137–146, 152, 153, 157, 159

U
Uncivil behavior, 7, 127–129, 131

V
V*a*KE (Values *and* Knowledge Education), 6, 7, 42, 63–72, 81, 107–123

INDEX

Values, vii, 1, 4–7, 11, 12, 14, 17, 19, 26, 33, 34, 44–46, 48–52, 54, 57, 58n1, 63–72, 82, 90, 94, 96, 103, 107–123, 131, 133, 134, 138–141, 143–145, 146n1, 151, 152

Vocational education, 90, 146n1

Printed in the United States
By Bookmasters